Nations and Citizens
in Yugoslavia and
the Post-Yugoslav States

Nations and Citizens in Yugoslavia and the Post-Yugoslav States

One Hundred Years of Citizenship

Igor Štiks

Bloomsbury Academic
An imprint of Bloomsbury Publishing Plc

BLOOMSBURY
LONDON • OXFORD • NEW YORK • NEW DELHI • SYDNEY

Bloomsbury Academic

An imprint of Bloomsbury Publishing Plc

50 Bedford Square	1385 Broadway
London	New York
WC1B 3DP	NY 10018
UK	USA

www.bloomsbury.com

BLOOMSBURY and the Diana logo are trademarks of Bloomsbury Publishing Plc

First published 2015
Paperback edition first published 2016

© Igor Štiks, 2015

Igor Štiks has asserted his right under the Copyright, Designs and Patents Act, 1988, to be identified as Author of this work.

This work is published subject to a Creative Commons Attribution Non-commercial No Derivatives Licence. You may share this work for non-commercial purposes only, provided you give attribution to the copyright holder and the publisher. For permission to publish commercial versions please contact Bloomsbury Academic.

No responsibility for loss caused to any individual or organization acting on or refraining from action as a result of the material in this publication can be accepted by Bloomsbury or the author.

British Library Cataloguing-in-Publication Data
A catalogue record for this book is available from the British Library.

ISBN: HB: 978-1-4742-2152-8
PB: 978-1-3500-0763-5
ePDF: 978-1-4742-2153-5
ePub: 978-1-4742-2154-2

Library of Congress Cataloging-in-Publication Data
Štiks, Igor, 1977- author.
Nations and citizens in Yugoslavia and the post-Yugoslav states : One hundred years of citizenship / Igor Štiks. – 1st published 2015.
pages cm
ISBN 978-1-4742-2152-8 (hardback)
1. Citizenship–Yugoslavia. 2. Citizenship–Former Yugoslav republics. 3. Yugoslavia–Politics and government. 4. Former Yugoslav republics–Politics and government. I. Title.
JN9677.A2.S85 2015
323.609497–dc23
2015002045

Typeset by Integra Software Services Pvt. Ltd.

*To Jelena Vasiljević
and our son, Ivor Vasiljević Štiks,
born into families whose members were
agents, victims and survivors of
the one hundred years
I describe in this book*

Contents

Preface and Acknowledgements	x
Introduction: A Balkan Laboratory of Citizenship	1
A century of dis/integrations	1
Citizenship and citizenship regime	4
In Yugoslavia, and after: Citizenship as research field, citizenship as battlefield	11
Citizenship as a political history of Yugoslavia and the post-Yugoslav states	17
Part 1 From National Integration to the First Disintegration	**23**
1 Brothers United: The Making of Yugoslavs	25
Brothers as aliens: From Yugoslavism to Yugoslavia	25
Brothers as citizens: The belated birth of Yugoslav citizenship	30
Precarious birth, fragile existence and the brutal death of the first Yugoslavia	34
2 Revolutionary Brothers: The Communist Formula for Yugoslavia	37
Yugoslav communists: Solving the national question	38
Wartime: Enemies or brothers?	47
From brothers in arms to federated citizens	50
Part 2 From Socialist Re-Integration to the Second Disintegration	**53**
3 Brothers Re-United! Federal Citizenship in Socialist Yugoslavia	55
Centralist federalism, 1945–1967	55
Bifurcated citizenship	62
Self-management, decentralization and citizenship	66
4 Brothers as Partners: Centrifugal Federalism, Confederal Citizenship and Complicated Partnership	71
Centrifugal federalism, 1967–1974	71
From federal to confederal citizenship	79
Broken partnership: From confederal citizenship towards crisis	82

5	The Bridges Over the Miljacka: The Long Farewell to Yugoslav Citizenship	89
	Yugoslavism: Fading of an idea	90
	Yugoslavia: Only a matter of interests?	93
	Code red: Turning citizens into enemies	97
Part 3	From Nationalist Disintegration to War	101
6	Partners into Competitors: Divisive Democracy and Conflicting Conceptions of Citizenship	103
	Democracy and nationalism	104
	Citizens as voters: Democratize and divide	110
	A secret handshake between nationalism and electoral democracy	116
7	Where is My State? Citizenship as a Factor in Yugoslavia's Disintegration	119
	So, why did it happen?	119
	Relevant factors of Yugoslavia's disintegration	121
	The citizenship factor	128
8	Enemies: Citizenship as a Trigger of Violence	133
	The dark side of 1989: Violence in post-socialist Europe	133
	Triggers of violence: Citizenship, borders and territories, and the role of the federal military	138
	Conclusion: The price of war	146
Part 4	From Ethnic Engineering to European Re-Integration?	149
9	From Equal Citizens to Unequal Groups: The Post-Yugoslav Citizenship Regimes	151
	The citizenship conundrum in post-socialist Europe	152
	Ethnic engineering after Yugoslavia: The included, the invited, the excluded and the self-excluded	156
	Enemies into neighbours: Unconsolidated and overlapping citizenship regimes	165
	Concluding remarks: From ethnic engineering to ethnic democracies	168

10 Partners Again? The European Union and the
    Post-Yugoslav Citizens   173
    The EU's direct and limited influences   174
    Five ways to (mis)manage the post-Yugoslav citizenship regimes   176
    Partners, or just neighbours?   183

Epilogue: The Citizenship Argument – Why Are We in This Together?   187

Notes   194
Bibliography   203
Index   215

Preface and Acknowledgements

There is something strongly personal about my interest in citizenship. At different periods in my life I have been classified as a citizen (of states but also of sub-state and supra-state units), as temporarily stateless (or with no valid papers to certify my citizenship), as a refugee, as a legal (but also illegal) immigrant and as a permanent and temporary resident. The different statuses I enjoyed brought with them different rights and duties, possibilities and limitations that were sometimes compatible, but sometimes mutually exclusive. The *personal* experience finally influenced my *academic* curiosity as well. In 2001, I enrolled in the Philosophy department of the University of Paris 8 where I did my DEA thesis with Rada Iveković on European citizenship and the possibilities of a supranational emancipatory political identity. A friend's remark that the issues I discussed in my thesis could be quite applicable to Yugoslavia as well – the problems related to its construction and disintegration – made me rethink my research aspirations.

I decided to change my focus and face directly some accumulated and, in my mind, long neglected questions. I thus turned towards the problems of citizenship in polities that we knew as *Yugoslavia* as well as in the states that were built in the geographical perimeters where Yugoslavia once stood. I was fortunate to work with Jacques Rupnik at Sciences Po Paris and Andrew Wachtel at Northwestern University. They were not only supportive advisors who knew when to, intellectually speaking, let me wander freely and when to put me back on a productive track, but also generous friends with whom I spent some unforgettable moments. On the personal side, I am forever indebted to Marijana Kramarić for her affection and support during this period.

This book would have never been possible without my postdoctoral work as senior research fellow at the School of Law of the University of Edinburgh. I owe this privilege to Jo Shaw, the principal investigator of the CITSEE research project ('The Europeanisation of Citizenship in the Successor States of the Former Yugoslavia', ERC 230239), within the framework of which I found a stimulating academic environment but also an enriching comradeship with other CITSEE-affiliated researchers. My collaboration with Jo Shaw meant a constant exploration not only of citizenship as theory and practice, in and outside Southeast Europe, but also of all available instruments to acquire research excellence and, furthermore, to communicate our results to both academic and non-academic audiences. Our friendship was forged thanks to many scholarly endeavours and numerous travels, inevitably filled with huge quantities of humour.

Last but not least, the ideas and arguments running throughout this book were shaped thanks to constant conversations with my wife Jelena Vasiljević. To her inspirational, profound and transformative presence in my life and work, to our love and to our son, this book is dedicated.

Introduction: A Balkan Laboratory of Citizenship

A century of dis/integrations

One could say that Yugoslavia was a legitimate child of its century. It lasted almost exactly as long as Eric Hobsbawm's 'short twentieth century' which spanned the years between the outbreak of the First World War in 1914 – following, in the words of Lawrence Durrell, that fatal 'echo of a pistol-shot' in Sarajevo – and the disintegration of the Soviet Union in late 1991. Yugoslavia, like many other states that surged to the surface of history after the 'collective suicide' of European nations between 1914 and 1918, was conceived and variously imagined during the preceding 'long nineteenth century'. The 'state of the South Slavs' was especially sensitive to the geopolitical seismic shocks between 1918 and 1991. It came into existence *twice* and vanished *twice* following two 'hot' wars and the end of one 'cold' one. Initially it left behind five states whose number has risen to seven at the time of writing. Between the assassination of the Archduke Franz Ferdinand on the Latin Bridge in June 1914 and the centenary commemorations of this event at the same spot in 2014, the political makeup of the region kept relentlessly changing following almost unpredictable shifts of international and internal borders. Between and across these borders various political communities (co)existed and (dis)integrated. This book is an attempt to describe and understand these political communities and their transformations by focusing on both the tension between the *status* of their members, comprising their legal equality, and the *quality* provided by political participation that turns members into citizens. That *status* and that *quality* combined is what constitutes modern citizenship.

By invoking 'a laboratory of citizenship' I am by no means the first one to have applied a scientific language to describe the history of this region. Almost four decades ago, a senior scholar of Yugoslavia, Dennison Rusinow, summarized the socialist 'Yugoslav experiment' in the following terms:

The history of Yugoslavia during the quarter-century since the experiment with a 'separate road' began in 1949 has therefore actually 'proved' nothing expect the astounding flexibility and adaptability of the Yugoslavs, both leaders and led, and an impatient, apparently inexhaustible and often bewildering willingness to experiment. (1977: 344).

If to the socialist experience we add the 'first' Yugoslavia (1918–1941), this 'impatient, apparently inexhaustible and often bewildering willingness to experiment' resulted not only in two Yugoslavias over more than seven decades but also in six different constitutions. The disintegration of federal Yugoslavia can also be taken as yet another political experiment followed, after massive human, economic and social destruction during the post-socialist 'transition', by continuous attempts at another kind of integration, this time into the European Union (EU).

By following *one hundred years of citizenship* in Yugoslavia and the post-Yugoslav states, this book shows how these political communities and their members were made, unmade and re-made. In this region, various successful and unsuccessful political formulae have been tried, each of them vividly testifying to various forms of modern citizenship, the ways to establish and practice them, their multiple political and social outcomes and dramatic narratives of their creations and collapses. The study of citizenship in various political entities in this region between 1914 and 2014 is not only an illuminating angle from which to narrate and analyse their histories but also, more generally, an insight into the fine mechanics and repeating glitches of modern politics.

We can claim that individuals as social and political beings are profoundly shaped by citizenship, by the status it bestows upon them, by the privileges and restrictions it can entail and indeed by the loss of citizenship, whether voluntarily or not. Being born in one place and not the other, in one particular period and not the other, of particular parents and not of some others, is highly significant. The aleatoric fact of our birth can have a decisive influence on our life chances, individual development, social circumstances and finally our political participation and emancipation. Having this in mind, let us engage in a thought experiment and imagine something not entirely impossible, an individual born in 1914, somewhere in what will become Yugoslavia, who lived long enough to see the centenary commemorations of the First World War. Even without changing his or her place of residence, he or she would have changed his or her state citizenship on numerous occasions. Moreover, citizens of the contested regions and on the country's borders frequently found themselves at the mercy of different masters. Several times in their lives they woke up to see a different flag on the main square; border changes turned previous ethnic and religious majorities into minorities and vice versa. In addition, citizenship laws and administrative practices themselves were often redefined rendering existing states and laws fragile and liable to change, and creating citizens with ambiguous statuses, rights, identities and loyalties.

In December 1918, at the end of the First World War, former Austrian, Hungarian, Serbian and Montenegrin citizens, and numerous individuals with undetermined civic statuses, came together to form the Kingdom of Serbs, Croats and Slovenes, a unitary state governed by the Serbian royal family. In 1941 Yugoslavia was occupied by the Axis powers and partitioned, and the former citizens of the evaporated Kingdom experienced different wartime fates. They had been subjected to different foreign occupying authorities (German, Italian, Hungarian and Bulgarian) as well as to the governments of domestic collaborators (the fascist Croatian state and Vichy-like regime in Serbia). These authorities treated them quite differently, in general as a function of their ethnic, religious or 'racial' origins. Some were offered fragile privileges; others suffered expulsions and genocide. In 1945, the Resistance movement led by the Communist Party and its leader Josip Broz Tito liberated the country, mostly by its own forces and, against all odds, revived Yugoslavia. This 'new' or 'second' Yugoslavia was based on a federal principle of internal organization, which also introduced a new type of citizenship. The average Yugoslav citizen was simultaneously citizen of a republic in which he or she resided, or to which she or he was related through her or his parents, and of the new federal state. The Yugoslav Federation and, by extension, its citizenship(s) experienced multiple changes over the years, as did relations between citizen and state as well as the form and content of citizens' political participation.

Our imaginary citizen thus reaches retirement in a modernized and developed society that was about to experience, after the death of Tito, various economic and political crises. She or he is 77 when she/he loses her/his federal citizenship and the country disappears. The former Yugoslav republics used their republican citizenship laws to establish their initial citizenries, but they often left the door open for ethnic kin living in the neighbouring countries or abroad and closed many doors to former compatriots and 'brothers'. This abrupt change of citizenship status was especially difficult for those living in zones of conflict, those of mixed origins or of an ethnic background different from the majority governing the territory they inhabited. But this will not be the final experiment in the 'laboratory of citizenship'.

Since 2000 we have again seen new redefinitions of these states and their citizenships, but also the emergence of new independent states such as Serbia and Montenegro in 2006 and partially recognized Kosovo in 2008. New states usually write new constitutions and new citizenship laws, and the already established states often amend them. Since all of the states that formerly made up Yugoslavia have declared their willingness to join the EU – and the EU has, on numerous occasions, declared itself committed to their eventual membership – one can observe new reforms in the domain of state-building and citizenship, as well as the introduction of a new supranational EU citizenship for those already accepted into the Union (Slovenia in 2004 and Croatia in 2013).

This brief historic overview suffices to illustrate that our imaginary citizen who celebrates his or her own centenary in 2014 is someone who has lived multiple political lives. This book aims at telling her or his story by illuminating political constitutions and functioning of the communities she/he belonged to and those which she/he was excluded from and, finally, the reasons behind their many changes. In order to achieve this goal, we should explain first what do we mean by modern citizenship, how it was conceived, how it was practiced and how it developed historically, as well as why the concept of citizenship regime is crucial for understanding what it actually means to be a citizen.

Citizenship and citizenship regime

Citizenship as status and quality

Generally speaking, modern citizenship is a legal link between a state and individuals, involving rights guaranteed by the state to its citizens and duties citizens owe to their states. Those having citizenship of a given state form a 'community of citizens' that defines itself at the basic level by the exclusion of non-citizens. It is precisely this exclusionary character of citizenship that emancipates the citizen vis-à-vis his/her co-citizens and distinguishes him/her vis-à-vis the others, non-citizens residing in the same state, or foreigners living elsewhere and sometimes visiting. In any given territory there is always a hierarchy of statuses among the present population. Although various dimensions of discrimination, especially social and economic ones, do not in general disappear just because a group of persons share a common citizenship, legally having citizenship status should guarantee formal equality before the law and the right to equal political participation and self-governance of citizens. However, children, migrants, the disabled or members of the LGBT (lesbian, gay, bisexual and transgender) community can often be more accurately described as 'semi-citizens' (Cohen 2009) because of restrictions – of various types – placed upon their enjoyment of full citizenship rights (restrictions that, in the case of children, are merely temporary). Residents, refugees, asylum seekers and even tourists should benefit from basic levels of rights protection (although for illegal immigrants this is likely to be reduced to immediate humanitarian assistance at best), and residents can aspire to various sorts of civic, economic and social rights – but they cannot fully participate as equal political subjects. This is true even in situations when some states allow certain categories of residents (EU citizens, third-country nationals, etc.) to participate in local elections or even in the national elections (e.g. Irish and 'qualifying' Commonwealth citizens in the United Kingdom). In this sense citizenship could be considered a *privilege* that can be earned mostly by birth (being born into a community), but also by marriage and residence (being incorporated into a community), by work (by contributing to a community's wealth), by sacrifice and merit (by serving a community, usually militarily) or, nowadays, by the interest a community expresses in an individual (e.g. sportsmen, scientists or investors).

The dialectic between inclusion and exclusion turns out to be fundamental to citizenship. The privilege of membership makes the community of, at least formally, free and equal citizens bear similarities to a *club* (Walzer 1983: 41), in which members are preferably united around a common political idea or at least the decision to live together. When it comes to states based on ethnocultural membership, Walzer compares them to a *family*. Nevertheless, once the club's membership becomes hereditary, clubs start to resemble families, although the rules of inclusion in some instances might be less centred on the conception of 'blood' and heritage that defines ethnocultural identities. The 'birthright lottery' or citizenship as inherited property (Shachar 2009) is actually how the vast majority of people become citizens of a certain community. Therefore, we are often born into a political community or communities by pure genetic luck – that some would melodramatically call 'destiny' – and by inheriting citizenship privileges from our parents.

I underlined above that citizenship *status* comprises rights but also duties (paying taxes, observing laws, military service or various serving roles during states of emergency, for instance), whereas the *quality of citizenship* is based in ideally equal political participation of citizens (thus not *only* members or *nationals*) that is, in turn, crucial for a sense of membership and a shared political identity.[1] The dynamic and tensions between the two are constitutive for citizenship. Ideally, the two should coincide but this has not always been the case. We can think of people having citizenship status but not experiencing citizenship as a quality – for instance, those subject to dictatorial regimes, or state-imposed class or social discrimination – and about those experiencing the quality of citizenship – EU citizens in other EU states or international activists involved in global mobilizations and struggles – without having formal citizenship of a place where they happen to live or act. Moreover, dual and multiple nationals, migrants, various statuses that a nomadic individual can possess in different places at the same time, political activities that are transcendent and cannot be limited to state boundaries, among others, blur and complicate the relationship between citizenship as status and citizenship as quality. We can conclude that when it comes to citizenship status the Arendtian formula of 'right to have rights' is indeed applicable, but the *quality* of being a citizen should be understood as both 'the right to claim rights' (Isin 2009: 371) and participation in the social, political and economic matters of one's community.

Transformations of citizenship

The very idea and first practices of citizenship have their roots in ancient Greek city-states and later in the Roman Empire, though their concepts differed greatly. The Greek model was characterized by community belonging and direct participation of free and equal citizens, those who did not serve anyone or work for anyone (Meiksins Wood 1995: 204). However, the fruits of Greek democracy were enjoyed only by a tiny portion of the actual population, involving the males who inherited citizenship status. In the Greek conception of citizenship, the sphere of freedom and politics was separated from the private sphere (the household was left to women and children) and the sphere of labour and commerce (involving slaves and *metics* as non-citizen residents). On the other hand, the Roman notion of citizenship bestowed status and legal personality upon those possessing the title of Roman citizen across the Empire and citizenship was mostly understood as the right to own, to possess and to manage 'things', regulated by law.

A citizenship would surface again in the townships and guilds of the late Middle Ages and with early capitalist development.[2] However, we cannot talk about *modern* citizenship, defined by at least a formal juridical equality of all citizens, before the late eighteenth century and the early nineteenth century. Democratization of political rights was the focal point of all struggles of the last two centuries and their principal framework was the nation-state; the hyphen between the two words implied a congruence between a political community (nation), its political and administrative institutions (state) and, inevitably, territory. However, the ideas about what defines a 'nation', how its 'state' should be organized (monarchy or republic, democracy or dictatorship, socialist or capitalist, etc.) and where exactly its territory is or should be differed and still differ sharply, often resulting in internal and international conflicts.

The modern national citizen is thus a product of both juridical status guaranteed by his/her state and of *nationalization* of individuals transforming them into members of their nations by providing various degrees of (ethno) cultural identity. This *double coding* was applied, although differently, in almost all cases of nation-building (Habermas 2000: 113). This process could also be described as the mass production of *national citizens* out of individuals previously fragmented into a variety of class, ethnic, regional, linguistic, religious and corporatist groups. The social, economic and political life of *homo nationalis* is therefore marked by everyday interactions with state institutions, ranging from education and health systems, to army conscriptors and tax collectors. The state provides citizens with tools for work, communication and migrations, and with limited or, at times, extended social mobility. In order for industrial capitalism to function properly, it requires an 'anonymous, fluid, and mobile' population (Gellner 1983: 138).

The life of the national citizen is marked by a developed range of duties (most prominent being military conscription and tax obligations), the control of his/her movements (Torpey 2000), sanctions for transgressing social rules and laws and surveillance if he/she is categorized as belonging to socially excluded or 'dangerous' groups (Foucault 1975). It is not surprising then that the constitution of modern national citizenship went hand in hand with 'the invention of the passport' (Torpey 2000) and various techniques of establishing a person's identity (Groebner 2007). States monopolized the 'legitimate means of movement' (Torpey 2000) and established control of movements of citizens and non-citizens alike through a system of international passports, internal passports and identification cards. Although the practice of issuing documents confirming one's identity has its roots in the late Middle Ages and early modern Europe (Groebner 2007), the systematization of identity documents that started in the late eighteenth century developed throughout the nineteenth century to become a generalized practice by the early twentieth century.

The development of modern citizenship was intimately related to the progressive expansion of rights. In 1949, T. H. Marshall gave a famous lecture on *Citizenship and Social Class* in which he divided citizenship according to three types of rights it provided: *civic, political* and *social*. However, these rights are of recent origin and correspond to three distinct phases in the history of capitalist societies and their expansion in the West or, more precisely, in England. In the eighteenth century, citizenship meant *civic* rights, entailing individual freedom, the right to own property and the right to justice. *Political* rights would start to expand only a century later and the process would end in the early twentieth century. *Social* rights including economic, educational and social privileges, whose goal was a more egalitarian national society, were only acquired by the mid-twentieth century (1950: 10–14). A growing list of rights related to citizenship is primarily due to the long struggles of those excluded from political rights (working class, women, colonized, etc.), whereas social rights would only appear with the advent of capitalist welfare or socialist states. It is only in the second half of the twentieth century with further democratization and de-colonization that most parts of humanity started to enjoy various degrees of full citizenship, although for so many individuals on earth effective benefits of citizenship were and often are reduced, revoked or out of reach altogether.

The logic behind T. H. Marshall's 'trinity of rights' implied a progressive growth of rights. However, since the late 1970s, we have witnessed a progressive dismantling of the welfare state model as a result of the simultaneous processes of deregulation, privatization and individualization (Bauman 2005). The 'neoliberal' process, involving a wide range of economic and social policies, has brought us into a situation in which social rights are no longer seen as guaranteed by citizenship. With the collapse of the state socialist regimes came an abrupt end to many social rights they provided to their citizens; in post-socialist societies, free market economy and liberal democracy, and thus expansion of political and civic rights, came eventually together with neoliberal reduction of social rights. Since the 1970s, we can also observe the parallel rise of cultural or group rights as well as the shift from distribution to recognition (Fraser 1995). Recognition of minority rights transformed the traditional identity dimension of national citizenship, although at the same time states often promote an integrationist agenda and restrictive citizenship policies (Joppke 2007).

If the reduction of social rights removed the possibility of substantial and not only formal equality among citizens, proliferation of demands for recognition of cultural rights reminded us of the blind spots of the imposition of unified national citizenship and signalled the shift towards differentiated citizenship. In other words, not only that global markets and neoliberal capitalism have shaken the social fabric of national political communities but the very idea of sharing belonging and identity, often seen as necessary or at least desirable for a stable national community, seems undermined (see Shaw and Štiks 2013b).

Furthermore, national citizenship is under attack from both supranational economic and political processes, transnational reconfigurations of communities, armed with new communication technologies and subnational mobilizations. The regional communities such as the EU bring another understanding of citizenship. Although limited in its political influence European citizenship brought some new rights and possibilities for citizens of the EU member states, especially extended electoral rights (see Shaw 2007). At the same time, some of its current members are facing prospects of secession or calls for more autonomy from their regions (in the United Kingdom, Spain or Belgium), whereas seven current EU members were not so long ago part of larger multinational federations.

As a result of changing international borders, economic dynamics, political dis/integrations, intensive migrations, the proliferation of diasporic groups and identity-based politics, political communities have become increasingly complex and overlapping. The rise of dual and multiple citizenship, as well as a wide range of statuses that a person could possess (especially a migrant and nomadic one), complicates the classic relationship between an individual and a state as well as the definition of rights and duties. Resident citizens share to various degrees their political community with non-citizen residents, non-resident citizens and even by non-citizens who are also non-residents (usually in cases of ethnic diasporas). Naturally, migration flows result in a proliferation of partial citizenship for migrants (Bauböck 2011) and pose the question of who has the right to participate and who is a stakeholder in a given community (Bauböck 2008). Some of the old characteristics of citizenship such as membership, belonging, identity and rights have been decoupled or are under tension (Soysal 2000). Global economy and technology have also created within nation-states different *zones* with varying economic and social privileges, from concentrated wealth to slums (Ong 2006). All these transformations of contemporary citizenship mean that individuals will continue to face changing political authorities, the unpredictable logic of inclusions and exclusions, territorial recompositions as well as to enjoy, or be deprived of, multiple statuses and memberships as well as vacillating rights, duties and responsibilities.

What is citizenship regime?

In order to understand what happens to individuals, citizens and non-citizens alike, in certain parts of the world and at a given period, and how the different components of citizenship interact with each other within a certain social, political, economic and international context, there is a need to supplement the concept of citizenship, in its various forms and dimensions, with the concept of citizenship regime.[3] A 'citizenship regime' comprises the citizenship laws, regulations and administrative practices regarding the citizenship *status* of individuals, including existing mechanisms of political participation (*quality*). More precisely, a citizenship regime is based on a given country's citizenship legislation defining the body of citizens (citizenry), on administrative policies in dealing with citizenship matters and the status of individuals on a given territory and, finally, on the official or non-official dynamic of political participation, inclusion and exclusion. 'The concept encompasses a range of different legal statuses, viewed in their wider political context, which are central to the exercise of civil rights, political membership and – in many cases – full socio-economic membership in a particular territory' (Shaw and Štiks 2010: 6).

Every citizenship regime is influenced by other, often neighbouring citizenship regimes, and, conversely, in the age of intensive migrations and the proliferation of dual and multiple citizenship, every national citizenship regime necessarily extends beyond its own borders. In addition to that, a citizenship regime is constituted, and thus conditioned, by a specific legal set-up that includes not only domestic laws and regulations on citizenship matters but also international conventions and norms. A citizenship regime should also take into account concrete, practical and everyday interactions between citizens and non-citizens with a given state regulating citizenship matters on a given territory. This will include the rules and processes governing the acquisition and loss of membership statuses, external citizenship and various internal 'quasi-citizenship' statuses.

However, the formal set of relationships needs to be placed within the wider context of constant political contestation and of concrete struggles over the content, range and enjoyment of citizenship rights and forms of participation. Formal possession of citizenship does not guarantee a wide range of rights or their actual enjoyment, and equal participation. On the other hand, depending on circumstances, those without formal citizenship might still in practice enjoy certain citizenship rights as well as a certain degree of participation as a result of their residence status. Thus both expansion and reduction of rights and participation of citizens and non-citizens alike depend on the actual functioning of a citizenship regime, which is always a result of social and political interactions, dynamics and struggles. Finally, it is not just formal rules that define citizenship regimes, but also formal and informal ideologies, personal and collective narratives, individual and group beliefs, social rituals and practices and everyday experiences.

It is especially important to bear in mind the concept of citizenship regime suggested here while analysing citizenship in Yugoslavia and post-Yugoslav states between 1914 and today. Only a fine understanding of the functioning of all these elements of citizenship regimes in this region will help us grasp the reasons behind their numerous changes and often tragic transformations.

In Yugoslavia, and after: Citizenship as research field, citizenship as battlefield

Citizenship is one of the central political concepts that, surprisingly, attracted only marginal attention during the existence of Yugoslavia and, until recently, after its disintegration. During the Yugoslav times one can only find legal commentaries by local experts on the matters of citizenship status regulations, the content of law and on the administrative practices (Jovanović 1977; Tepić and Bašić 1969). One possible reason for the almost total marginalization of the concept of citizenship by local scholars could be found perhaps in unfortunate translations of *citizenship* and *nationality* in the local languages. Citizenship as the status of being a citizen of a state (what is in international documents often described as *nationality*) is translated as *državljanstvo* (a status related to the state, *država*), whereas *nationality* (*nacionalnost*) itself actually means the ethnocultural belonging of a person, or ethnicity. The only other possible translation of citizenship is to use the polysemic word *građanstvo* (related to the city, *grad*) that at the same time could describe public activities of citizens ('active' citizenship), a special social group (city dwellers) and a specific class (bourgeoisie). *Državljanin* is a citizen of a state, whereas *građanin* again is the term used for public political and social activities but also for city inhabitants (as opposed to those coming from rural areas). In local languages, save for Slovenian where *državljanstvo* is the term for both status and activity, *državljanstvo* is thus understood as formal status, something related exclusively to legal and administrative matters.

At the same time, *građanstvo* creates a terminological confusion and ideological polemics. A liberal understanding of the political role of *građani* and the idea of *građansko društvo* (civil society) is confronted with left-leaning and Marxist understandings of class struggle and emancipation. Therefore, in socialist Yugoslavia several categories (working people, working class and citizens) were often mentioned alongside each other in legal documents and public discourses with a specific understanding of their roles in the self-managing socialist community. In short, the problem of translation of political concepts should not be neglected here: if, for instance, French *citoyenneté* is usually understood as active public participation, even as a progressive emancipatory force of citizens taking matters of public interest into their own hands, *građanstvo* in the South-Slavic languages would not necessarily have the same meaning and, moreover, would depend on who is actually using it. To avoid misunderstandings, in this study we are interested in the dynamic legal–political relationship and tensions between citizenship as status and citizenship as political and social participation and activity (the *quality* of being a citizen) or, in other words, between *državljanstvo* and various forms of *građanstvo* (non-related to the *bourgeoisie* as a social or hegemonic class).

Citizenship as status started to attract scholars after the ethnocentric exclusiveness of the new post-Yugoslav citizenship laws and practices proved to be not only a serious obstacle to their democratization but also a grave violation of basic human rights for a significant number of individuals. It is small wonder that the research on citizenship was undertaken by mostly legal scholars and some human rights activists rather than political analysts. Starting in the second half of the 1990s one finds works dealing with the right to nationality (Čok 1999), citizenship laws in a comparative manner and their political ramifications in the post-Yugoslav states (Pejić 1998), studies relating the citizenship issue to constitutional design and political changes in general (Dimitrijević 1998; Hayden 1999; Verdery 1998) and three volumes on the citizenship laws and practices in Yugoslavia's successor states prepared by legal experts, supported by international bodies and international NGOs (non-governmental organizations) (Dika, Helton, and Omejec 1998; UNHCR 1997 and, much later, Imeri 2006). Since 2009, the project on 'Europeanisation of Citizenship in the Successor States of the Former Yugoslavia' (CITSEE, University of Edinburgh), with which I have been associated as a researcher, has produced numerous country case and thematic studies related to citizenship in post-Yugoslav and wider Balkan space.[4] By now a body of scholarly work on citizenship *after Yugoslavia* (see Shaw and Štiks 2013a and the CITSEE working papers' series) has grown considerably.

However, if we put aside the collections of laws published in Yugoslavia with introductory texts written by legal experts, the body of works on citizenship *during Yugoslavia* is reduced to a valuable legal assessment of Yugoslav citizenship in its federal and republican forms (Medvedović 1998), a commentary on Yugoslav citizenship related to post-Yugoslav development (Drouet 1997), a chapter on citizenship and civil society written in a book on Yugoslavia's disintegration (Allcock 2000) and my own work on the matter that serves as the basis for this book (Štiks 2006, 2013). A student of citizenship in socialist Yugoslavia thus must turn to related and complementary studies on Yugoslav constitutional development (see Dimitrijević 1995; Hondius 1968), federal structures and institutions (see Bunce 1999; Cohen 1989; Ramet 1992) and the general functioning of the Yugoslav political system and citizens' role and participation in it (see Burg 1983; Djilas 1991; Jović 2003a; Rusinow 1977).

Above I offer possible (both terminological and ideological) explanations of why local scholars marginalized the question of citizenship. Another unanswered question is why citizenship in Yugoslavia fell below the radar of international scholars. Since the reason cannot be terminological, it is to be found in ideological positions on the matter (adopted by local scholarship in the post-socialist period) and the widespread opinion among scholars that citizenship as such is intimately related to liberal democracy or, in other words, to political participation of citizens through free elections in a multi-party system. Therefore, citizenship in socialist countries, characterized by one-party rule, could not be *genuine* citizenship, or so the argument went. Rather, it was considered to be little more than a pure legal category bereft of any real political value and thereby unworthy of serious political analysis. A similar opinion is widely held with regard to two related fields, namely socialist constitutions and socialist federalism. If 'really existing' citizenship, constitutions and federalism are the exclusive reserve of liberal democracy, then citizenship, constitutions and federalism in socialist countries exist only 'on paper': 'in a very strict sense only a democracy can be a federal system' (Stepan 2004a: 32). This belief prevented a number of scholars from effectively exploring what citizenship, constitutions and federalism – and the relationship between them – actually meant in socialist regimes and how they helped shape the political system, the nature of political participation, the political dynamic in these societies and, finally, their disintegration. By dismissing socialist institutions as basically *illegitimate*, one fails to realize what actually happened to these institutions once democratization gave them 'legitimacy' and how they operated and, eventually, accelerated disintegrative processes. The important role that institutional arrangements of socialist countries played in the final years of these regimes (see Bunce 1999) proves that we should not neglect their significance.

This is especially the case of Yugoslavia and its disintegration process. By rejecting the view that citizenship is exclusively owned by liberalism and by showing multiple transformations of citizenship in socialist Yugoslavia that will have direct consequences on the process of transition to liberal democracy and free market economy, this book aims at bridging this obvious gap. The Yugoslav and post-Yugoslav examples show how citizenship is not only a contested concept and a research field but indeed a real battlefield, both academic and political. To perceive citizenship as only the right to elect and be elected at multi-party elections, as the right to vote and to openly express political opinions within a strong civil society and independently of state control, is to imagine an idealistic vision (unspoiled by socio-economic concerns) of citizenship in a perfectly functioning liberal democracy. It also means limiting citizenship studies only to this wishful model presented thus as the normative ideal and cutting out the formation and functioning of political communities in different periods, different parts of the world (not only in the Western hemisphere) and under different ruling and ideological regimes.

Socialist citizenship, or citizenship in socialist countries built in accordance with the general ideology of Marxism–Leninism, was conceived and practised often in direct opposition to liberal democracy and 'bourgeois parliamentarism'. Scholars have mostly failed to take a closer look at the theory and practice of socialist citizenship and equally failed to detect what exactly the 'rights and duties' of socialist citizens were in those countries led by the single, or as in Yugoslavia, federalized party playing the ideological role of the political avant-garde of the working class. As the ideological victor, liberal democracies successfully managed to sideline other political models and other democratic experiments different from the representative system run by biparty or multi-party system of periodic elections. Therefore, we are left without a serious account on how, acting in accordance with their main ideological principles, socialist countries – as is the case with any other polity – defined their own rules of political inclusion and exclusion. Access to the socialist *agora* was generally, but differently in different socialist states, open to members of the party, to members of a variety of trade unions, different organizations and movements such as youth organizations, or, in Yugoslavia, the massive Union of the Working People of Yugoslavia and, finally, to self-managed economic collectives and associations.

Invoking T. H. Marshall's model of historic development of modern citizenship, Gershom Shafir notes that socialist dictatorship performed badly when it came to *political* and *civic* rights, but performed very well when it came to *social* rights (1998: 15). I would add to this that many state socialist regimes also performed well in the areas of *cultural* rights for ethnonational groups, and also of women's rights. The expansion of citizenship and social rights after the Second World War aimed at annulling or changing modern citizenship's historic relation to capitalism, understood already by T. H. Marshall, which manifests itself as the situation in which 'in modern capitalist democracies, socio-economic inequality and exploitation coexist with civic freedom and equality' (Meiksins Wood 1995: 201). During *les trente glorieuses* in the Western welfare state, in state socialist countries not only social but properly speaking *socialist* rights were the most prominent characteristic of citizenship. Socialist rights aimed at rapid bridging of the inequality gap by annulling the detrimental social and economic logic of capitalist markets and replacing them with a wide state-controlled redistribution system. Among other rights, socialist rights guaranteed full employment, a publicly funded education and health system, housing rights and, in Yugoslavia, workers' self-management as social ownership and workplace democracy coupled with the elaborated delegate system of representation in the political sphere (Kardelj 1977: 156–187; Višnjić 1977):

> The basis of all freedoms and rights of working people and citizens in our socialist society is the right to self-management. This is a new and direct democratic socialist right, which is possible solely in the conditions of the social ownership of the means of production and the ruling position of the working class in the society. This right is unquestionable and inalienable and as such belongs to all working people and citizens. (Kardelj 1977: 119)

One often forgets the main ideological premise of these societies, namely their orientation towards the future and the overarching goal of achieving 'really existing socialism' and, eventually, communism. They claimed (in theory at least) to be more democratic, more humane, more legitimate and morally superior to the capitalist regimes. Actually, all of these systems experienced a deep crisis of legitimacy, not because they failed to construct or reconstruct classical liberal democratic institutions but because these regimes failed to achieve what they had promised and what they claimed to be doing, namely radical social emancipation, the liberation of men from inhumane exploitation and a genuine (unlike oligarchic 'bourgeois') democracy that entails, among other things, respect for basic human rights.

As social engineers, Yugoslav communists turned an agrarian country of mostly poor and illiterate people into an urbanized industrial society of relative social equality and rapid social mobility. Moreover, they could argue that they actually surpassed the liberal democratic model by their decentralized system of delegates (Kardelj 1977: 97–102) and by the self-managing system of workers' ownership, with all its successes and failures, as the largest experiment ever undertaken in industrial or workplace democracy (see Pateman 1970). Citizens were not only citizens once in four years but, ideally, on an everyday basis via their workplaces that, furthermore, they legally owned. The reality, already signalled by Yugoslav scholars at the time, was not always as rosy. It resulted often in concentration of power in the hands of managerial class, usually related to their own republican party leaderships, that pushed for more liberal market reforms creating competition and inequalities among producers and, which turned out to be politically more explosive, among republics (see Suvin 2014; Unkovski Korica 2015).

Socialist Yugoslavia seems to serve also as a counterexample when it comes to federalism: it was for the majority of its existence a relatively functional multinational federation that could be even branded a confederation after the constitutional changes between 1967 and 1974 that offered substantial autonomy not only to its constituent republics but also to the autonomous provinces in Serbia. Needless to say, the party itself was not as monolithic as in the USSR and Czechoslovakia but rather was partitioned along republican and provincial lines. If Yugoslavia was not politically pluralized, the Communist Party was internally pluralized. This proves that a federal institutional organization, dormant or not, matters and that once in place, these institutions are or could be politically important and 'can become catalysts for unexpected (and unwelcome) change' (Gibson 2004: 9).

However, in spite of the structural differences between multi-party and single-party federalism, federalism in ex-socialist countries, and certainly in Yugoslavia, 'structured the relations between state and society in important and enduring ways' (Irvine 1997: 12). As Valerie Bunce concluded, '[t]he fact remains that federalism in practice created nations and states-in-the-making in Yugoslavia, Czechoslovakia and the Soviet Union' (Bunce 1997: 354). In the last paragraphs of his valuable book on socialist Yugoslavia, Dennison Rusinow concludes that, by the 1960s, Yugoslavia had become a system that 'could no longer reasonably be called totalitarian or even a Party autocracy'. In his opinion, Yugoslavia was a 'polycentric polyarchy involving a network of elites to which access was usually open to all except a few minorities excluded by geographical, cultural or self- or externally-imposed ethnic or ideological isolation'. Back in 1977 Rusinow was convinced that 'Yugoslavia would become merely another slovenly, moderately oppressive, semi-efficient, semi-authoritarian State run by an oligarchy of contending elites, a society in which many people are free and participant and many are not. Like most States' (1977: 346–347).

In 'most states', citizenship should nonetheless turn members into citizens that share a strong degree of mutual loyalty and the commitment to a common future. John Allcock, a rare international scholar of Yugoslavia interested in citizenship, explains the failure of Yugoslavia as principally a failure of modernization related to the lack of civil society and of a sense of citizenship, both of which are, in his view, characteristic of modernity. 'At the heart of the failure of the Yugoslav state to modernise has been its inability to institutionalise citizenship' (2000: 301–302). Obviously, Allcock here has in mind the belonging and identity dimension of citizenship rather than the firmly institutionalized two-tier citizenship in federal Yugoslavia (of which he does not seem to be aware). Allcock knows that citizenship played a certain political role in Yugoslavia (2000: 303), but he maintains, similarly to Sabrina Ramet (2006: 603), that it failed to produce a strong sense of Yugoslav political identity and a pan-Yugoslav political culture.

These goals basically presuppose the functioning unifying nation-state model and the solidarity and cohesion provided by cohesive national citizenship. Such integrative measures had failed already in the inter-war Yugoslavia (see Chapters 1 and 2). After the mid-1960s, the practice of what I call centrifugal federalism and bifurcated citizenship in socialist Yugoslavia (see Chapters 3 and 4) was diametrically opposed to any attempt to integrate South Slavs into a single nation precisely because of the resentment occasioned by the inter-war experience. Nevertheless, I do agree with Allcock, Ramet and Linz and Stepan (2001 [1992]) that a stronger dose of all-Yugoslav political culture vis-à-vis ethnonational fragmentation would have made the breakup of the country less probable and would have created a potential for political mobilization around the idea of supranational political community. However, we cannot ignore the fact that the democratization of Yugoslavia occurred within an intentionally already highly decentralized federation where, as is later argued in this study, republican citizenships became more important *politically* than federal citizenship as such. I show in this study not only why Yugoslavia in the 1980s was in a deep crisis of its economic and political model (Chapters 4 and 5) and why from 'an oligarchy of contending elites' it found itself run, again, by 'an oligarchy of contending elites', only this time legitimized by poorly organized multi-party elections (Chapter 6), but also what was the role of citizenship in the process of its disintegration (Chapter 7).

Citizenship as a political history of Yugoslavia and the post-Yugoslav states

Citizenship can be also defined as a tool of any state or nation-building process as it is supposed to provide for elementary solidarity and legal equality among the individuals who form a community within which they mutually recognize themselves as co-citizens. The history of Yugoslavia and the independent states that were built upon or out of its ruins provides an instructive and rare example of how citizenship can be used as a *tool* for different and even opposing goals (Štiks 2013). Citizenship was a tool of national integration in the first Yugoslavia (1918–1941), a tool of socialist re-unification after the failure of the previous national integration and the wartime inter-ethnic conflicts (1945 to the mid-1960s), a tool of cooperation among nations and republics in a socialist multinational (con)federation (beginning in the late 1960s and continuing until 1990), a tool of fragmentation and dissolution (1990–1992) and, finally, of ethnic engineering. Since 2000, the process of joining the EU has been dominating the region and the EU is one of the most powerful external factors in shaping post-Yugoslav citizenship regimes. Although generally citizenship policies are more inclusive than in the 1990s, one can observe that citizenship is still used as a tool of reconciliation and re-integration but also as a tool of ethnonational consolidation and further divisions.

The first Yugoslavia was born at the end of the First World War when the military situation and political circumstances opened up the possibility of the realization of a nineteenth-century idea: that culturally and linguistically similar South Slavs should form their own national state. To paraphrase Massimo D'Azeglio's famous judgement on the Italian *Risorgimento*, after the creation of Yugoslavia it was necessary to create *Yugoslavs*, out of South Slavs and numerous minorities. Therefore, the Yugoslav Kingdom was conceived as a unitary state with a single citizenship (introduced only in 1928) and as one nation, though composed of three 'tribes', Serbs, Croats and Slovenes (see Chapter 1).

It very soon became clear that it was easier to create Yugoslavia than Yugoslavs. The powerful regional nationalist movements each aspired to form an independent state or, short of that, required more autonomy for their units within Yugoslavia. The unitarist project, in the context of the political hegemony of the centre (Serbia), was resisted from the beginning by separate national groups (especially Slovenes and Croats) that had different political and historic memories and different and sometimes opposing political goals. Demands for autonomy and federalism of smaller groups and units were supported by a rising political force, namely the Communists. After initial disputes on the nature of Yugoslavia, Yugoslav communists adopted federalist Yugoslavism as the formula to solve the 'national question' in Yugoslavia. Yugoslavia was destroyed by the Axis powers in Spring 1941 which unleashed fascist terror, inter-ethnic killings and fierce war for liberation, which brought to the fore the popular resistance movement led by the Communist Party and its charismatic General

Secretary Tito. Their 'solution' for Yugoslavia combined the preservation of the country in the federal form, inter-ethnic reconciliation and national and social emancipation (see Chapter 2).

Yugoslavia re-emerged on the political map of post-war Europe as a federation of six republics. One of its crucial innovations from the very outset was to add citizenship to the republics' attributes of statehood. Citizenship in socialist Yugoslavia was from the very beginning defined as having two levels and it was legally and politically bifurcated into federal and republican citizenships. As part of the package of the 'just' solution to the national question, bifurcated citizenship in post-war federal Yugoslavia was a tool of the socialist re-unification of the country. It meant both a commitment to the idea of a South-Slavic state and the acknowledgement that its brotherly nations should develop fully and independently but preferably – as advocated between 1945 and the mid-1960s – in the direction of a higher socialist unity (see Chapter 3).

However, from the mid-1960s, first within the party and later in the far-reaching constitutional changes in the late 1960s and early 1970s it was acknowledged that over the years the South-Slavic brothers had evolved into independent partners. Yugoslavia's internal structure and the relations among the republics were defined by what I call *centrifugal federalism*, a process of gradual but irreversible empowerment of the subunits at the expense of the centre. It was the *device* that transformed Yugoslavia from a centralist federation into a confederation. It also transformed bifurcated citizenship in Yugoslavia from a tool of re-unification of 'brothers' into a tool of cooperation among equal partners (see Chapter 4).

In spite of decentralization and centrifugal tendencies, one has to take a long view over the whole century to understand why the Yugoslav idea or *Yugoslavism* was one of the most powerful mobilizing forces in this region and how it started to lose its attraction and, finally, its political weight after the death of Tito in 1980. No citizenship regime is only legally defined; without a certain ideological conviction that certain numbers of individuals should live in common political community, no matter how organized, no political entity is really possible or enduring. The progressive abandonment of the idea of Yugoslav political identity and citizenship was an introduction to Yugoslavia's dissolution (see Chapter 5). At the end of the 1980s and the beginning of the 1990s citizenship became one of the factors behind Yugoslavia's disintegration, an additional tool of dismantling of its multinational federation. It critically influenced the democratization process (see Chapter 6), disintegration (see Chapter 7) and even the outbreak of violence (see Chapter 8). Citizenship was, of course, one of many factors, but it is one which has not yet received sufficient attention (see Chapter 7).

Democratization came to Yugoslavia via its republican backdoors and never reached its federal institutions. The right to participate in the liberal democratic game of free elections and post-electoral formation of coalitions, with minorities and majorities, was at first extended to all residents of the republics. However, trans-republican ethnic solidarity began to dominate the Yugoslav political space. It involved the vision of an ethnocentric state that would reassemble most, if not all, ethnic members in one state. It is therefore not surprising that, in the context of the Yugoslav political crisis, the election results revealed strong support for ethnic leaders and ethnic parties (see Chapter 6). The ethnonational conception of citizenship prevailed and fuelled violent conflicts over the redefinition of national borders within which the ethnonational states were to be formed on the basis of the absolute majorities of the core ethnonational groups. Democracy, on this view, was seen as workable only if it was essentially ethnonational and, conversely, the ethnonational group or ethnic nation was understood as the only workable framework or basic unit for democratization (see Chapters 6 and 7). In the context of disintegrating federation and inter-ethnic mistrust, fuelled by nationalist forces and aggressive media propaganda, one can detect, in my view, three main triggers of violence: the question of territory and borders, the role of the failing federal army and, finally, citizenship or, in other words, the search of citizens for a political community in which they would secure their rights and equality and for a state that would guarantee their protection. These three triggers of violence were to various degrees present in all violent conflicts in the post-socialist space (see Chapter 8).

What initially presented itself as ethnic solidarity and a nationalist vision of recomposition of previously existed communities into neatly divided ethnocultural groups governing 'their' territory was soon enshrined in legislation. Almost all of the successor states of the former Yugoslav federation have used their respective citizenship laws as an effective tool for ethnic engineering. Citizenship laws played a key role in determining the citizenry of the new states. Where there were equal citizens of the Yugoslav federations, in the post-Yugoslav states we find four unequal groups: the included, the invited, the excluded and the self-excluded (see Chapter 9). All former citizens, regardless of their ethnic backgrounds, who were registered in the citizens' republican registers were automatically transferred into new registers. Those were the *included*. However, some – ethnic kin in the neighbouring republics and overseas – were also *invited* to join the citizenry of the new states. And, while some were invited, some long-term residents were *excluded*. Their situation was often even more complicated if they were of different ethnicity to the core ethnic group of the republic where they lived. Finally, some decided to *self-exclude* themselves from the new citizenship regimes, with the idea of forming one's own ethnically based state and/or joining their kin state and its citizenship.

Since 2000, we have generally witnessed greater inclusiveness and less discrimination on ethnic grounds, as well as increased sensitivity to the political aspirations of minorities. However, citizenship is still a *tool* of ethnic nation-building, divisions and discriminations in this region of overlapping and interdependent citizenship regimes (see Chapter 9). In the context of the aspirations to join the EU, we can observe how the EU (mis)manages these citizenship regimes, legislation and administrative practices in these states as well as general political behaviour (see Chapter 10). Regardless of an eventual integration into the EU of all post-Yugoslav states, which would add the European citizenship framework for their citizens, one is tempted to ask if and how one-time brothers, yesterday's enemies and today's neighbours will become tomorrow's partners.

Part One

From National Integration to the First Disintegration

1

Brothers United: The Making of Yugoslavs

The revolver came from Serbia, but the finger that pulled the trigger that would kill Franz Ferdinand and thus announce the end of one world and the birth of another acted upon two strong beliefs. If one can judge from his statement, underage Gavrilo Princip, like so many of his peers, was foremost convinced that South Slavs should be liberated from a foreign yoke and unite in their own state; this belief was strongly though not articulately mixed with another conviction that the world about to come must be the world of profound social transformation. Two motives with which our story of 'one hundred years of citizenship' begins will be repeated in many different forms during this century: should South Slavs have their own common state? Or form separate ones? And, regardless of the answer, should political transformations entail more social equality or only a change of the rulers at the top of the existing hierarchy? Every idea often has deep roots and various historic materializations. One of the two ideas that materialized in that finger that eventually pulled the trigger on 28 June 1914 had started its long voyage to Sarajevo almost a century before.

Brothers as aliens: From Yugoslavism to Yugoslavia

In contrast to the separate national projects that aspired, as did almost every nationalist movement, to the maximum degree of congruence between their (ethno)national groups and their respective states (Gellner 1983), i.e. movements that were both nation-building and state-building projects, Yugoslavism was ambivalent on this point from the very outset. Could Yugoslavism be described as a classical nationalist movement aiming at the creation of a distinct Yugoslav nation ideally living in its own sovereign state? If so, in this sense, it was not different from separate ethnic nationalisms but merely had a broader ethnic basis encompassing almost all South Slavs. Or, was it just a political project of South

Slavs which aimed at achieving the separate national and political emancipation of each group within a common and, therefore, more *viable* state?

It used to be easy to know when you were in Eastern Europe, as Andrew Wachtel pointedly reminds us in his original definition of this region without clear borders, because 'Eastern Europe is that part of the world where serious literature and those who produce it have traditionally been overvalued' (Wachtel 2006: 4). Wachtel refers here to the traditional societal position held by writers across Eastern Europe. Their engagement was of paramount importance during the nation-building period ('fathers of the nation'),[1] in sharp contrast to the West (although sub-state nations there, such as Scotland, defy the rule) where the dominant civic type of nationalism propelled mostly political figures to the forefront of the nation-building process (though the role of the intelligentsia was always crucial). The South-Slavic lands were no exception to the general rule in Eastern Europe: modern nations were first imagined in the minds of small groups of writers, linguists and intellectuals against the trend of actual political conditions and, for these times, against all odds. As mentioned earlier, South Slavs were loyal to different masters and often distant capitals. Moreover, they were linguistically fragmented into a number of South-Slavic dialects; their respective bourgeoisies were thin and illiteracy was very high. Within such a politically dormant population, a number of regional intellectuals of Croat, Slovene and Serb origins, such as Ljudevit Gaj, Janko Drašković, Vuk Karadžić, Petar Preradović and Stanko Vraz, influenced by national movements in Germany, Italy and elsewhere in Eastern Europe, set in motion the 'Illyrian awakening' in the 1830s.

The guiding idea of the 'Illyrianists' who falsely believed that South Slavs were the descendants of an eponymous ancient Balkan people – that idea was also present earlier in Napoleon's short-lived *Provinces Illyriennes* – was in harmony with the unquestioned principle of ethnic and linguistic nationalism: various groups speaking the same language and which manifested similar ethnic characteristics most probably constitute *a* people that should be united, culturally and politically, and, eventually, govern itself. However, the first task was precisely to create the common standard language that would then displace the web of dialects, some of which (e.g. the Croatian kajkavian, štokavian and čakavian dialects as well as Slovenian) had already developed rich literary traditions. Croatian writer Ljudevit Gaj and Serbian linguist Vuk Karadžić agreed on the necessity of one standard language for all South Slavs, the unavoidable loss of local richness notwithstanding, the basis for which they had found in the widespread štokavian dialect.

Although this decision corresponded to the dialect spoken by the majority of future Yugoslavs, the question of common language has remained a sensitive issue to this day. It revolves around the issue of whether it is the single language with regional varieties (the view held by all serious linguists), or actually every constituted nation speaks a similar but *different* language (the position held by nationalist linguists; on these disputes see Kapović 2010: 127–156; Kordić 2010). One can easily guess that today's nationalists still inhabit exactly the same nineteenth century mental trap as the 'Illyrians'. For them also, peoples/nations are divided by separate languages and, consequently, separate nations must speak separate languages even if this requires introducing artificial differences. The others more or less subscribe to Croatian writer Miroslav Krleža's ironic statement that Serbs and Croats are two peoples divided by one language and one God. In other words, political reality should be separated from the question of language that should develop freely and in mutual interaction of its different varieties.

Back in the 1830s, the above-mentioned intellectuals had a gigantic task. They were a tiny minority of the literate population with no political or institutional power. Imposing a new standard language without an army or an administration seemed the fruit of the pretentious imagination of overly ambitious intellectuals coming from deep, underdeveloped provinces of large empires. Nonetheless, the first serious consequence of imposing the standard language was the unbridgeable divide between Slovenes on the one hand (who with a few exceptions notwithstanding, generally opposed giving up the literary use of their own language) and Serbs and Croats on the other. They later accepted the štokavian standard, albeit bifurcated into the *ijekavian* (Croatia, Bosnia, Montenegro) and *ekavian* (Serbia) versions, and were often reluctant to give up the particularities of their local vocabularies and syntax. It is important to note that the 'awakeners' had enormous difficulties in naming the newly created standard language; a perennial problem for all subsequent generations. In the nineteenth century, in order to avoid using either a Serbian or Croatian name, and lacking alternatives that would satisfy everyone, they often called the language *narodni jezik* (people's language), or *naški* or *naš* jezik ('our' language). In subsequent periods it was named 'Serbo-Croatian' – christened as such in 1824 by a German linguist Jacob Grimm and accepted by Illyrians in the 1830s and later (Kordić 2010: 127) – and 'Croato-Serbian', 'Serbian and Croatian' and 'Croatian or Serbian', until the 1990s when Yugoslavia's successor states decided to name the language spoken on their territories solely by the name of their countries or their ethnic majorities; therefore, Croatian, Bosnian, Serbian and, more recently, Montenegrin. International institutions today refer to these languages, for practical purposes, as BCS or BCMS and former Yugoslavs when speaking among themselves refer to it as *naš jezik*, like the people who 'imagined' them almost two centuries ago.

Today one is tempted to conclude that Yugoslavism never enjoyed even an initial advantage over the various South-Slavic nationalisms. Over the course of the nineteenth century Serbia constituted itself as autonomous and was in 1878, together with Montenegro, recognized as an independent state. This, coupled with growing Slovenian and Croatian nationalist movements in the Habsburg lands and the Ottoman presence in most of the Balkans, proved to be an insurmountable obstacle to South-Slavic *national* unification. In Croatia in the second half of the nineteenth century, however, some of the most important cultural, political and literary figures such as the poet and politician Ivan Mažuranić, and even clerical leaders such as Bishop Josip Juraj Strossmayer and Father Franjo Rački, continued to work on the Yugoslav project. Strossmayer, for instance, was the founder or initiator of the *Yugoslav* Academy of Arts and Sciences, established in 1866 in Zagreb, and the University of Zagreb, established in 1874, as well as the generous benefactor of other South-Slavic intellectuals. He saw Zagreb as the cultural capital of South Slavs, regardless of possible political outcomes. Nevertheless, Croatian Yugoslavs had to face the emergence of the concurrent Croatian nationalism embodied in the powerful Party of the Rights.[2] This Party, led by influential Ante Starčević and Eugen Kvaternik, rejected any future unification of Croats with other South Slavs and based their programme solely on Croatian nation and state building. Separate Croatian nationalism had long-lasting partners in the Catholic Church – in spite of some notable exceptions such as Strossmayer and Rački – the Croatian petty-bourgeoisie and among peasants. Although intellectually and culturally strong, the pro-Yugoslav group remained largely isolated from the wider masses. It experienced a second wind with a new generation of young Croatian politicians such as Ante Supilo, Ante Trumbić and Josip Smodlaka, who perceived political unification with Serbs as a means of preserving Croatian statehood and securing its national independence in the context of Hungarian and German dominance.

The decisive moment for the Yugoslav idea thus seemed to be its appropriation by competing nationalist programmes (Rusinow 2003: 13). Nevertheless, this moment was significantly delayed in independent Serbia and arrived only just prior to the First World War. The exception to this was the short-lived cooperation between the Serbian politician Ilija Garašanin and Strossmayer.[3] It has been reported that Garašanin, mostly known as the author of the secret Serbian expansionist programme 'Načertanije' [The Draft], suggested to Strossmayer the liberation of the South Slavs from the Turkish yoke and 'unification of all South Slavs in one federal state' (Prpa-Jovanović 1997: 46). If Garašanin was ready to make such an opening towards Habsburg South Slavs, Serbian politicians after him almost completely ignored Yugoslavism as a political project, or considered it only as a means of creating a larger and stronger Serbian state. Serbian Yugoslavism had to confront 'Greater Serbianism', the project of unifying the štokavian regions under Serbian rule (and excluding the kajkavian regions of Croatia and Slovenia).

At the turn of the century, in the decisive years preceding the First World War, several mutually exclusive conceptions of South-Slavic unity were thus proposed simultaneously. In the Habsburg West, there were demands for cultural and linguistic rights, political unification of the Habsburg South Slavs with or without Serbia, as well as some support for Austro-Marxist ideas. In the East, in Serbia, two orientations confronted one another: an 'eastern' one advocating the unification of Serbs and Bulgarians (adopted by Garašanin as well) and a 'western' one demanding either a Greater Serbia or a large South-Slavic State with Serbia as its dominant region or Piedmont (Rajaković 1992).

It remains, nonetheless, questionable as to whether Yugoslavism really competed with other separate national projects or whether it was just their temporary *complement* under existing historical and political circumstances. Rusinow (2003) argues that Yugoslavism never truly passed through all three main stages of the classic nation-building process in Eastern Europe as defined by Czech historian Miroslav Hroch. The first stage of the model proposed by Hroch is marked by the appearance of a handful of intellectuals and writers; the second stage is characterized by the transmission and propagation of the national idea by 'patriots' who form movements and political parties; and, finally, in the third and final stage, the national programme acquires mass support. Against this scheme, the First World War and the subsequent fall of the great empires opened an unprecedented window of opportunity for the Yugoslav programme to come into being without requiring a preceding mass support. Without mass movements, the question that needed to be answered was the following: under what political form should this nation- and state-building programme, that suddenly had a chance to be realized, be implemented? In 1917, the Corfu Declaration on the creation of a parliamentary constitutional monarchy of the Serbs, Croats and Slovenes was signed by, on one side, the Yugoslav Committee composed of mostly prominent Croatian artists and politicians such as Trumbić and sculptor Ivan Meštrović, and, on the other, the Serbian government in exile presided over by Nikola Pašić. By that time, and especially a year later with the creation of the Kingdom of Serbs, Croats and Slovenes in December 1918, two types of Yugoslavism – *unitarist* and *federalist* – had already opposed one another and would continue to plague political relations in the inter-war Kingdom to the point of almost totally defeating, after merely two decades, the idea of Yugoslavia as state.

Brothers as citizens: The belated birth of Yugoslav citizenship

Advocates of an 'integral' Yugoslavism, backed up by Serbia, established a clear agenda. Yugoslavia was envisioned as a centralized state engaged in an integral Yugoslav nation-building process that could come in two forms: either smaller Yugoslav 'tribes' would join the larger Serbian nation or a new national identity should be created and, eventually, supersede all earlier 'tribal' identities. With regard to the latter version of the process, we must mention the efforts made to create a 'synthetic' Yugoslav culture based on recognizable but complementary elements of each separate culture. This approach is most famously represented in the works of Ivan Meštrović (for a detailed analysis see Wachtel 1998: 67–128). On the other hand, a vision of a decentralized and multinational Yugoslav state that would naturally take the form of a federation of distinct nations was opposed to any form of *integralism*. The former Habsburg subjects, for whom the end of the Austria–Hungarian Empire presented a historic opportunity to regain national independence in union with other South Slavs, were unsurprisingly in favour of the federalist Yugoslavism. After all, they had some experience in federalist politics and in limited autonomy and were not keen on transferring all their powers to the new centre. It is often said that Yugoslavia was a child of Croatian ideas and Serbian military power. As in other similar coalitions, the actual number of military divisions was the determining factor.

The first moments of disillusionment with the political and economic life in the common state dominated by the Serbian monarchy soon developed into a permanent crisis.[4] The first Constitution of 1921, also known as the St. Vitus' Day Constitution (*Vidovdanski Ustav*), essentially consolidated Belgrade's dominance. It was adopted by a simple majority and was rejected by, among others, Croat parties and Communists. The Croatian grievances with Yugoslavia were channelled into massive support for Stjepan Radić's Peasant Party that

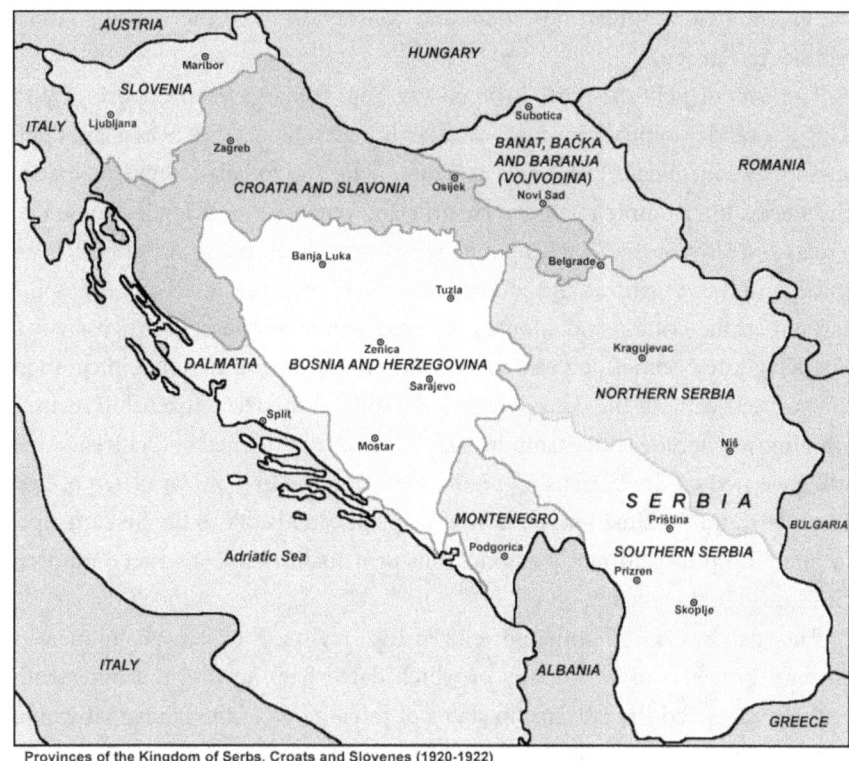

Provinces of the Kingdom of Serbs, Croats and Slovenes (1920-1922)

Figure 1.1 The Kingdom of Serbs, Croats and Slovenes 1920–1922 (Source: Wikimedia Commons).

vacillated from 'the Peasant International' to which Radić subscribed in Moscow in 1924 to a conservative-nationalist party. Since its birth, Yugoslavia had been under heavy pressure from its internal economic and political imbalances. It seems that 'Croatians and Slovenes expected their economic position to win them political authority, while the Serbs expected their political authority to strengthen their economic position, mainly through the power of taxation' (Prpa-Jovanović 1997: 54). The assassination of Radić by a Montenegrin deputy in the Yugoslav Parliament in 1928 only aggravated the already soaring tensions over the national question in Yugoslavia. Dejan Djokić warns, however, that it would be a mistake to view Yugoslavia's problems only through the prism of the conflict between Serbs and Croats. These difficulties were equally a result of the clash between centralist and anti-centralist visions of Yugoslavism, and were a consequence not only of inter-tribal but also of *intra*-tribal political conflicts (2003: 139, 145; also Djokić 2007). One should also add that these events in Yugoslavia were also taking place in the context of a collision between the growing Communist movement and conservative and increasingly fascist regimes in Europe.

The overall political crisis in inter-war Yugoslavia gave an opportunity to King Alexander to proclaim royal dictatorship on 6 January 1929 as a last-ditch attempt to consolidate Yugoslavia as nation-state and to balance and supersede embittered inter-ethnic relations. He officially renamed the Kingdom of Serbs, Croats and Slovenes as 'The Kingdom of Yugoslavia' (the name had already been widely used), reorganized the country into nine provinces based on geographic and not ethnic criteria and adopted the programme of integralist Yugoslavism. The King knew something else as well: no programme of national integration can succeed without the consolidation of a unified modern citizenship regime. For almost a decade, citizenship in Yugoslavia was undefined and citizens were still governed by the citizenship regimes left in place by now obsolete polities. To understand the situation, we have to step back in history to the first attempts by ailing Empires and newly autonomous principalities to construct a modern citizenship in this region.

The patchwork of different citizenship regimes, based on numerous citizenship laws and acts, many of which dated back to the mid-nineteenth century, regulated the citizenship status of inhabitants of the lands that would form the 'first' Yugoslavia in 1918. The 1879 Hungarian law on citizenship (Article 'L' (50)) was applied in Croatia, Slavonia, Vojvodina, Medjimurje and Prekmurje and Rijeka, whereas the Austrian laws on citizenship (Articles 28–32) from the 1811 (1867) Austrian Civil Code were in force in Dalmatia, Austrian Littoral, including Istria, and Slovene lands. In Serbia, citizenship was defined and regulated by the 1844 Civil code of the Kingdom of Serbia (the articles 44, 45 and 48) and by the 1844 'Regulation on Serbian Naturalization and Release of the Serbs from their Fatherland [*otačastvo*]' (Tepić and Bašić 1969: xxxvii). Curiously, Montenegro did not have a proper citizenship law; only a regulation on exceptional naturalization of foreigners was legally codified in the Constitution of The Principality of Montenegro. In Bosnia-Herzegovina, during the last decades of the Ottoman rule, the *Tanzimat* reforms brought the first taste of modern citizenship with the adoption of the Nationality Law in 1869 (Sarajlić 2010: 2–3). After the Austrian occupation and annexation, articles 3 and 4 of the 1910 Land Statute for Bosnia-Herzegovina regulated the question of 'Bosnian-Herzegovinian belonging'. After the Balkan wars, the Ottoman subjects in Kosovo, Sandžak and Macedonia came under either Montenegrin or Serbian rule. It is difficult to speculate about their formal status during these wars and in the First World War. The region was overrun by the Axis powers in 1915 – the

Serbian army retreated through Albania to Corfu – and was a theatre of some of the bloodiest war operations.

Following the founding of the Kingdom of Serbs, Croats and Slovenes in 1918, the citizenship issues that arose due to the dismemberment of Austria-Hungary and the subsequent creation of new states were mostly settled by the peace treaties and inter-state treaties concluded by the Kingdom with its neighbouring countries.[5] Peace treaties with Austria and Hungary established that a person who had the 'homeland right' or domicile (*Heimatrecht* in German; *zavičajno pravo* or *zavičajnost*[6]), which signified permanent municipal residence and a legal link between the individual and municipality or county where he or she lived – on former Austrian–Hungarian territory should have citizenship of the country currently exercising its authority on that very territory (Čepulo 1999: 797–806; Jovanović 1977: 11–12, 15). The treaties also established the right of option for adult persons and, more important after the dissolution of the multiethnic empires and during consolidation of new nation-states, the right of option for members of ethnic minorities to live in their kin-state, i.e. basically to *emigrate* to their kin-states. The peace treaty with Bulgaria specified that Yugoslav citizens would become permanent residents of the territories that were incorporated into Yugoslavia and would also be offered the right of option. Following the Rapallo Treaty with Italy, ethnic Italians from Dalmatia acquired the right of option for Italian citizenship without obligation to emigrate.

The above-mentioned laws and regulations on citizenship – enacted by the defunct Habsburg Empire and the post-Ottoman kingdoms in the making – remained in force in the Yugoslav lands for a decade after unification. On 21 September 1928, the Kingdom of Serbs, Croats and Slovenes finally enacted its own citizenship law that established a single Yugoslav citizenship (article 1).[7] The law had retroactive application. Its intention was to determine who had actually acquired and who had lost Yugoslav citizenship between 1 December 1918 and 31 October 1928 (article 53). Yugoslav citizens consisted of all persons who on the day of unification had citizenship in the Kingdom of Serbia, the Kingdom of Montenegro, the Kingdom of Croatia and Slavonia and all others whose citizenship had been regulated by the Peace Treaties. Individuals in Kosovo, Sandžak and Macedonia became Yugoslav citizens if they lived in these territories until 1918. The municipal belonging or *zavičajnost* was the crucial instrument to establish Yugoslav citizenship for Slovenia, Croatia, Slavonia, Dalmatia and Vojvodina, and the land belonging was required in Bosnia and Herzegovina. The law also provided that 'every citizen must have *zavičajnost* in one of the Kingdom's municipalities'. Proof of *zavičajnost* was a necessary requirement for the Kingdom's authorities to issue a certificate of Yugoslav citizenship (article 4). Interestingly, *zavičajnost* remained an important legal device up until 1947–1948. It constituted the basis for the determination of individuals' republican citizenships in federal Yugoslavia.

Precarious birth, fragile existence and the brutal death of the first Yugoslavia

The King's dictatorship managed to construct a single citizenship regime as well as to administratively unify the country, but along the way the unification project acquired a lot of enemies. The King's efforts were, eventually, a failure. Ten years of negative political experiences under the Serbian crown led to the King's dictatorship being almost automatically associated with Serbian hegemony. It betrayed Croatian hopes for more autonomy and provoked complaints by Serbs whose democratic institutions had been suspended. In short, it was too little, too late. It was too little for Slovenians and Croats whose strong national consciousness required urgent political recognition; it was too late, because the prospects for an effective cultural and political Yugoslav unity had already faded. King Alexander's assassination in Marseille in 1934, perpetrated by Croatian and Macedonian right-wing extremists, brought an abrupt end to his autocratic rule. In the years preceding the Second World War the leading politicians – with the Serb and Croat political elites in the driving seat – would engage in a number of attempts at reforming and preserving the state (see Djokić 2007: 171–268).

However, the national question did not disappear from the agenda; it remained and threatened, under the pressure of Nazism and Fascism, the very existence of Yugoslavia itself. In August 1939, on the eve of the Second World War, the Yugoslav government, led by Dragiša Cvetković, and leader of the Croatian Peasant Party, Vlatko Maček, signed the Agreement (*Sporazum*), the purpose of which was the satisfaction of Croatian demands for greater autonomy. It established a semi-independent Croatian *Banovina*. If this spelled the end of integral Yugoslavism and the beginning of the 'federalization' of Yugoslavia, as argued by Djokić (2003: 153), it failed to properly address the Slovenian and Macedonian questions, nor did the *Sporazum* offer any comprehensive plan for restructuring Yugoslavia. It was, again, an insufficient solution delivered too late.

The first Yugoslavia disappeared during eleven days in April 1941, swept away by yet another *blitzkrieg* by the Axis powers. Yugoslavia was divided between the occupying powers (Germany, Italy, Hungary, Bulgaria) that on the remaining territory established the puppet fascist Independent State of Croatia (NDH), together with a collaborationist regime in Serbia, and attached Kosovo to the Italian-occupied Kingdom of Albania. It did not seem plausible at the time that Yugoslavia would ever again be resurrected. However, and against considerable odds, two years later the Resistance movement led by the Communist Party of Yugoslavia (CPY) offered, amidst bloody inter-ethnic conflicts perpetuated at a massive scale by Croat fascists against Serbs, Jews and Roma, and followed by a series of massacres by different factions of Serb collaborationists, extremists and royalists against Muslims, Croats and Jews, a new federalist formula for a future (preferably socialist) re-unification of liberated Yugoslavia.

However, as I show in the following chapter, the road between the 1919 founding congress of the CPY and its pivotal wartime role in re-establishing Yugoslavia was far from straight. It is crucial to unearth this ideological and political development to explain how it was at all possible to resurrect Yugoslavia as political project after the initial failure. Without this ideological and political background, that has been often neglected by scholars of Yugoslavia, the idea behind federal Yugoslavia and its federalized citizenship, the evolution of its federal institutions over next four decades as well as the dynamic of its disintegration, cannot be properly understood.

2

Revolutionary Brothers: The Communist Formula for Yugoslavia

Eric Hobsbawm once remarked that 'each Communist party was the child of the marriage of two ill-assorted partners, a national Left and the October revolution. That marriage was based both on love and convenience' (2001: 3). In other words, it was the marriage between the specific national circumstances that required a corresponding political strategy and the imperative of a Moscow-led world revolution and, as was often the case, its own particular state interests. The two agendas did not always go hand in hand and the outcome of any clash between them was usually detrimental to the political position of national Communist parties within their own societies. The Communist Party of Yugoslavia was not an exception to the rule until its break with Stalin in 1948. However, classic (im)balances between nationalism and internationalism in the communist struggles in South-Slavic lands took the form of a complex relationship between separate ethnic nationalisms (Serb, Croatian and Slovene), Yugoslavism that would later on be turned into a specific South-Slavic inter-nationalism, Balkan regionalism and global internationalism.

In order to properly answer the question of why Yugoslavia was *re*-unified as a socialist multinational federation in 1945 and how an entirely different conception of citizenship was actually developed through decades of theoretical and political struggles, one must first examine the history of two intellectual and political traditions that shaped the discussions, opinions, political meandering and, ultimately, the decisions of Yugoslav communists: on the one hand, Marxist tradition and the debates within the Marxist movement on the national question and the form of the socialist state, and, on the other, Yugoslavism as the ideology of South-Slavic national and political unity.

For more than a century and a half the relationship between Marxism and nationalism was at different times either conflicted or complementary. The conflicts between the two ideologies that grew significantly around the same time in the nineteenth century were a matter of principle. The complementarities between them, on the other hand, were more the product of historical and political realism. Nationalism was not a phenomenon destined to wither away so soon, as Marxists had predicted and hoped, and ignorance of this bitter fact would prove politically harmful. Marxists thus had to learn how to come to terms with nationalism and even how to manipulate it for their own ends (Connor 1984: 6). In addition, nationalists of various stripes equally learned how to manipulate demands for social justice and equality for their own agenda.

South-Slavic Marxists found themselves, ideologically and politically, in a rather confusing situation. From the very outset, they had to face two opponents who appeared in the guise of nationalism and had to be either fought or accommodated: the separate South-Slavic ethnic nationalisms on the one hand and, on the other, Yugoslavism that aspired to unite linguistically and culturally similar South Slavs in a common state. On the plane of ideology, Marxists had to overcome the philosophical incompatibility between the internationalist class struggle and local nationalist demands which cut across class lines. In the South-Slavic lands, the task was even more complex as two parallel nationalist movements – one seeking higher Yugoslav unity, the other arguing for the separate political autonomy of ethnic groups – often complemented one another, but at other times were in open conflict. Moreover, the political and territorial ambitions entailed by the various ethnic nationalisms often collided with each other. Eventually, as elsewhere, a marriage of necessity brought the two together. Yugoslav communists had to acknowledge that nationalism was a potent political force. They thus continued searching for a political project that could successfully combine both social and national emancipation in the context of developed and often mutually exclusive national projects of neighbouring groups. In this chapter, I show how the Yugoslav communists 'discovered' the successful federalist formula for the socialist re unification of Yugoslavia after the Second World War as well as how, as with any 'successful' formula, its discovery was preceded by numerous fruitless experiments.

Yugoslav communists: Solving the national question

The roots of the formula: Marxism and the national question

The Austro-Marxist approach to nations and nationalism, developed within multinational Austria–Hungary, would leave a long-lasting influence on Yugoslav communists, especially Tito and Edvard Kardelj. Yugoslav communists inherited many ideas on the national question either directly from Austrian Marxists (the South Slavs being part of the Austrian Socialist party) or via Moscow (Stalin himself was significantly influenced by Austro-Marxists as well). Generally, the experience of Austria–Hungary in which both Kardelj and Tito were born and raised provided a number of solutions already, from duality of the Monarchy and special federal arrangements, including sub-state and provincial autonomies, to dual citizenship (the separate citizenship regimes of Hungary and Austria). It comes as no surprise that the national question was debated within large multinational empires, such as Czarist Russia and Austria–Hungary, where the workers' movement already suffered from deep divisions along ethnonational lines. This problem forced the leaders of the Austrian Social Democrats to take the national issue into serious consideration. Their efforts to do so would result in some of the most influential contributions to the debate on the national question, some of which retain their relevance even in contemporary political circumstances.[1]

In 1897, the Austrian Socialist Party (also called *Gesamtpartei*) was transformed into a federative organization of six national parties (Ukrainian, Czech, Polish, German, Italian and Slovene) with a common executive committee.[2] Two years later, at the Congress of Brno, the programme regarding the national question was adopted in favour of transforming Austria into 'a democratic federation of nationalities'. Karl Renner was first to develop the idea of non-territorial national cultural autonomy and the 'personality principle' which argued that membership of a national association would be a matter of personal choice (Nimni 2000: xxv). Seriously concerned by the negative effects that the conflict between Czechs and Germans could have within the Socialist movement, young Otto Bauer wrote his celebrated volume *The Question of Nationalities and Social Democracy* (1907). In Bauer's view, the 'unitary nation [is] a community of education, work, and culture' (Bauer 2000 [1907]: 118). Bauer stresses the importance of 'common history' that constructs the national character and introduces, via his concept of 'a common area of habitation' (115), the *territorial* principle (which later influenced Stalin's own definition of the nation) as a necessary element of a nation's survival. However, 'communities of character' survive in spite of their being geographically separated – diasporic communities serve as proof – if they remain in contact with their culture, which as in Bauer's time, and even more today, is facilitated by modern means of communication.

Lenin's entry into the Marxist debate on the national question turned out to be decisive for the communist movement. On the issue of nations and nationalism, Lenin remained torn between his conflicting roles as *a Marxist philosopher* who pays respect to his intellectual tradition, *a socialist politician* seeking the most effective political strategy in pre-revolutionary and wartime Russia, and *the leader of the Revolution* confronted on a daily basis with complicated and changing circumstances. Lenin as philosopher stuck to classical Marxist theory, which posits a direct causal link between the bourgeoisie and the nation. In his *Critical Remarks on the National Question* (1913), Lenin stresses the utter incompatibility between Marxism and nationalism and advances a theory of two cultures in every nation, one of the dominant bourgeois class and the other one of the exploited masses. On the other hand, Lenin as a socialist politician realized the monumental political mistake socialists had been making by neglecting the national problem for so long. As with Marx and Engels before him, Lenin had to answer the question of *when* the matching of the two would be mutually beneficial (his answer being when they fight absolutism and build a bourgeois-democratic state), and under what circumstances the combination would endanger socialism (the answer here being when a mature bourgeoisie uses nationalism against the proletariat). Lenin thus distinguishes between the nationalisms of oppressing nations and those of the oppressed. Lenin therefore presented himself an ardent advocate of the right of nations to self-determination and secession. Lenin the philosopher and Lenin the political realist reconciled on the following point: although nations will eventually wither away, for the moment being they hold a strategic political importance that must not be neglected.

In 1913, the Party sent Stalin to Vienna to study Austro-Marxism and to write a response to Renner's and Bauer's theories. As often happens in these kinds of intellectual and ideological encounters, Stalin's critique revealed a high degree of contamination by the ideas of his adversaries. For him, 'a nation is a historically constituted, stable community of people, formed on the basis of a common language, territory, economic life and psychological make-up manifested in a common culture' (Stalin 1953 [1913]: 307). Lenin's distinction between two kinds of nationalisms is notably absent from his theory. Eventually, Stalin's most lasting contribution to the debate would remain the territorial principle.

Soon after the principle of self-determination was practically applied through the creation of national Soviet republics – regardless of the actual degree of their independence – the Bolsheviks were obliged to consider formal relations between these subunits and the centre. Federalism, confederalism and autonomy were debated with (again contradictory) goals in mind: how to reconcile political centralism with the territorial and political autonomy of self-determined nations? This turned out to be a perennial problem for them and all future multinational socialist federations.

Before Yugoslavia

Before April 1919 when the Communist Party of Yugoslavia (CPY) was established under the short-lived name of the Socialist Workers Party of Yugoslavia (Communists), the socialist movement in the South-Slavic lands was fragmented along existing borders and had a late start by comparison with its West European counterparts. The Social-Democratic Party of Croatia and Slavonia was established in 1894. As Dalmatia was under the tutelage of Vienna, and not of Budapest as Croatia proper and Slavonia, contacts between socialists in the south and north of today's Croatia were weak. The significantly named *Yugoslav* Social Democratic Party was established in Slovenia in 1896. On the other side of the southeastern Habsburg border, across the Danube, the Serbian Social Democratic Party was founded in 1903. In spite of this fragmentation, there was a widespread awareness of the need for closer cooperation between socialist-minded South Slavs. Nevertheless, political, economic and social differences between the Habsburg South Slavs and Serbia were impossible to ignore. These differences, in turn, influenced their respective socialist programmes as well as their views on the national question, a question that was obviously a different matter in multinational Austria–Hungary than in the nascent Serbian nation-state.

At first, Croatian socialists demanded no more than broader autonomy and did not radically question the existing relations with Budapest and Vienna (Djilas 1991: 40). But already at their second congress they called for full autonomy for Croatia, Slavonia and Dalmatia (Shoup 1968: 15). They insisted on cooperation with Serbian comrades, opposed anti-Serbian sentiments in Croatia, and believed that the diverse 'tribes' should be united into one Yugoslav nation. Serbian socialists, looking at the matter from Belgrade, acknowledged certain *national* differences (Djilas 1991: 44). They were, for the most part, internationalist and anti-imperialist – in other words, opposed to Austrian expansion in the Balkans – and advocated a Balkan federation. In 1910, the Social Democratic Parties of Serbia, Bulgaria, Romania and Greece indeed formed the Balkan Social-Democratic Federation. Serbian socialists continued to advocate a Balkan federation (with Macedonia as an entity) throughout the First World War, but the conflict between Serbia and Bulgaria made the idea unrealistic. By 1918, the left-wing of the Party called for a more viable Greater Serbian state that would incorporate Bosnia, Herzegovina and Dalmatia (Shoup 1968: 18).

Austria–Hungary's annexation of Bosnia-Herzegovina in 1908 sparked the first conflicts between Croatian and Slovenian socialists and their Serbian colleagues (Djilas 1991: 45). For Croats and Slovenes, the annexation actually meant strengthening of the South-Slavic bloc within the Monarchy, whereas Serbs perceived it as an imperialist move that would affect Serbia's own (deemed more legitimate) aspirations in Bosnia. The following year a conference of Habsburg Yugoslav socialists ('Konferencija socijalista Jugoslavena') took place in Ljubljana. At the end of the conference the highly significant 'Tivoli resolution' was adopted.[3] In the resolution, Yugoslav socialists stressed the 'colonial character' of the position in which Yugoslavs living in Austria–Hungary found themselves. The Yugoslav socialists seemed to support the Bauerian idea of autonomy for each nation in the sphere of national-cultural questions within an Austria–Hungary united as an economic region, regardless of historical boundaries. They stated three main goals of their programme: (1) the national unification of all South Slavs regardless of existing differences in name, religion, grammar and dialect or language; (2) a national constitution regardless of all artificial state, legal and political boundaries, together with a common national autonomous life for each group as 'a free unit' within a totally democratic confederation of peoples; (3) the struggle for the total democratization of the Dual Monarchy.

At the outbreak of the First World War, South-Slavic socialists were divided between several mutually exclusive possibilities for South-Slavic political independence in the twentieth century. Aleksa Djilas sums up four of the general socialist proposals as follows: (1) South Slavs would form an autonomous unit within a decentralized and liberal-democratic Habsburg monarchy (clearly without an independent Serbia and Montenegro); (2) Austria–Hungary would be transformed into a Danubian federation within which South Slavs will have their own unit (with or without Serbia and Montenegro); (3) a Balkan federation would be created with or without Habsburg South Slavs (the option advocated in Serbia) and finally, (4) an independent decentralized Yugoslav state (1991: 44). Obviously, only the fourth proposal prescribed the unification of all South Slavs within their own national state. If in the pre-1914 world it was not the most realistic vision on the table, the dramatic twists and turns of the Great War allowed it to be realized in a form that Yugoslav socialists would accept only half-heartedly. Although it did result in the actual unification of South Slavs, their independent state acquired a monarchical and conservative form.

Communists in the first Yugoslavia

Although the Yugoslav socialists were generally in favour of the new state, in April 1920 the Communist International (Comintern) presented a 'Manifesto' to the Balkan communists that called for the immediate destruction of the unjust 'Versailles' order in the Balkans and for the emancipation of oppressed nations. This implied the dismemberment of Yugoslavia, the very term being viewed by the Comintern as nothing more than another name for 'the rule of the Serbian bureaucratic and landowning oligarchy'. The solution proposed for Yugoslav nations implied their incorporation into a 'Federation of Socialist Balkan (or Balkan and Danubian) Soviet Republics'. 'Somewhat paradoxically, the Communist Party of Yugoslavia elected to endorse the goal while ignoring the prescribed means' (Connor 1984: 133). In other words, the CPY wanted Yugoslavia as such to become a member of the future Soviet Federation. Their silent defiance was confirmed in the programme adopted at the Vukovar congress only two months later in June 1920. They kept this line until the Comintern started to employ more serious measures of persuasion, which, in turn, provoked a significant theoretical and political split among Yugoslav communists.

In the founding congress' 'practical action programme', the Party advocates 'one national state with broadest autonomy of regions, counties and municipalities'. It demands, however, the 'protection of national minorities' and, interestingly, 'total juridical and political equality of non-citizens and citizens' (in Kobsa et al. 1978: 179–180). In line with classic Marxist teaching, it hails unification and centralism (but not of the bourgeois kind!) since larger economic units are beneficial to general development and, eventually, the communist revolution (Djilas 1991: 59). The communists thus oppose separatism in favour of local autonomy, insist on the primacy of class struggle and generally, until 1923 perceive the national question as yet another bourgeois trick. In 1920 the Party did extraordinarily well in the municipal elections (especially in larger cities such as Belgrade where the communist Filip Filipović was elected mayor) and in the elections for the Constituent Assembly in November of the same year, a success that propelled the CPY to the position of the third strongest party in the Parliament. However, only a month later, the CPY was outlawed by the Royal 'Pronouncement' ('Obznana'), resulting in a rapid decline in the Party's membership and political influence over the next decade.

During the years in which the national question plagued Yugoslav politics and society, the Communists' obstinate blindness to the problem only accelerated their political marginalization. In July 1922, a 'Resolution on the political situation and the Party's primary tasks' was adopted at the First CPY conference. It acknowledged that the theory of national unity, as presented by the Serbian bourgeoisie, only served the interests of Serbian imperialism. For the Party, the principle of self-determination was the only solution to all 'national and tribal' oppression, but full national and economic liberation would become possible only through revolution and within a Balkan Socialist Federal Soviet Republic (in Kobsa et al. 1978: 185). A year later the major and determining conflict on the national question erupted between the right-wing and the left-wing of the Party.

The right-wing of the Party approved the Party's earlier stance on the national question. Its leader Sima Marković portrays the national question as a matter of conflict between the Serbian, Slovenian and Croatian bourgeoisies over economic resources; the 'national' conflict thus 'blurs' what was essentially a class struggle. The Party should insist on pure class struggle, the national question being reduced to nothing more than a 'constitutional question' that could be solved by the democratization of political life and amendments to the 1921 Constitution. These would guarantee equality of Serbs, Slovenes and Croats and secure the political autonomy of the regions. Marković interestingly saw Yugoslavia as a union of sovereign nations though not of sovereign states (Djilas 1991: 69), and, therefore, he opposed federalism as an arrangement that would, as many Marxists feared, only fragment the working class (Marković 1985 [1923]). The right-wing's anti-federalist, but also anti-unitarist position provoked a backlash from the left-wing of the CPY that favoured the federal solution (Banac 1988: 54–55). The left-wing endorsed the Leninist principle of 'self-determination to secession' and rejected Marković's constitutional measures and his insistence on class struggle, since, in their opinion, the national question involved all classes. They argued that separatist nationalisms could be tolerated, provided caution was exercised regarding the 'purposefulness' of secession in each case (Cvijić 1978 [1923]: 202–203). The most prominent contributors from the left-wing faction were Đuro Cvijić and the expressionist Croatian writer August Cesarec who, in an article from August of 1923, recognized the historical importance of the South-Slavic unification but, on the other hand, rejected its present monarchic form in favour of a republican federation (1978 [1923]: 193–196).[4]

The federalists had the upper hand at the Third CPY conference in Belgrade in January 1924. The adopted 'Resolution on the National Question' for the first time links national and social emancipations in the Party's revolutionary strategy, a blend that would turn out to be critical two decades later. The Resolution accused the Serbian bourgeoisie for its initial failure at the creation of the Yugoslav nation (in Kobsa et al. 1978: 221–225). The creation of one nation in Yugoslavia was aborted at its birth, which set in motion ever-deepening national antagonisms and eventually produced three independent nations (Serbs, Croats and Slovenes). The Serbian bourgeoisie was to blame for its colonial expansionist policy against Macedonia (which had been subjected to 'Serbianization') and Albania dating back to before the First World War, its exploitation of Slovenia and Croatia (and even of their respective bourgeoisies) and the destruction of Montenegro's, Bosnia's and Vojvodina's autonomy. On the other hand, the *separation* of nations might not always be 'purposeful'. Therefore, to recognize the right to secession in the abstract would not prevent the Party's agitation against it in particular cases, because – the Resolution curiously argues, a belief that will persist somehow until the last Yugoslav Constitution of 1974 – 'the fuller the freedom to self-determination, the weaker is separatism'. The 1924 Resolution would go on to have enormous significance for the later history of Yugoslavia. The Party acknowledged the end of the Yugoslav nation-building project and emphasized the state-building of the future federal Yugoslavia. Nevertheless, during the two following decades Yugoslav communists hesitated between the total rejection of Yugoslavia – the position they adopted under the Comintern's instruction between 1924–1925 and 1934–1935 – and variations of the federalist solution.

The open factional conflicts over the national problem within the CPY forced the Comintern to react half a year later at the Fifth congress of the Communist International and to openly criticize the right-wing of the CPY. The right of nations to self-determination in the South-Slavic lands, as interpreted by the Comintern, basically meant the immediate dismemberment of royalist Yugoslavia or, what would have effectively amounted to the same thing, its profound reorganization. Stalin himself confirmed this position in March 1925. At the Fifth Plenum of the Executive Committee of the Communist International, a conflict erupted between Stalin and Sima Marković.[5] Stalin argued that the national programme of the Party must include the right of nations to self-determination and secession, or national territorial autonomy for those nationalities that would like to stay in Yugoslavia. He not only left the door open for the eventual survival of Yugoslavia as a state, but offered a very important instruction for its future organizational structure: Yugoslavia itself, he maintained, would be transformed into '*a federation of autonomous national states based upon the Soviet system* [emphasis added]' (in Kobsa et al. 1978: 229–231). Yugoslav communists followed the Comintern's orders. Until 1934–1935, the immediate dismemberment of Yugoslavia and creation of independent Slovenia, Croatia and Macedonia remained the Party's line.

From rejection to defence of Yugoslavia

The Comintern radically changed – overnight, as it were – its policy towards Yugoslavia at the end of 1934 and confirmed this new direction in 1935. Faced with Hitler's rise to power and the necessity of a strong anti-fascist coalition, the Comintern's leadership realized that encouraging Yugoslavia's dissolution had actually been serving its enemy's strategy. The CPY once more obediently followed the new line and keenly returned to the federalist formula, which was generally more acceptable to the aspirations of its rank and file. In Yugoslavia itself, the Party had lost a huge number of members and many faithful communists were either in prison or in exile. It is clear that Moscow's arcane global policies played a pivotal role in forcing the CPY to reject Yugoslavism between 1924 and 1934, but this harmful shift took place at a moment of widespread disillusionment with the Yugoslav project among non-Serb nationalities and of general discontent with King Alexander's dictatorship and his policy of integral Yugoslavism. In this context, the CPY actually rejected Yugoslavism – already understood not as nationalism but as South-Slavic inter-nationalism – in the name of an internationalism within the Balkans or even a greater regional and, eventually, world socialist federation. In spite of a whole decade of, from the perspective of later events, embarrassing behaviour vis-à-vis Yugoslavia, the CPY remained the only true *Yugoslav* political party that had any relevance throughout Yugoslavia itself (Djilas 1991: 78).

In the spring of 1934, the Comintern still encouraged the secession of Slovenia, Croatia and Macedonia from Yugoslavia. In June 1934, the CPY signed a pact with Italian and Austrian communists on the creation of a united and independent Slovenia (Shoup 1968: 39). The first signal of the change to follow was issued in December of 1934 at the CPY's Fourth National Conference. The Party suddenly stopped calling for the immediate break-up of Yugoslavia and made a historically important decision for the CPY itself (contributing in a way to its final dissolution more than a half century later) and the future socialist Yugoslavia; it obliged itself to establish separate Communist Parties of Slovenia, Croatia and Macedonia. The CP of Slovenia was indeed founded in April of 1937 with the creation of the CP of Croatia following in August that year.

The true turning point came the following year. In March 1935, the Central Committee (CC) of the CPY ceased labelling Yugoslavia an 'imperialist creation'. Instead, it stressed regional autonomy, most importantly for Croatia, but this time avoided any call for the dissolution of Yugoslavia. In June 1935, at the Split plenum of the CPY's Central Committee, the shift was publicly announced.

Yugoslavia should be preserved as a federation of autonomous national units. In 1937, the CPY dropped the term 'self-determination' from its operational vocabulary and continued to condemn separatism. But only a year later, Moscow sent another confusing signal after signing the Nazi-Soviet non-aggression agreement in August 1939. The CPY was instructed to adopt a pacifist and neutral attitude towards Yugoslavia, instead of supporting or agitating against it.

In October 1940, six months before the invasion of Yugoslavia by the Axis forces, the Fifth Conference of the CPY took place in Zagreb. Its Resolution echoes the deep national grievances and discontents that required the Party to put at the top of its political agenda 'the most important and acute task – the struggle for the national equality of the oppressed peoples and nationalities of Yugoslavia' (Tito 1978: 4). Whereas the Resolution rehearses well-known phrases, Tito's speech at this Conference deserves a closer look.[6] Tito criticizes the former Party leaders (Sima Marković and Milan Gorkić had both already disappeared in Stalin's purges)[7] for not understanding the national question. 'And all the time, the answer was there, in their own hands, had they only known it'. But what was this answer? To this question, Tito offers a rather intriguing formula: 'national autonomy, the condition for social revolution; diversity of national cultures – the condition for political uniformity'.[8] Tito significantly points to the Soviet Union as, in his opinion, 'the model for the multinational state, the model for what Yugoslavia with its varied *races* must become' [emphasis added]. In the next sentence, he fleshes out the Party's exclusive ownership of 'the solution' of the national question in Yugoslavia: 'Never forget, comrades, that the party which dares to bring this solution to Yugoslavia must become its master. And never forget that we, and we alone, have this solution'.

Wartime: Enemies or brothers?

Tito was right. Only the Party, on the eve of war, combined the solution of the national question with social emancipation. In other words, through a mutually reinforcing coalition, the federalist formula for a future multinational state could work only if combined with socialist revolution, and *vice versa*. The structural changes within the Party between 1937 and 1941, the political lessons learned, as well as the precious experience collected in prisons, in the battlefields of Spain, in the underground and in coalition with non-communist 'progressive' forces within the Popular front, had made the Party's rank and file ready for war, both ideologically and operationally. Since his appointment in December

1937, Comintern-educated Tito managed swiftly to discipline and unify the Party. The new leadership attracted many new members, especially among the young intelligentsia, coming from all Yugoslav ethnic groups. The Nazi invasion of Yugoslavia in April 1941 and the Soviet Union in June 1941 served as a trigger for the armed resistance against the occupiers and their local allies.

By November 1943 and the historic Second Session of the Anti-Fascist Council of National Liberation of Yugoslavia (AVNOJ), the Resistance movement of diverse anti-fascist forces, led and dominated by the CPY, emerged as the only credible partner of the Allies in the war against Hitler. The reasons for such a rapid ascension from being a relatively weak movement to the leading political force of the Resistance (and of the country after its liberation in May 1945) are surely manifold, but there is a general consensus that 'the brilliantly successful national policy' developed by the Communists was 'instrumental in their victory' (Shoup 1968: 60). We do not have enough space here to describe the details of the movement's constantly changing fortunes during the war, the shifts in the Party's strategy or the brutalities and crimes committed by the occupiers and local actors during the inter-ethnic and political civil war that ravaged Yugoslavia between 1941 and 1945, or, for that matter, the post-war revenges of the winners. I will mostly concentrate on the process that engendered the successful formula for post-war Yugoslav unification under Communist rule.

'Possible but not probable' would have been a good answer, had anyone asked in 1941 about the chances for Yugoslavia's resurrection. The odds that Yugoslavia would be resurrected under Communist rule seemed even more far-fetched. The CPY faced powerful occupiers as well as their local nationalist collaborators such as the White Guards in Slovenia, the notorious Ustashe in Croatia responsible for mass killings of Serbs, Jews and Roma and diverse Serbian pro-fascist formations. The Party was also facing competition from the Chetnik movement, led by general Draža Mihailović and loyal to the royal government in London. However, the Chetniks' programme for the restoration of royal Yugoslavia and a territorially and politically reinforced Serb position within the unitarist state did not have much appeal to non-Serbs, who were generally disenchanted with Yugoslavia under the Karadjordjevićs' rule. The Chetniks' general passivity against Germans and Italians, their loose military organization, a series of crimes committed against non-Serb populations (most notably in Eastern Bosnia against the Muslim population) and hostility to the Partisans that brought them ever closer to the occupiers (with whom they openly collaborated in certain regions), discredited the Chetniks as a resistance movement worthy of the Allies' support. On the other hand, the

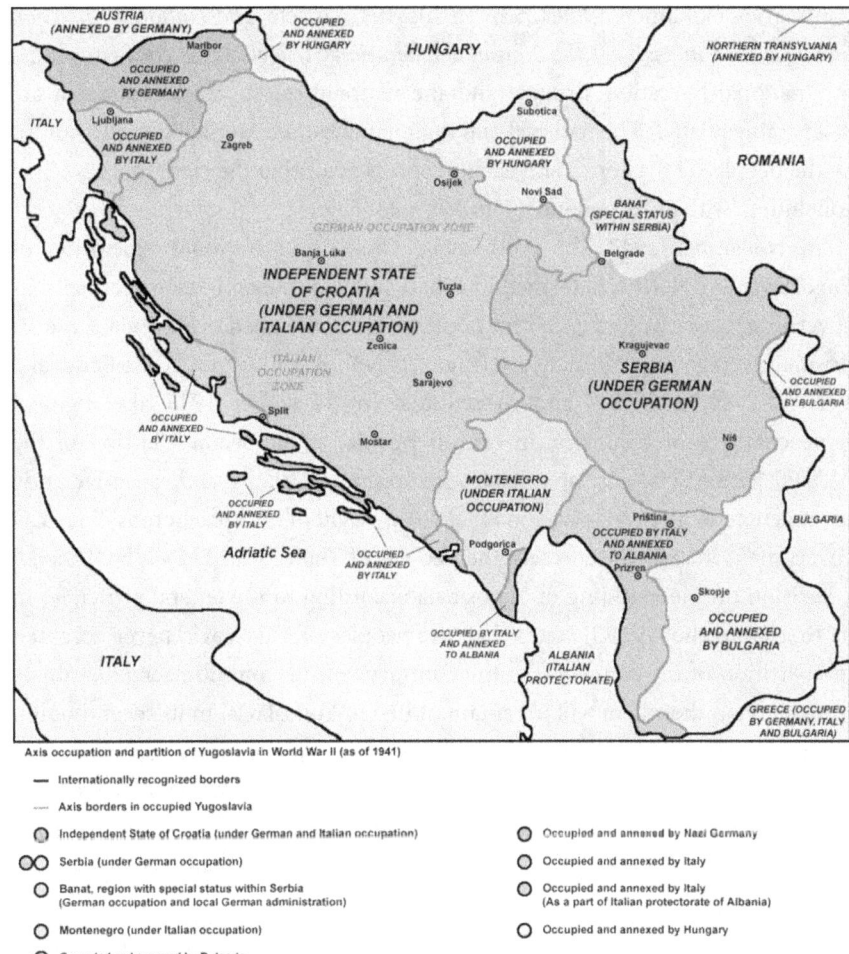

Figure 2.1 Axis occupation and partition of Yugoslavia in 1941 (Source: Wikimedia Commons).

federalist formula that implied both the restoration of Yugoslavia and the national emancipation of non-Serb nations matched perfectly well with the broad platform of the anti-fascist resistance movement and the promise of social change. This potent vision of a future political community, built on the ashes of the first Yugoslavia, secured for Tito's Partisans the necessary support base to survive, fight and eventually win the war.

The CPY proved its commitment to the federal solution by establishing, as early as August 1941, separate military commands for each region. The actual organization of the resistance struggle respected ethnic as well as historical boundaries (Vucinich 1969: 250). In his 1942 article *The National Question in Yugoslavia in Light of the National Liberation Struggle*, Tito confirmed that the 'national-liberation struggle and the national question in Yugoslavia are inseparably related'. The national and regional questions would be 'easily' solved by the people, Tito asserts, 'and each people is acquiring the right to do so', Tito concludes, 'with arms in hand' (Tito 1983: 43–53).

In November 1942, the Anti-fascist Council of National Liberation of Yugoslavia (AVNOJ) was formed in Bihać. In 1943, the anti-fascist councils, as governing legislative and executive bodies, were constituted in Slovenia, Croatia, Bosnia-Herzegovina, Montenegro (together with Boka Kotorska) and Sandžak,[9] and, in 1944, in Serbia and Macedonia. In November 1943, the regional representatives met in Jajce, in central Bosnia, at the Second Session of the AVNOJ. The AVNOJ declared itself the supreme legislative and executive body of nascent federal Yugoslavia and revoked any right of the 'treacherous' Yugoslav government in exile to represent the peoples of Yugoslavia. The AVNOJ issued a decision on the 'building of Yugoslavia according to the federal principle'. In its first point the AVNOJ states that 'the peoples of Yugoslavia never accepted the partition of the country'. On the contrary, 'in the common armed struggle [they proved] their firm will to remain united in Yugoslavia'. In its second point, federalism was evoked again as the governing principle of future Yugoslavia that would provide for the full equality of Serbs, Croats, Slovenians, Macedonians and Montenegrins, or, in other words, 'the peoples of Serbia, Croatia, Slovenia, Macedonia, Montenegro, and Bosnia and Herzegovina'. It is interesting to note that in one of the founding documents of the future socialist Yugoslavia the very definition of peoples – the Yugoslav ethnic nations[10] and/or the peoples of the constitutive republics – is imprecise and ambiguous. Two years later, on the second anniversary of the Jajce decisions, these programmatic points were translated into practice: the monarchy was abolished and replaced by the Federal People's Republic of Yugoslavia.

From brothers in arms to federated citizens

The federalist Yugoslavism, as I have shown in the previous and in this chapter, pre-dated Soviet multinational federalism. Only after Moscow's shift in policy towards Yugoslavia in 1934, was the Soviet model, so to speak, re-discovered as an existing and functioning ideal of how federalist Yugoslavism – the type of Yugoslavism that had always commanded a majority following among the

Party's members – could be translated to political reality. It is erroneous thus, in my opinion, to see 'new Yugoslavia' as a pure imitation of, or the product of blind adherence to, the Soviet model. Nevertheless, Soviet guidance was indisputably present during the initial post-war years, and Yugoslav communists looked towards Moscow for many practical solutions. How multinational federalism should actually function was one of them. Power was highly centralized and in several occasions Tito himself had to issue a public reminder of the real meaning of federalism in Yugoslavia. Immediately after the liberation of Zagreb in May 1945, Tito referred to its 'administrative' character: 'The borders of the federal states in federal Yugoslavia are not borders which divide, but borders which unite. What is the meaning of federal units in today's Yugoslavia? We don't consider them a group of small nations; rather they have a more administrative character, the freedom to govern oneself' (see Haug 2012: 110–114).

At the founding congress of the CP of Serbia in 1945, Tito, as if taken by a sudden premonition, once more warns that '... it is not our intention to create states within Yugoslavia which will make war on one another ... It is only a matter of administrative division' (in Banac 1988: 110). However, the first signs of discontent with the new federation soon arose. 'The Partisan federation was too centralist for most non-Serbs and too diffuse for the Serbs' (Banac 1988: 99). The underlying assumption was that the communist federalist formula – that famous formula that only they possessed! – would satisfy elementary national demands, whereas the real agenda – after which the national question would be finally 'eliminated' – is the socialist revolution led by the Party.

In this chapter, I have tried to provide an answer to the general question as to why Yugoslavia was brought back to life as a multinational and socialist federation, after a politically disastrous experience in the inter-war period and its complete disappearance during the Second World War. Almost a 100 years of Marxist debates on the national question resounded heavily within different fractions of the CPY; this led to their contrasting understanding of the Marxist approach to the Yugoslav case. Ultimately, the Soviet model, built on the Leninist–Stalinist interpretation and concrete decisions taken during the October Revolution and the ensuing Civil War, as well as the Comintern's political decisions, had the upper hand. However, this model was not simply *imported* from the Soviet Union. The federalist position was advocated within the Party by its left-wing in the first half of the 1920s and, despite the Comintern caesura between 1924–1925 and 1934–1935, remained the dominant position among Yugoslav communists vis-à-vis Yugoslavia as state. What I call in this chapter 'the federalist formula for the socialist re-unification of Yugoslavia' proved, eventually, to be an effective tool and possibly the most decisive element of the communist-dominated Resistance's victory in the Second World War. The formula would be constantly questioned, both by its partisans and adversaries, in multiple constitutional and institutional changes and never-ending debates on how to organize the political and economic life of a multinational federation, decisively for Yugoslavia's existence as state between 1989 and 1991.

In a nutshell, Yugoslav communists made three important wartime promises: liberation, a solution to the national question and social emancipation. The first promise was kept in 1945, but the attempts to keep to the other two, inextricably bound together, were to determine the fate of Yugoslavia. National and social emancipations were perceived as conditional upon each other: there could be no socialism without a satisfactory solution to the national question, and, conversely, no satisfactory solution to the national question could be possible without a successful socialist revolution. This implied that every crisis of socialism (economic or political) would cast doubt on the Yugoslav communist solution to the national question. National grievances, on the other hand, inevitably put in question the legitimacy of the socialist regime. In the next chapter, I sketch a history of socialist Yugoslavia as the story of constant efforts to keep these two wartime promises. To keep them meant also to preserve Yugoslavia as a framework for both socialism and the national emancipation of Yugoslav nations and nationalities. The widespread dissatisfaction with the socialist regime and the economic crisis experienced in the 1980s implied also dissatisfaction with the existing solution to the national question and, unavoidably, with Yugoslavia itself.

Part Two

From Socialist Re-Integration to the Second Disintegration

3

Brothers Re-United! Federal Citizenship in Socialist Yugoslavia

Centralist federalism, 1945–1967

The first phase of federalism in post-war Yugoslavia can be named 'administrative federalism' by borrowing Tito's own definition of the federal units as having only an 'administrative character'. However, the matter was not at all purely administrative. It involved the re-creation of the Yugoslav polity and at the same time a laborious construction of sub-state entities and their own political communities. The creation of separate republican citizenship was part and parcel of this intensive construction of modern states within a larger federation. New Yugoslavia was established as a federation of six republics (Slovenia, Croatia, Bosnia-Herzegovina, Montenegro, Serbia and Macedonia), one autonomous province (Vojvodina) and one autonomous region (Kosovo), both within Serbia. The republics were established according to ethnic but also historic criteria that resulted in one major exception (Bosnia-Herzegovina) to the general rule that units should be ethnonational homes for their titular nationalities. Another exception was autonomous Vojvodina within Serbia, established because of its separate history from Serbia proper and its multiethnic composition that would, however, soon be dominated by a Serb majority. Due to its large ethnic Albanian population, Kosovo was formed as an autonomous region (*oblast*) – a lower status than that of a province (*pokrajina*) – and was immediately under martial law after the war. Montenegro might be seen as a cross between a historic state and an ethnically based republic. The debate on whether Montenegrins are a separate nation (they were recognized in socialist Yugoslavia as titular group in their own republic) or a regionally defined part of the larger Serbian nation (the belief still held by one third of contemporary Montenegrins who identify themselves as Serb) is still ongoing.

In this context, it is important to mention the political destiny of the Muslim-populated Sandžak region divided between Serbia and Montenegro. During the war Sandžak had its own land assembly that was on an equal footing with other land assemblies. A separate Sandžak land assembly was a political concession to the region's Muslim population that was not significantly present among the Partisans. After the war the region faced several possible scenarios: unification with Bosnia-Herzegovina and autonomy (the solution favoured by the Muslims of Sandžak), unification with either Serbia or Montenegro or division between Serbia and Montenegro. The last option eventually prevailed in the spring of 1945 as Sandžak was judged by the Anti-Fascist Council of National Liberation of Yugoslavia (AVNOJ) to have no 'national basis' for autonomy. As for the 'borders that unite', disputes and conflicts erupted immediately after the war between Croatia and Serbia over the Srem/Srijem region that had been put under Croatian command during the war but was mostly Serb-populated, between Croatia and Montenegro over Boka Kotorska (historically part of Habsburg Dalmatia but mostly ethnically Montenegrin) and over Sandžak (see Banac 1988: 100–108).

In early 1946, the first post-war Constitution was adopted and the country established itself as the Federal People's Republic of Yugoslavia (FNRJ). Its first article reads as follows:

> The Federative People's Republic of Yugoslavia is a federal people's state republican in form, a community of peoples equal in rights who, on the basis of the right of self-determination, including the right of separation, have expressed their will to live together in a federative state. (*Constitution of FPRY* 1947)

Its article 9 proclaims that 'the sovereignty of people's republics (…) is limited only by the rights which by this Constitution are conferred on the Federative People's Republic of Yugoslavia'. The following article (10) deemed *unconstitutional* 'any act directed against the sovereignty, equality and national freedom of the peoples of FPRY and their people's republic'. As explained in article 1, each republic had the right of self-determination 'including the right of separation'.

This point caused confusion over whether this right had been already used or whether it remained there for eventual future use. The leading Yugoslav Marxist Moša Pijade explained in a letter to Colonel Vlado Strugar that the republics had already exercised their right to unite and not to secede (see Hondius 1968: 141–143). Therefore, the right of secession 'is only in connection with the origin of the FNRJ and not in order to ensure that our republics still have today the right of separation'. Pijade insists that it was an irreversible act of unification (Djilas 1991: 167), the act brought into being during the common resistance struggle. Pijade obviously considered the recent armed struggle politically more significant than a referendum: spilled blood in the place of a cast ballot!

Although the republics were nominally sovereign, their power was curtailed by the Constitution itself that clearly underlined the prevalence of the centre. Article 9 provided that certain rights belonged exclusively to the Federation, whereas article 11 stated that the republican constitutions were to conform to the federal constitution (see Djilas 1991: 161; Shoup 1968: 114). In the case of a discrepancy, the federal laws were supposed to supersede those of the republics. The Constitution also established a bicameral federal Parliament that consisted of the Federal council representing the population (50,000 inhabitants for one deputy) and the Council of Nationalities to which every republic sent 30 delegates, whereas Vojvodina had 20 and Kosovo 15 seats.

In light of the future constitutional and political development of Yugoslav federalism, it is interesting to note that the 1946 Constitution established separate republican ministries of education without a similar federal body. This immediately created a problem over the school textbooks in the sensitive areas of history and literature, the pillars of any Eastern European nation-building: Montenegro, Bosnia and Macedonia required the common approach, whereas Croatia, Slovenia and Serbia opposed it (Lampe 2000: 237). The educational

Figure 3.1 Yugoslavia 1945–1991 (Source: The Cartographic Section of the United Nations).

curricula were never unified and the differences in content and interpretations of events or literary works only grew in the following years (see Wachtel 1998).

The 1946 Constitution is largely seen as a copy of the Soviet 1936 Constitution. Edvard Kardelj himself admitted that this was the inspiration. 'For us the model was the Soviet Constitution, since the Soviet federation is the most positive example of the solution of relations between peoples in the history of Mankind' (in Hondius 1968: 137). Nevertheless, in spite of Kardelj's enthusiastic praise for the Soviet model and the widespread opinion that the 1946 Constitution was a clear case of plagiarism – an opinion that was more often than not automatically repeated by many scholars of Yugoslavia – there are some significant differences.

One can agree with Hondius that '[t]he Yugoslav Constitution was partly an original product, partly a copy of the Stalin Constitution' (1968: 150). The origins of Soviet and Yugoslav federalism were quite different. The long-existing tradition of federalist Yugoslavism eventually matched the Soviet model of a multinational federation, but the USSR was an ideological union of different nationalities – thus its non-national and non-geographic name – whereas Yugoslavia was established as a South-Slavic (supra)national state. One of the most conspicuous differences between the two is evident in the guiding principle according to which the subunits were formed: Yugoslavs did not follow the Soviets by applying exclusively ethnonational standards, but created historic (Bosnia-Herzegovina, Vojvodina and to a large extent Montenegro) as well as ethnonational subunits and paid more attention to history, though not always, than their Soviet role models in determining their borders. Among the more specific departures from the Soviet model was the granting of larger fiscal powers to the republics (Lampe 2000: 234; Rusinow 1977: 17). Also, by 1948 each republic had its own communist party. However, Yugoslavs did not follow the Soviets in granting to some republics the right to have their own foreign ministries and their own armies. Yugoslavs would soon distance themselves even further from their Soviet teachers only two years later when the romance with Moscow came to its abrupt end. This would push them to develop new original formulae for 'really existing socialism' in a multinational federal country.

The ideological brainstorming between 1948 and 1953 resulted in the 1953 Constitutional Law that significantly altered the 1946 Constitution. Article 1 defines the FPR of Yugoslavia as a 'socialist federal state of sovereign and equal nations' (*Ustavni zakon* 1988 [1953]). However, the following article (2) clarifies that 'all power in the FPRY belongs to the working people'. The 'working people' of Yugoslavia, as a newly constructed supreme sovereign body, was obviously supposed to supersede the individual, although still 'sovereign and equal' nations. The confusion over supremacy and sovereignty would mark future constitutional attempts as well. The working class and the working people would be often mentioned as sovereign alongside with Yugoslav nations, the republics and, finally, all citizens. We can see here that four different legitimacy principles were in conflict, which is important to bear in mind for later developments. 'Working people' was supposed to include all working citizens of Yugoslavia, not only the working class as the pillar of a socialist regime. In addition, initially five and later six nations were sovereign as well and had the right of self-determination. Furthermore, six republics including their citizens, regardless of ethnicity, were also sovereign and had the same rights (later the right of secession as well). Finally, the Federation as such represented the totality of all citizens. It was clear from the start that the very constitutional definitions of these overlapping 'sovereign' bodies invited different ways of imagining political community or communities and thus constant and necessarily conflicting re-interpretations.

The 1953 Constitutional Law itself did not include the right of self-determination and secession of the republics. This elision corresponded to Moša Pijade's influential and original interpretation that the single-use right of self-determination' had not been exercised as a right to secede but to unite.[1] The right itself thus became obsolete. This significant change was rooted in the widespread belief among the Yugoslav political elite that the national question had been solved once and for all and that the Yugoslav socialist consciousness was about to develop. The Yugoslav constitutional architect Edvard Kardelj explained the constitutional changes by a new development that had brought into being a 'unified Yugoslav community' that would overcome the national consciousness of individual nations but would not become a new nation (in Djilas 1991: 180). Nevertheless, the lawmakers were not unanimous on the question of sovereignty: the centralists wanted the question to be avoided altogether and the true character of the Yugoslav Federation to be finally recognized, whereas those coming from the republics sensitive to federalism (Macedonia, Croatia) defended the constitutional notion of republican sovereignty (Shoup 1968: 191–192).

The establishment of the Council of Producers (*Vijeće proizvođača*) in place of the Council of Nationalities (*Vijeće naroda*) confirmed the new ideological line centred on socialist self-management. Historians of Yugoslavia (Djilas 1991: 179; Lampe 2000: 261) usually interpret this, together with the loss of the right of secession, as a step towards the withering away of the republics. The Constitutional Law also appointed Tito as president of the FNRJ and established the Federal Executive Council (SIV). The Federal Council (*Savezno vijeće*) itself consisted mostly of the members representing their constituencies (one deputy for 60,000 Yugoslavs), whereas republican or provincial authorities delegated a total of 60 members. The Constitutional Law made possible the direct election of deputies. Nonetheless, the deputies were mostly indirectly elected and delegated to the Parliament, which signalled the Party's orientation – under Kardelj's influence – towards a total rejection of direct political representation judged to be too 'bourgeois' (Rusinow 1977: 77).

These constitutional changes, as noted above, were primarily motivated by the conflict with the USSR and the ideological competition between the two socialist states. Fostering of Yugoslav unity, on one hand, seemed necessary in the face of the Soviet threat, but, on the other, was a product of the sincere belief that once the national question had been solved by the internal federal organization of Yugoslavia, all energy should be invested into the building of a single socialist society. The insistence on an all-Yugoslav unity of the working class echoed the Marxist imperative that, in spite of the administrative and political divisions within the state and the Party, the unity of the working class and the Party itself should not be jeopardized.

Only eight years later preparations for a new constitutional experiment began under the leadership of the unavoidable Kardelj who joined forces with the Croatian leader Vladimir Bakarić and other more liberal politicians (Rusinow 1977: 155). The fruit of this two-year labour was a new, ambitious Constitution that was adopted in April 1963. It sought to codify all Yugoslav political, social and economic experiments with socialism after the official introduction of self-management in 1950 and the 1953 Constitutional Law. The country was significantly renamed the *Socialist Federal Republic of Yugoslavia* (SFRJ). The term 'state' was replaced with 'social community' and 'socio-political community'. The text itself consisted of nine principles followed by 259 articles (*Constitution of SFRY* 1963). It is important to note here the first basic principle and its significant wording:

> The peoples of Yugoslavia, on the basis of the right of every people to self-determination, including the right to secession, on the basis of their common struggle and their will freely declared in the People's Liberation War and Socialist Revolution, and in accord with their historical aspirations, aware that the further consolidation of their brotherhood and unity is to their common interest, have united in a federal republic of free and equal peoples and nationalities and have founded a socialist federal community of working people, the Socialist Federal Republic of Yugoslavia (…)

Article 1 again redefined Yugoslavia as 'a federal state of voluntary united and equal peoples and a socialist democratic community based on the powers of the working people and on self-government' [a more common translation would be 'self-management', Ustav 1971].

As for the relations between the centre and the republics, one can say that the republics gained some significant concessions. The right to self-determination and secession was mentioned again in the first basic principle and the republics' legislative powers were broadened. The Constitution mentioned voluntary cooperation among the republics and institutionalized the practice that equal representation should determine the composition of the Federal Executive Council (article 226).

Nonetheless, it could be generally concluded that the power of the centre was confirmed. Rusinow notes that the republics – defined now as 'state socialist democratic communities' (art. 108) – had not been reinforced vis-à-vis the centre, but that enterprises, communes and other self-managing associations had been (1977). For Hondius the new Constitution proved the Yugoslav leaders' intention to start 'transition from the hierarchical to the organic state community' (1968: 311). In this sense, enterprises, associations and republics themselves were all seen as communities; the Federation being, in the words of legal scholar Jovan Đorđević, 'a community of communities' (in Hondius 1968: 312).

The Federal Assembly was radically reformed and divided into five chambers, four of which represented citizens by their economic or social-political function (economy, education and culture, welfare and health and organizational-political chamber), whereas the fifth was the reformed Council of Nationalities (now consisting of ten members from each republic and five from each autonomous province). To understand citizens' engagement, delegation and representation as well as political legitimacy, one has to take into account a special Yugoslav political model. Besides self-management at the workplace, direct elections were practised only at the lowest communal level. After that, the communal and republican assemblies delegated members to the Federal Assembly. As mentioned before, for Kardelj this was a radical departure from the bourgeois-democratic concepts of parliament and political representation (Kardelj 1977: 97–102, 119–133; Rusinow 1977: 152). Rusinow explains that the Yugoslav voter enjoyed triple representation: as a citizen-consumer in the political chambers, as a citizen-producer in the corporate chambers (if employed in 'working communities') and as a member of an ethnic group represented by a republic or province in the Chamber of

Nationalities (1977: 151). Bosnia-Herzegovina as a non-ethnic republic, but some other republics as well, paid special attention to the equal representation of all major ethnic groups in its bodies.

To sum up, the 1963 Constitution could be seen not as a turning point of Yugoslav federalism, but as a moment of hesitation. Although centralist federalism was underlined as the norm of the constitutional and political organization of Yugoslavia, the 1963 Constitution unleashed a political dynamic that would lead towards more decentralization and would even encourage liberal trends. This became evident after the fall of the leading centralist and chief of the state security apparatus Aleksandar Ranković in 1966 and the adoption of the first amendments to the 1963 Constitution already in 1967.

Bifurcated citizenship

On 28 August 1945, the law on citizenship of Democratic Federal Yugoslavia was enacted. It was slightly modified a year later after the adoption of the 1946 Constitution of the FNRJ.[2] The law had an important function in establishing the initial body of citizens of the 'new' Yugoslavia. Yugoslav citizenship was primarily based on the principle of origin (*ius sanguinis*; see Jovanović 1977: 22; Medvedović 1998: 27–29; Tepić and Bašić 1969: xxxvi). Its article 35 provided that everyone who had been a Yugoslav citizen on 28 August 1945, under the 1928 citizenship act of the Kingdom of Yugoslavia, would become a citizen of the Democratic Federal Yugoslavia. Some of its provisions revealed an intention to underscore the South-Slavic character of the country and also to revoke citizenship from internal ideological wartime enemies who either collaborated with the occupiers or had emigrated abroad. Since it was often impossible, due to the widespread destruction caused by the war, to prove former Yugoslav citizenship, article 25 proclaimed that anyone belonging to one of the 'peoples' of Yugoslavia (i.e. to one of the South-Slavic ethnic groups), those born and raised on the territory of Yugoslavia and permanent residents of the FPRY would be considered citizens of the FPRY. Article 9 also facilitated acquisition of Yugoslav citizenship for persons belonging to 'any of the peoples of the FNRY' and coming from regions outside its current borders, i.e. to any of the South-Slavic nations, but not for members of *nationalities* considered to have their national home outside Yugoslavia.

Furthermore, in 1948 the law on citizenship was revised in order to exclude from Yugoslav citizenship all citizens of German ethnicity residing abroad on the basis of their 'disloyal conduct toward the national and state interests of the peoples of the FPRY'. In the same year, an unusually named law on the deprivation of citizenship was enacted as well.[3] By these two legal provisions, an unwanted minority – a vast majority of almost 500,000 Germans living mostly in Slavonia and Vojvodina – together with ideological adversaries were excluded from the initial citizenry of the new Yugoslavia.

The status of another largely unwanted minority – namely, ethnic Italians residing in the coastal parts of Slovenia and Croatia – was regulated by separate acts and treaties between Yugoslavia and Italy. A special act related to Yugoslav citizenship – the law on citizenship of Persons Residing on the Territory Annexed to Yugoslavia according to the Peace Treaty with Italy[4] – was adopted in 1947 following the Paris Peace Treaty between Yugoslavia and Italy. According to this act, persons who as of 10 June 1940 were residents of the territories annexed by Yugoslavia were to lose their Italian citizenship and acquire Yugoslav citizenship. Ethnic Italians had a one-year period to opt for Italian citizenship – in effect, to opt for whether they wanted to live in Yugoslavia or Italy. In addition, an equivalent offer of Yugoslav citizenship was made to the Slavic population from the contested border region between Yugoslavia and Italy.[5]

The first law on citizenship immediately established a two-tier or bifurcated citizenship in post-war Yugoslavia. Article 1, paragraph 2 of the 1945/46 law on Yugoslav citizenship stated that: 'Every citizen of a people's republic is *simultaneously* a citizen of the FPRY and every citizen of the FPRY is *in principle* a citizen of a people's republic.' Article 48 of the 1946 Constitution of the FPRY established that 'every citizen of a republic enjoys in every republic the same rights as the citizens of that republic'. The 1953 Constitutional Law (article 12) contains the same provision. The 1963 Constitution, however, coupled these rights with duties (article 118), a measure that was also incorporated into the 1974 Constitution of the SFRY (Jovanović 1977: 22).

As mentioned in the previous chapter, the republic-level citizenships of the constitutive republics were established on the basis of municipal membership or *zavičajnost* (Jovanović 1977: 14–17, 26) and Yugoslav citizens were allowed to have only one, clearly established republican citizenship. The municipal units of the republican Ministries of the Interior started evidencing republican citizens as of 1947 (1977: 45–46). Although it is a widespread opinion – among those rare scholars who examined this issue – that republican citizenship was an almost irrelevant administrative and legal measure in socialist Yugoslavia, it is clear that from the very beginning it had a political function. According to the Voting Registers Law of 10 August 1945 and of 17 July 1946, only citizens of a particular republic had the right to vote in that republic and in the voter's registration form their republican citizenship had to be stated (*Zakon o biračkim spiskovima* 1947: 32). Citizens from other Yugoslav republics who happened to *reside* on the territory of that republic were not allowed to vote there. Republican People's Assemblies were supposed to be elected only by citizens of these republics, although some republics, such as Croatia, in the following years allowed both its citizens and its residents to participate in the election of delegates for the Croatian Parliament (Hondius 1968: 184). Yugoslav citizenship and permanent residence in a republic were general conditions for participation and voting at the first democratic elections in 1990 as well.[6] These electoral rules were fashioned by republican socialist authorities and with respect to valid federal laws that guaranteed all Yugoslav citizens the same rights and duties throughout the still existing Federation. However, one cannot fail to see that Yugoslav citizens entered liberal politics through the republics whose citizenship they possessed (the large majority of voters) or in which they permanently resided, and not as federal voters. This would have serious political consequences during the decisive years of 1990 and 1991 (see Chapters 6 and 7). After the break-up of Yugoslavia, republican-level citizenship became essential in determining the initial citizenry of the new states. In other words, republican citizenships became the only strong criterion for political inclusion or exclusion (see Chapter 9).

Another striking feature of bifurcated citizenship in Yugoslavia – another element that since the beginning had been silently reinforcing the power of the republics vis-à-vis the federation – was that only the republic-level registries of citizens existed in Yugoslavia between 1945 and 1991.[7] Thanks to the republic-level registries, after the dissolution of Yugoslavia, all former Yugoslav republics were in a position to adopt the policy of legal continuity between previous republic-level citizenship and citizenship of the new state.

During the era of socialist Yugoslavia, three laws on Yugoslav citizenship were enacted (in 1945/1946, in 1964 and in 1976) following the major constitutional changes in 1945/1946, 1963 and in 1974. They also defined the relationship between federal and the republic-level citizenship. The 1945/1946 changes provided federal citizenship for Yugoslav citizens who were concurrently – 'in principle' – citizens of constituent republics. In turn, all citizens of constituent republics were *simultaneously* citizens of the FNRY. The 1964 law, however, provided for a *united* Yugoslav citizenship (article 1), made republican citizenship conditional upon federal citizenship and declared that republican citizenship would be lost with the loss of federal citizenship (article 2, paragraph 2).[8] The 1976 law on Yugoslav citizenship contained a similar provision and added an article (22) on how to resolve disputes caused by the republics' varying laws on citizenship.[9] These norms regulated the citizenship status of a newborn child either according to the citizenship laws valid in the republic of which the child's parents were citizens or, if the parents did not have the same citizenship, according to the citizenship laws of the republic where the child was born. The norms also offered an option for parents of different citizenships to agree on the citizenship of their child as well as, if the parents could not agree, a possibility for naturalization of the child in the republic of his or her birth. What was mostly an administrative hurdle for new parents, if they migrated within Yugoslavia or came from different republics, was exactly what would turn to be of outmost importance for their children (often unaware of their republican citizenship) when the country disappeared. Those whose families kept in order their 'archives' managed to navigate more or less successfully the post-Yugoslav administrative labyrinths and traps. Those who were not that lucky had a much more difficult path towards full citizenship status in the new states.

The republic-level laws on citizenship were fashioned in order to be in harmony with the federal law on citizenship. In general, they were similar, but they also varied to a certain extent from one republic to the next. They were adopted in three waves, in 1950, in 1965 and in the period between 1975 and 1979. In order to understand their role and the nature of the changes, I briefly present below the case of Croatian citizenship, a case that fairly represents the citizenship-related legislation of other Yugoslav republics as well.

In 1950, the law on citizenship of the People's Republic of Croatia provided that the basic principle for acquisition of Croatian republican citizenship was *ius sanguinis*.[10] However, and this is where the administrative procedure imagines different scenarios, if parents of a newborn child had different republican citizenships, the child could acquire Croatian citizenship if both parents agreed. If they did not agree and they had residence in Croatia, the child would automatically acquire Croatian citizenship. If the parents did not have residence in Croatia but the father had Croatian citizenship, the child would become a Croatian citizen as well. The 1965 law on citizenship of the Socialist Republic of Croatia brought some changes to the procedure.[11] Croatian citizenship was automatically granted if a child was born in Croatia and both parents had Croatian citizenship. In all other cases, parents had to agree on the child's citizenship. In the 1977 law on citizenship of the Socialist Republic of Croatia, we observe some new changes related to the acquisition of citizenship.[12] *Ius sanguinis* remained the automatic criterion for acquiring Croatian citizenship;

if both parents were Croatian citizens, the child would automatically become a Croatian citizen. However, if only one parent were a Croatian citizen, the parents then had to agree. In cases in which the parents did not agree or did not sign a statement during the two months following the birth of their child, Croatian citizenship was automatically accorded to the child if the parents had permanent residence in Croatia. If the parents did not have permanent residence in Croatia, the child would acquire Croatian citizenship if his/her birth was registered in Croatia's registry of births.[13]

Those were the legal attempts at establishing clearly who belonged to what federal entity. The administrators were doing their job, more or less accurately, while the 'ordinary citizens' came across complex citizenship matters only when dealing with the administrative offices and tended generally to forget about them the moment they solved their pressing problems. In their almost complete ignorance of these matters, the nature and functioning of their citizenship regimes, understood here in its legal and political dimensions, was changing not only by laws or administrative measure but also by the political and constant constitutional processes, the dynamic intra-party politics (or the separate republican parties' competition), as well as by wider socio-cultural debates in a rapidly modernizing society such was Yugoslav. Above I explained the importance of the changing nature of Yugoslav federalism for better understanding of what it meant to be a Yugoslav citizen. Equally important for Yugoslav citizenship was the system of self-management and the unrelenting process of decentralization.

Self-management, decentralization and citizenship

The constitutional changes cannot be seen or analysed separately from the general trend of decentralization that modestly began in the early 1950s. The expulsion of Yugoslavia from the communist family by its *pater familias* Stalin forced the Yugoslav leadership to find theoretical justifications for their rebellious position. In this politically precarious situation and in the midst of purges launched within Yugoslavia against *Stalinists*, Milovan Djilas re-read Marx's early writings and found the principle of socialist self-management that implied anti-bureaucratism and anti-*etatism*, both of which were associated with Stalin's USSR. In Djilas' own account of events, he recalls that in the spring of 1950 he suggested that Marx's idea of the free association of producers should be implemented in Yugoslavia. He explained this to Kardelj and to the leading Yugoslav economist Boris Kidrič (while sitting in a car in front of Djilas' villa). The idea was hotly debated in the Party's inner circles for months and was finally embraced by Tito (Rusinow 1977: 50–51). As early as 26 June 1950, the National Assembly adopted the first laws on self-management that would become the trademark of Yugoslav socialism. In short, they claimed control of the economy for the workers and direct democratic control over political bodies for the citizens, with the ultimate goal of the 'withering away of the state', i.e. the creation of a classless and stateless communist society.

The first decentralization measures were tested in the politically less charged economic field. By April 1951, only railways, the postal service and river and air transport were left to central control (Lampe 2000: 256). Self-management meant social ownership of the means of production by those who actually produce. However, the central state did not give away its leverage. The heavy taxation of profits meant that it kept a grip on self-managing production units. However, the process had started and it required constant changes and reforms that would in the decades to come become increasingly market oriented (Unkovski-Korica 2015). It would also empower local actors, factory managers closely related to the republican elites and the republics themselves. Little wonder that Yugoslavia soon faced an economic competition between republics as well as sharp inequalities in economic performance and standards of living between the more developed republics and provinces such as Slovenia, Croatia and Vojvodina and those less developed such as Bosnia, Kosovo and Macedonia. In spite of solidarity mechanisms such as the funds for the underdeveloped republics, Yugoslavia soon experienced its most complex political conflicts over economic issues. Self-management, in spite of frequent criticism that it actually never empowered workers enough or that managers and party cadres actually ran the workplaces and in spite of all its imperfections in a developing country, remains, however, the biggest experiment in economic democracy ever undertaken. As such it attracted international attention during its existence (e.g. Pateman 1970: 85–102; Zukin 1975) and continues to do so (Lebowitz 2013; Suvin 2014: 219–359; Unkovski-Korica 2015), especially in the context of intensive thinking about economic alternatives to neoliberal capitalism, the growing importance of workers' cooperatives and some concrete steps in introducing self-management in different forms in certain Latin American states. Self-management was based on the idea that people should not only govern political structures and be equal in rights in front of the law but also that equality and democratic control should necessarily, for democracy to flourish, be introduced in the workplace where most of the people spend most of their time. In this respect, we can claim that self-management was an important part of the Yugoslav socialist citizenship regime in its political empowerment of citizens-workers.

More far-reaching political changes followed the introduction of self-management. In 1952, at the Sixth Congress of the CPY in Zagreb, the Party was renamed the *League of Communists of Yugoslavia*. Djilas claims that this was again his idea; only later did he remember that it was what Marx had called the First International (Rusinow 1977: 75f). The *nomen* was an *omen* of departure from the Leninist style of monolithic party structure and a signal of general democratization that included the delegation of all power to the 'base' (communes and factories). The LCY was supposed to maintain for itself the leading ideological role within the general socialist movement and to remain apart from both the state and the economy. This had far-reaching effects, particularly visible more than a decade later with political decentralization and economic liberalization. Rusinow notes that three new Executive committee members who replaced the Party's politburo were also the heads of republics (Vladimir Bakarić of Croatia, Lazar Koliševski of Macedonia, and Djuro Pucar of Bosnia) and four members neither lived in Belgrade nor executed any federal political functions. 'This, too, was a more important real harbinger of future developments than the formal downgrading of the status of the republics in the Constitutional law' (1977: 76).

Party congresses often announced future constitutional changes. Therefore, at the next Seventh Congress in 1958, the LCY recognized 'individuality, equality, and the right to self-determination of all Yugoslav peoples (…) as well as their unity on the basis of federal state structures'. Although the right of self-determination was mentioned again and was to be re-introduced to the Constitution five years later, the Party was still insisting on 'socialist, Yugoslav consciousness' and its development in a 'socialist community of peoples' (in Shoup 1968: 207).[14]

The next Eighth Congress of the LCY in 1964 turned out to be decisive for the decentralization of Yugoslavia that would soon proceed at an ever-growing pace. Only a year after the 1963 Constitution was adopted – the Constitution that displayed strong centralizing elements! – decentralization or, more precisely, federalization of the Party was put in motion, which signalled the move towards what I call 'centrifugal federalism' (see Chapter 4) and the corresponding constitutional changes. The statute adopted at the Eighth Congress emphasized the 'independence' of the republican parties and provided that in the future the republican congresses would assemble *before* the central congress of the LCY. They were supposed to determine 'the policies, positions, and tasks' of the republican Leagues of Communists that should be 'in harmony' with the policy of the LCY (Lampe 2000: 286; Shoup 1968: 213). It is important to note that the national question was the central topic of the reports delivered by leading political figures, including Tito, Kardelj and Veljko Vlahović (in Kobsa et al. 1978: 354–359), with the exception of Aleksandar Ranković.

At the congress, Kardelj significantly talked about 'national economic independence' as a 'special way of self-management of the working people'. He openly supported decentralization and stated that self-managing peoples should enjoy the fruits of their own labour as individual workers (Budding 2008: 103). Kardelj explicitly equated peoples with republics and, more importantly, with individual workers. Some new elements clearly entered into his theory justifying the national existence of the republics on economic grounds, which was, according to Paul Shoup, a reversal of his original intent. The motives behind both Tito's and Kardelj's abandonment of their earlier insistence on broader Yugoslav consciousness are to be found in the strong resistance that this policy met, the importance of Croatia and Slovenia in fighting the opposition to economic reforms and the fear of Ranković's centralist faction (Shoup 1968: 225).

Simultaneous to these changes within the Party was a renaissance of parliamentary life after the adoption of the 1963 Constitution and the ensuing elections. '[It] became, virtually overnight, more exciting and effective than in any other Communist single-party State' (Rusinow 1977: 152). The movement seemed to be orientated towards real parliamentarism, but as Burg concludes, the actual direction was towards *immobilisme* (Burg 1983: 76). This, however, proves that certain institutional measures dynamized – even beyond expectations of their creators – the political life in Yugoslavia and, to the surprise of many conservative communists such as Ranković, actually pushed liberal decentralizing trends forward. They also empowered local players, a development that would become decisive in the years to come (see Rusinow 1977: 154–156). According to Sabrina Ramet, the reforms that took place between 1963 and 1965 established a balance-of-power system in Yugoslavia. And the fundamental principle of this system was that no single actor (republic) had sufficient power to dictate terms unilaterally to the others (Ramet 1992).

The opposition to progressive decentralization of the Party and the state was finally crushed during the Fourth Party plenum at Brioni in 1966 with the fall of Aleksandar Ranković, the chief of the omnipresent state security for twenty years since the war. The defeat of Ranković and his followers signalled a huge push for liberally oriented anti-centralists. The Party itself was immediately reformed. Its former power was reduced and its administrative organization cautiously refashioned to prevent the accumulation of power in certain organs or, even worse, in the hands of influential individuals. Tito's leading position was, of course, not questioned and he continued to lead the Party, but this time as president and not as secretary general as before. Dennison Rusinow stresses the significant events taking place at the end of 1966: Ranković and his group were pardoned (although harsh measures were required by some Party organs), Milovan Djilas was released from prison, and the Slovene government resigned after a proposed bill on social insurance taxes was overturned in the Slovene republican assembly. This was, as Rusinow points out, the first time that a Communist government in a one-Party system resigned because of a parliamentary non-confidence vote (see 1977: 197–202).

If, as I noted, the 1963 Constitution was a moment of constitutional hesitation, the ensuing four years could be branded as a period of intensive decision-making intended to provide the country with a political stability that would emanate from its subunits and not from its centre. The events from the Eighth Party congress in 1964 to its Fourth plenum in 1966 and the first constitutional amendments in 1967 generated the centrifugal logic of distribution of political and institutional power. In his study on 'conflict and cohesion' in socialist Yugoslavia, Burg reiterates that the Yugoslav leadership tried to produce a system of conflict regulation in order to prevent inter-republican, i.e. inter-ethnic, conflicts. The strategy of decentralization was actually conceived as a strategy to preserve the integrity of the Yugoslav state, but it eventually produced deeper divisions and created conflicting blocs that were, in turn, more often than not identified with ethnic groups (1983: 3–4, 6). This description reveals clearly the logic of centrifugal federalism to which we turn in the next chapter.

4

Brothers as Partners: Centrifugal Federalism, Confederal Citizenship and Complicated Partnership

Centrifugal federalism, 1967–1974

Introducing centrifugal federalism: The constitutional amendments, 1967–1971

Between 1967 and 1974 Yugoslavia entered a period of intensive constitutional change that started with a series of amendments to the 1963 Constitution and ended with the adoption of a new Yugoslav Constitution in 1974, its fourth in thirty years. One could claim that these changes transformed the country into a confederation of its republics. The centrifugal dynamic of transferring ever more powers from the federal centre to the subunits soon reached the point of making the centre dependent on consensus among quasi-independent republics, empowered even with certain prerogatives usually reserved for sovereign states in the international system.

Centrifugal federalism started to determine political life in Yugoslavia in April 1967 with the adoption of the first six constitutional amendments. Curiously, these far-reaching changes were adopted at the initiative of the Bosnian leadership that, unsatisfied with a decision of the Managing Board of the federal fund for allocation of resources for underdeveloped regions, had convened a special meeting of the Chamber of Nationalities (Burg 1983: 67–68). This usually passive institution got, politically speaking, a second wind and demanded changes in the Constitution that would assure a more important political role for the republics and a more potent political role for the Chamber itself. The reforms were clearly going in the direction of reducing the power of the Federation (see Haug 2012: 203–212; Hondius 1968: 325–326; also Burg 1983; Ramet 2006; Rusinow 1977).

The first constitutional amendment revitalized the Chamber of Nationalities. Beforehand, this Chamber had mandatorily convened only when constitutional changes were debated. Now it acquired an equal status to the Federal Chamber itself. This, in turn, enhanced the power of the republics and, surprisingly, of the autonomous provinces. At the urging of Kosovo and Vojvodina, the minimum number of delegates entitled to convene the session of the Chamber was reduced from ten to five, which happened to be the number of delegates of each autonomous province. Subsequently, this allowed them to act more independently from Serbia. One amendment (4) clearly confirmed the decentralization trend. From then on, the republican public prosecutors were to be appointed by the republican assemblies and not by the federal public prosecutor, which was the direct result of the fall of Ranković a year earlier. The state security apparatus was consequently put under not only federal but also republican control as well (amendment 4, point 1), whereas only the Yugoslav army was left under the exclusive jurisdiction of the centre.

Although these steps were relatively modest in scope, voices discussing the confederalization of Yugoslavia were immediately heard (see Burg 1983: 67; Hondius 1968: 329; Rusinow 1977: 226). Hondius, who finished his study just after the adoption of the amendments, could not have known that this was only the beginning of the progressive confederalization of what he then already called the 'genuine federation' (1968: 329).

The new amendments adopted in 1968 and 1971 not only confirmed the general trend but also went even further. They inevitably brought back to the table 'the national question' or, more ominously, suggested that it was not properly 'solved'. 'Once the amendment process has been initiated,' Burg emphasizes, 'it opens the door for further debate not only over relationships between the constituent units but also over relationships between the nations that inhabit them' (1983: 68). 'It was an irony of history,' Hondius concludes, 'which, in 1967, made Bosnia and Hercegovina take the initiative for the first meeting of the Chamber of Nationalities, which led eventually to a confirmation of the link between peoples and Republics' (1968: 343). More than two decades later, Bosnia, as the only true multinational republic, became the greatest victim of the principle that independent states, after the collapse of Yugoslavia, should be the homogenous nation-states of their ethnic majorities with their borders redrawn accordingly: the principle that would brutally attempt to eliminate its only true (Bosnian) exception.

In December 1968, another set of amendments (numbers 7–19) further empowered the Chamber of Nationalities. The Federal Chamber of the Federal Assembly was abolished with all competences delegated to the Chamber of

Nationalities now consisting of twenty deputies from the republics and ten from the provinces. Since all federal legislation had to be approved by the Chamber of Nationalities, it automatically turned it into the most powerful chamber.

As mentioned above, the flip side of the process of the confederalization of Yugoslavia was the federalization of Serbia, which also started in 1967 and 1968 and was confirmed in the 1974 Constitution. Amendment 7 constitutionally redefined the autonomous provinces as constitutive units of the Federation; they were not mentioned as constitutive parts of Yugoslavia in article 2 of the 1963 Constitution. Vojvodina and Kosovo were basically made equal to the republics. The provinces acquired their own supreme courts and their borders could not be altered without their consent. The League of Communists of Serbia was reorganized and separate Leagues of Communists were established in Kosovo and Vojvodina. Also, all rights usually guaranteed to the constituent peoples of Yugoslavia were guaranteed to all ethnic non-South-Slavic minorities (in this case Albanian and Magyar minorities) such as the use of a national language in public institutions. Nevertheless, the provinces remained subordinated to Serbia's sovereignty. They had neither the right to secede nor the right to their proper citizenship laws, their own police or territorial defence forces. Technically speaking, Serbia was not partitioned into three areas (Vojvodina, Kosovo and Serbia proper). Serbia proper was mostly used as a regional term but was not a political entity, although only in Serbia proper could the Serbian authorities act without confronting the obstacles of the provincial autonomies. In other words, within Serbia, two regions acquired a large autonomy, but remained under Serbia's nominal sovereignty.

In his 2003 study, Dejan Jović dedicates a whole chapter to the reasons why Serbia accepted the constitutional changes between 1967 and 1974 that eventually amounted to its proper federalization (2003a: 157–207). Jović argues that Serbia's political elite accepted Kardelj's ideas on the constitutional changes in Yugoslavia precisely because it saw in these changes the realization of both Serbia's national interests and the general ideological interest of Yugoslav socialist society. The changes were supposed to guarantee the preservation of Yugoslavia with Serbia as equal partner to the other republics and ethnic groups within and without Serbia (eliminating the possibility that Serbia could be accused of dominating and exploiting the others). But if this rationale prevailed among anti-nationalist and liberal-minded Serbian communists, other segments of Serbian society, the cultural and literary scene and, later in the 1980s, the political establishment as well, immediately started to question Serbia's role in the federation, claiming that the constitutional changes were to Serbia's disadvantage.

A year later, in 1969, each Yugoslav republic acquired one of the most important elements of sovereignty and statehood, namely, a proper military force. The new defence law established republican territorial defence forces (*teritorijalna o(d)brana*)[1] – and put them under exclusive republican control. In June 1971, a new series of twenty-two constitutional amendments was adopted. The end result of these amendments was the further reduction of the federal authorities' powers. Amendment 20 – that was to be incorporated into the 1974 Constitution – confirmed the republics' sovereignty, including all sovereign powers except those reserved exclusively for the Federation, now reduced only to foreign affairs, the military, common monetary policy, the regulation of the unitary Yugoslav market and the preservation of ethnonational and individual rights. All federal organs were to be formed on the principle of republican and provincial parity including the State presidency (consisting of 23 members including Tito), the Federal Executive Committee (SIV), the Chamber of Nationalities, the Constitutional Court and the administrative personnel of the federal ministries (see Burg 1983: 204–206).

Another important innovation was the creation of five inter-republican committees within the SIV that were supposed to design common policies in the areas of development, the monetary system, foreign trade and hard currency, the market and finance. Together with the chairman of the SIV, they were composed of nine delegates who were solely responsible to the republics and provinces (Ramet 2006: 248). The work of the committees proved to be very efficient in spite of the new rule (amendment 33) on the harmonization of positions (*usuglašavanje*) and consent in economic matters. On the other hand, as Lampe observes, 'the Committees' very success in making working arrangements between the republics made the federation's legislation process and representatives, whether elected or delegated, seem irrelevant' (2000: 312).

Yugoslavia as confederation: The constitution of 1974

As a whole, the set of forty-two amendments adopted between 1967 and 1971 profoundly and irrevocably confederalized Yugoslavia. These changes provoked opposing reactions. The debates at the Faculty of Law in Belgrade in 1971 caused a scandal. It resulted in a two-year prison sentence (reduced later to nine months) for Mihailo Đurić, a professor of the Belgrade Law Faculty, who claimed that the amendments had changed the nature of the federation, reduced Yugoslavia to a 'geographical term' and created almost independent and mutually opposed national states. He thought that such a development would significantly affect the position of Serbs who live in great numbers outside Serbia and underlined an inadequacy of republican borders, especially in the case of Serbia.[2] In Croatia, on the other hand, the amendments were seen as only a first step towards the realization of Croatian national aspirations, many of which were formulated in the pages of *Hrvatski tjednik* (Croatian Weekly), published by the traditional Croatian cultural organization *Matica hrvatska* (Rusinow 1977: 283). By the end of that year, the Croatian Spring mass movement demanding independent state-like autonomy for Croatia in economic and political matters was crushed. Young Croatian leaders (Mika Tripalo, Pero Pirker, Savka Dabčević-Kučar), who tolerated the nationalist 'excesses' of Matica hrvatska and the student organizations, were removed from office and replaced with conservative communists from within the Croatian party. Soon after the purge of Croatian leaders and series of arrests of student leaders or public intellectuals, the young Serbian leadership – accused not of nationalism but of liberalism – was also removed. And although this reassertion of Tito's power, i.e. the power of the federal centre and the central organs of the Party, could make one think that the heyday of centrifugal federalism had come to an end, exactly the opposite happened. Centrifugal federalism was fully endorsed and the confederalization of Yugoslavia confirmed in the 1974 Constitution.

One of the longest constitutions in the world (406 articles!) defined the SFRY in its elaborate and complicated first article as:

> [A] federal state having the form of a state community of voluntarily united nations [peoples] and their Socialist Republics, and of the Socialist Autonomous Provinces of Vojvodina and Kosovo, which are constituent parts of the Socialist Republic of Serbia, based on the power and self-management of the working class and all working people; it is a socialist self-managing democratic community of working people and citizens and of nations and nationalities, having equal rights[3]. (*Constitution of SFRY* 1974)

The competing 'sovereigns' – the working class, all working people, citizens, nations and nationalities, republics, peoples of the republics – were again put in the same confusing sentence mixing overlapping political communities. In perfect harmony with the post-1967 spirit of confederalization, the republics were defined as 'states based on the sovereignty of people' and autonomous provinces as 'autonomous socialist self-managing democratic socio-political communities'. The republics were 'states' whereas the federation was only a 'state community' (Dimitrijević 1995: 58). Naturally, these states had the right to self-determination and secession. Serbian legal scholar Vojin Dimitrijević correctly points out that the Constitution provided this right 'without envisaging the corresponding procedure' (1995: 71). This would leave the use of this right open to contending interpretations in the final years of Yugoslavia.

Three-stage elections for local, republican and federal assemblies took place in April and May of 1974 through a complicated 'system of delegations and delegates' (for details see Rusinow 1977: 331; Višnjić 1977: 73–91). The voters directly elected only members of the tricameral communal assemblies (chambers for labour, local government and social-political issues) who then sent delegates to the similar tricameral republican and provincial assemblies that, in turn, sent delegates to the bicameral federal assembly consisting of the Federal Chamber (thirty delegates from each republic and twenty from each province) and the Chamber of Republics and Provinces (twelve delegates from the republics and eight from the provinces). In the first round, 820,000 delegates were elected from 12,000 communities and 60,000 work units; in the second, 500 communal chambers voted for delegates to the republican and provincial chambers; in the final third round, they elected delegates representing their republics and provinces in the two federal chambers (Lampe 2000: 313). Politically speaking, the system of elections at the lowest level and then three rounds of delegation towards the higher levels secured, in the words of Serbian political scientist Laszlo Sekelj, 'absolute control over the electoral procedure by informal, non-elected, non-institutionalized, and uncontrollable local oligarchies' (in Lampe 2000: 314).

In the federal organs, all decisions were made unanimously through a procedure of harmonization of positions among the republics, i.e. their delegations voting *en bloc* (not their members). Needless to say, the republics had the right of veto over all federal decisions which prevented the federal institutions from acting independently. This was, in Dimitrijević's opinion, 'the real and fatal flaw' of the 1974 Constitution (1995: 60). In 1981, another set of eight constitutional amendments was adopted in order to allow the proper functioning of the federal bodies such as the Federal Executive Committee (the federal government and its prime minister), the Presidency and the Constitutional court (see *Amandmani* 1988 [1981]).

The 1974 Constitution of the SFRY was meant to be the peak of the proclaimed politics of decentralization that started at the Sixth Congress of the Communist Party of Yugoslavia in 1952. Among scholars, observers and participants, a general consensus exists that 1974 Constitution confirmed the confederal structure of the Yugoslav state. Yugoslav politicians called it a 'cooperative federal system' and its main ideologist, Edvard Kardelj, qualified it already in 1971 as neither 'a classical federation ... nor ... a classic confederation, but... a socialist, self-managing community of nations' (in Ramet 1992: 63). This *fédéralisme dénaturé*, as a French observer put it (Drouet 1997: 85), based at the federal level on the rule of consent and unanimity, was characterized by the ever-growing dependence of federal institutions on constitutive republics. The centre had to operate through the republics to 'implement virtually all policies, to gather revenues and to establish connections with the citizenry' that, as Valerie Bunce reminds us, amounts to quite a precise definition of confederalism (1999: 111).

The unstoppable decentralization

In April 1969, general elections were held for communal, republican and federal chambers and assemblies.[4] However, it was also the year of a destabilizing economic affair, known as the road affair or the road building crisis (*cestna afera*) that hit Yugoslavia at its most delicate spot, namely the relations between the federation and its subunits. When the Federal Executive Council decided not to distribute the funds received from the World Bank for certain road building projects in Slovenia, unanimous and loud protests against the federal government erupted in Slovenia (Burg 1983: 88–100). Moreover, at the very beginning of 1970 the Tenth Congress of the LC of Croatia took a strong stance against unitarism and bureaucratic centralism in Yugoslavia. It was the beginning of the 'Croatian crisis' during which economic questions and debates – concerning relations between developed and underdeveloped republics, foreign currency and the economic independence of the republics vis-à-vis the federal centre – were inevitably perceived in ethnonational terms and as inter-ethnic conflicts.

The LCY's presidency adopted a resolution in April 1970 in which it mentioned the 'sovereignty' of the republics and provinces. In September 1970 in Zagreb, Tito announced the future reorganization of the Federation and the creation of the Presidency (see his speech in Kobsa et al. 1978: 445–449). New constitutional decentralizing reforms followed suit in 1971 and then finally peaked with the new 1974 Constitution. A year before, in 1973, a Party document defined Yugoslav federation as 'a function of the statehood and sovereignty of each republic and province'.[5] In the same year, Edvard Kardelj confirms the confederalization of Yugoslavia by stating that the power of the federation is not autonomous, but rather 'stems from the republics, and not vice versa' (in Jović 2003a: 146).

The political and constitutional decentralization of Yugoslavia was followed by a concomitant decentralization – along with a burgeoning self-sufficiency among the republics – in other domains such as economics, media, culture, science and education. The effects of decentralization were evident, for instance, in the independent electricity systems, in the absence of common policy in the important areas of science and education as well as in paradoxical situations such as when Serbia proper imported wheat while its autonomous province of Vojvodina exported it abroad (Udovički 1995: 294). In the media sector there was no federal TV station. Instead, there were independent republican TV centres that created a small amount of common broadcasting. These republican radios and televisions were predictably dependent on republican-level political centres and would become main venues of nationalistic propaganda at the end of the 1980s and in the early 1990s and would play a major political role during the war (Allcock 2000: 292; Thompson 1999). Andrew Wachtel describes the absence of a common educational curriculum in the fields of literature, culture and history (1998). The civil society sector was divided along republican lines as well, even more so after the mid-1960s (see Irvine 1997). In 1981, in a paper on the Yugoslav national question as 'unfinished business,' Dennison Rusinow drew an early and revealing comparison between Yugoslavia and the European integration process: 'The individual republics now have nearly as much control over their economic fortunes and cultural identities as the sovereign states in the European Economic Community (which means that their control is not unlimited or free of intra-Yugoslav and wider interdependence)' (1981: 10).

The radical decentralization and confederalization of Yugoslavia stripped the federal centre of its classic state prerogatives but, in turn, consolidated the *statehood* of the republics and reinforced their state apparatuses. The process can be described, in the words of Valerie Bunce, as 'Yugoslavia's losing "stateness" from the 1970s onwards and its republics gaining statehood during the same period' (Bunce 1997: 349). Interestingly, Tito seemed to be aware of this in 1971 when he warned the republics not to 'divide up statism' among themselves (in Jović 2003b: 176). Jović himself comments that Kardelj's anti-statist rhetoric actually strengthened *statism* in Serbia, Croatia and Slovenia (2003b: 180). Decentralization was thus contained only at the level of the federal state, but did not take roots at the republican level, except in the case of Serbia whose federalization mirrored the confederalization of the country as a whole. In other words, the de-*étatization* of the Federation went hand in hand with the *étatisme* of the republics. The State, as such, was not actually in the process of withering away in Yugoslavia. What eventually withered away was only Yugoslavia itself.

From federal to confederal citizenship

The hybrid structure of Yugoslavia resulting from the constitutional changes between 1967 and 1974 was also manifested in the constitutional definitions of federal and republican citizenship. According to article 249 of the last (1974) Constitution of the SFR Yugoslavia, citizens possessed a 'single citizenship of the SFRY' and every citizen of a republic was 'simultaneously' a citizen of the SFRY. The third line of the Article confirms that 'a citizen of a republic on the territory of another republic has the same rights and obligations as the citizens of that republic'. In fact, this created confusion in legal literature over the question of primacy between federal and republican-level citizenship. During the high time of socialist Yugoslavia, it was mostly law students who took an interest in this tricky question, the precise answer to which became of utmost importance when the dissolution of the federation occurred. If one takes into consideration the views of legal experts, it is evident that no consensus exists on the question of primacy. Some authors cite the simultaneity and identity of the two citizenships (Pejić 1998) or find, in the equality of the rights and duties of a citizen of one republic living in the other, evidence of 'the primacy of Yugoslav citizenship over those of different republics' (Drouet 1997: 84) and describe the pre-eminence of federal citizenship as 'an important guarantee for minorities facing the majority "nation" of one or another republic' (1997: 91). On the other hand, some authors argue that, although only federal citizenship was legal in the international arena and republican citizenship had an 'exclusively internal legal role', republican citizenship had primacy over SFRY citizenship according to respective provisions of the 1976 law on SFRY citizenship and the republican laws on citizenship (see Muminović 1998: 73; Rakić 1998: 59).

The 1976 law on citizenship of the SFRY brought with it another element that could confirm primacy of the subunits and the confederal nature of Yugoslavia's bifurcated citizenship. The Act regulated conditions for acquisition and termination of Yugoslav citizenship, but transferred the competencies for implementation of the citizenship legislation from the Federal Ministry of the Interior to the republican authorities (art. 21, para 2; Jovanović 1977: 50–51; UNHCR 1997: 8). These competencies included the registration and termination of Yugoslav citizenship. Furthermore, the republican supreme courts were deemed competent in citizenship matters (such as, for instance, complaints against decisions related to citizenship). A somewhat confusing and unique situation – namely that subunits decide on Federal citizenship – prompted the author of an explanatory introduction to the law on Yugoslav citizenship to question the existence of any role for the federal authority in this domain (Jovanović 1977: 51). Unsurprisingly for a confederated structure like the one Yugoslavia progressively became after the mid-1960s, the citizenship-regulating norms showed some similarities to the norms of international law in cases of legal collisions among sovereign states (Jovanović 1977: 53). Jovanović finds, however, that there is still some room for the Federal authorities on this issue considering that they alone are responsible for citizenship matters in the international arena, but he admits that the only safe conclusion to be drawn is that the new 1976 law does not regulate the matter.

Another striking feature of confederalized citizenship in Yugoslavia was that, following the fact that only republican-level registers existed, only republics (and even autonomous provinces of Vojvodina and Kosovo) were entitled to issue Yugoslav passports with their own numbers (preceded with the letters signalling the republic or the autonomous region of origin). This resulted in a plethora of various Yugoslav passports. For instance, passports issued in Kosovo had the letters KA before the number and were printed in Albanian, Serbian and French; Yugoslav passports issued in Macedonia[6] were only in Macedonian and French (but not in Serbo-Croatian!).

The almost non-existent awareness of the *dual character* of citizenship in Yugoslavia was shared equally by the citizens and even by legal scholars (Medvedović 1998: 49–52). Since republican citizenship did not have any practical consequences within the Federation – some would even call it a 'phantom citizenship' (Pejić 1998: 185) – and since federal citizenship was the stronger guarantor of the rights of citizens living outside of their native republics, a fact that also stimulated the free movement of people between republics, *residence*[7] became the most important practical factor in the everyday life of Yugoslavs. Yugoslav citizens were, in principle, able to choose their republican citizenship depending on their residency or employment. The law on Yugoslav citizenship, and the republican laws on citizenship, allowed citizens to change republican citizenship. It is interesting to note that after 1964 it was even possible to do so without further formalities. On the other hand, after 1976 change of citizenship was still allowed by republican laws but only under certain conditions and after a legal procedure (Medvedović 1998: 49). Since republican citizenship was of no significant practical relevance, citizens usually did not change their republican citizenship status if they moved to another republic, and sometimes they did not even register change of residence or bother to sort out the republican citizenship of their children. Internal Yugoslav migration established strong personal and family ties across republican borders, while economically motivated migrations and the resettlement of federal administration personnel resulted in a considerable number of individuals living outside of their republic of origin. To a certain degree, this would affect the balance of ethnic groups in Yugoslav republics, the reality that the new citizenship regimes would try to amend as much as possible.

The progressive political empowerment of the republics over the federal centre finally altered the character of bifurcated citizenship in Yugoslavia from typical federal to confederal citizenship. This change was not explicitly reflected in citizenship legislation, although the above-discussed disputes over primacy show the tendency to legally codify the confederal structure of Yugoslavia in citizenship laws as well. After all, one could hardly imagine how citizenship could have been decoupled from the constitutional changes that transformed Yugoslavia between 1967 and 1974 into a confederation of republics. In other words, the political empowerment of the republics shifted the centre of a citizen's political activity towards his or her republic. Politically, it was basically a one-way street and the traffic flowed from the republics to the federal plateau where republican delegates and representatives discussed and deliberated *unanimously* on their relations and common affairs.

Interestingly, although republican-level citizenship was almost *practically* irrelevant for ordinary citizens in their everyday life, *politically* speaking it was republican belonging and citizenship that increasingly took the leading role. As Rusinow reminds us, powerful republican figures were reluctant to abandon their local republican bases and move to Belgrade to exercise only federal functions. After the death of Tito, the independent position of the republican communist elites towards the centre – actually, dependence of the centre on their practice of harmonization and agreement – became fully apparent.

At the federal political level, only republican 'groups' were allowed access through the system of republican delegations, whereas individual citizens could act only within their republics. Although it was possible to declare Yugoslav *ethnonational* belonging (*narodnost* or *nacionalnost*), those who did so were not recognized as nations or nationalities and were thus not represented. Although it seems paradoxical – this comes as little surprise in the confederated structure that Yugoslavia had become during the last quarter century of its existence – Yugoslavs did not have an exclusive territory on their own. One can safely conclude that the only 'group' within Yugoslavia that could be identified as truly Yugoslav, in the sense of using and practicing benefits of Yugoslav citizenship, were internal *migrants*. And many of them woke up one day in 1991 or 1992 as *aliens* or simply *stateless* in Yugoslavia's successor states.

Broken partnership: From confederal citizenship towards crisis

On 4 May 1980, Josip Broz Tito died in a hospital in Ljubljana. It was exactly 3.04 p.m. Every Yugoslav could easily remember both the day and the hour of Tito's death, since that moment was commemorated throughout the 1980s in all corners of Yugoslavia with wailing sirens. This was the tribute paid by Yugoslav citizens to the 'greatest son of all our nations and nationalities'. He left them locked in a system whose paradoxes and impasses, but also numerous beneficial possibilities, only he was capable of navigating. His successors would not possess the same skills. The slogan 'Even After Tito – Tito!' soon proved to be a useless mantra. Nevertheless, Tito's successors did try hard to make the machine work. The previous year they had lost the only man who could have served as a guide, Edvard Kardelj, statesman and theorist of Yugoslav self-managing socialism. A year later, in the Spring of 1981, civil unrest broke out in Kosovo, in a part of the country that was historically important for some Yugoslavs (especially Serbs) but whose mostly ethnic Albanian population had never felt at ease in the common house of the South Slavs.

This is how the last decade of Yugoslavia began. It was marked, among other things, by nervous attempts at systemic reforms, an economic downturn, the Kosovo crisis, foreign debt headaches, IMF-imposed standby arrangements and following austerity measures, massive strikes, the paralysis of federal institutions, conflicts within the federal LCY and inter-republican rivalries tainted with ominous nationalistic overtones. The fateful rise of Serbia's strongman Slobodan Milošević was followed by Slovenian resistance to his Kosovo policy and his recentralization attempts. Nevertheless, he got both of the Serbian autonomous provinces and Montenegro under his sway before 1990. The story of Yugoslavia's post-Tito *malaise* concluded with the disintegration of the LCY in January 1990 and the first separately scheduled democratic elections in the Yugoslav republics during 1990.

On the other hand, there was a bright side to the 1980s that inspired optimism. The regime's general weakness created an atmosphere of liberalization and many quickly learned how to orient themselves in politics, society, culture or the grey economy under a 'soft dictatorship'. Yugoslavia was still a highly respected member of the international community and historic leader of the non-aligned movement; citizens usually expressed a fairly high level of attachment to their country, tourism developed on the Adriatic coast, the Winter Olympic Games were hosted successfully by Sarajevo in 1984, Yugoslavs could travel freely and, important for their pride, *shop* abroad, and a sophisticated urban and alternative culture blossomed (see Debeljak 1994; Ramet 2002; Ugrešić 1996).

Many scholars have tried to answer the question of what went wrong in Yugoslavia. One has to start with the various failed efforts to reform Yugoslavia's confederal structure during the second half of the 1980s. They reveal that the republican elites had conflicting visions of the future of their regime and the country in general. Left without the final arbiter and effective federal structures that could serve as a bridge or mediator and confronted with economic inequalities between the republics, a growing debt crisis, as well as vocal demands for political and ideological transformation coming from developing civil society, the gap between these elites only grew in the years preceding the end of the socialist regime and the subsequent democratization of the Yugoslav republics.

Changes in Eastern Europe announced the end of state socialist rule and the advent of liberal democracy. Decentralization, centrifugal federalism and the earlier abandonment of the unifying Yugoslav political project naturally designated the constitutive units as future frameworks of democracy and people's rule. In short, liberal democracy was introduced into a confederated country whose very citizenship – as a general basis for any political activity – was itself politically confederated. Any political activity after the constitutional changes from 1967 to 1974 went from the republics towards the federation, and from the republican communist parties to the federal Party, and not *vice versa*, a fact that transformed the republics into primary political arenas.

Liberal democracy was thus introduced into a malfunctioning multinational confederation and resulted in a further fragmentation of the political space – more and more so along ethnic lines – which would jeopardize not only Yugoslavia as a state but also the prevailing consensus over its internal borders. I will show in the following chapters that insecurity surrounding the issue of citizenship – captured by simple questions such as 'what is the political community and state to which I belong?' and 'what state guarantees my rights and security?' – was one of the critical factors behind Yugoslavia's violent disintegration. Although rarely analysed and not articulated as the problem of citizenship, the citizenship factor must be added to the list of interactive elements that contributed to the Yugoslav drama (see Chapters 6–8). I describe how the ethnocentric conception of citizenship came to dominate political space and how the idea of creating ethnically homogenous states, the project that inevitably challenged the internal borders, unleashed a spiral of violence. But to understand this highly complex process whose well-known outcomes were far from inevitable, let us turn once more to the final decade of Yugoslavia.

Valerie Bunce identifies three elements necessary for a regime change: leadership succession, great reforms and international change (1999). All three were present in socialist Europe at the end of the 1980s. However, Bunce observes that regime change in Yugoslavia started earlier and, far from being concluded in a matter of 'ten days' or 'ten months' as in some Eastern European countries, it was played out over an entire decade following Tito's death. The potential emergence of a 'new Tito', or at the very least a pan-Yugoslav leader, was aborted by the confederal system itself. The period was thus characterized by a series of more or less unsuccessful successions of leadership and several attempts at economic and political reforms. Finally, once the international system started to change with Gorbachev's accession in 1985 and more dramatically in 1989, Yugoslavia seemed well prepared for regime change. Although many feared the outcome, regime change did not have to entail the dismemberment of the state itself. Although it seemed that everyone in Yugoslavia had acknowledged the need for change, the country experienced a chronic lack of consensus about these changes and common initiatives – with some notable exceptions – that would formulate this vision in pan-Yugoslav terms. Prior to Milošević's accession to power in Serbia in 1987, several groups formed along the dividing lines between conservatives and liberals or between *recentralizers* and *decentralists*. Liberal recentralizers were in power in Serbia, conservative recentralizers controlled Bosnia and Montenegro, liberal decentralists dominated Slovenia and Vojvodina while conservative decentralists held the reins in Croatia, Macedonia and Kosovo (Ramet 2006: 333). Another line of conflict separated those who defended the 1974 Constitution from those who advocated its reform (see Jović 2003a).

The disintegration process in socialist multinational federations began, Bunce argues, 'when crisis over power and reform weakened the regimes, mobilized publics, "republicanized" the state, and "nationalized" political protest' (1999: 98). In the Yugoslav case, the decisive events that would eventually lead to disintegration took place during 1986 and 1987. Slobodan Milošević and Milan Kučan, two crucial players from the final years of Yugoslavia, took over important political positions within their republican parties in 1986. By November of the same year, the Yugoslav republics achieved full fiscal sovereignty (Woodward 1995a: 74), a largely unnoticed event that only confirmed that the centrifugal machine of Yugoslav federalism was still in high gear. In September 1986, a draft of the famous (or infamous) Memorandum of the Serbian Academy of Arts and Sciences (SANU) leaked to the public. This document would later be widely considered a manifesto for the creation of a greater Serbian state on the ruins of Yugoslavia, a political programme espoused by both left-wing and right-wing Serbian nationalists and, finally, by its champion, Slobodan Milošević.

However, the Memorandum of the SANU was, in Dragović-Soso's view, less a programme for a Greater Serbia and more a litany of Serbian grievances against Yugoslavia. These grievances were formulated in literary circles and Belgrade salons and would resurge in newspapers or in theatre shows. The Memorandum referred to the 'ongoing genocide' against Serbs in Kosovo and employed other appalling language, which resonated strongly within Serb community (2008: 19). Nevertheless, the mere fact that this list of Serbian grievances against Yugoslavia's confederal and Serbia's federal structure was drafted by the members of the most prestigious Serbian intellectual institution and endorsed, with varying degrees of explicitness, by important intellectual figures within the biggest federal unit was in itself – regardless of the initial intentions of the drafters and their later open advocacy of a Greater Serbia – an aggressive attack on the communist solution to the national question, which was perhaps the greatest taboo in socialist Yugoslavia.

In the same year of 1986, the SFRY Presidency started to prepare new amendments to the 1974 Constitution which were intended to solve the Federation's paralysis and deal with 'hot' issues such as the relationship between the federation and its subunits, relations within Serbia itself and the unity of Yugoslav market. In January 1987, the Presidency's proposals included creation of a unified legal system, central control of the railroads, postal and telephone services and the unification of the Yugoslav economy. It is small wonder that proposals for a stronger Federation were welcomed in Serbia and largely rejected in Slovenia (Ramet 2006: 335–337).

On 24 April 1987, Slobodan Milošević came to the village of Kosovo Polje near the site of the 1389 battle between a diverse Christian coalition and the Ottomans that regardless of its real historical significance forms the core of the Serbian national myth. He arrived there as a largely unknown representative of the Central Committee to pacify inter-ethnic turbulence in the southern province. Thanks to Belgrade television, he returned to the Serbian capital as a new Serbian hero and the protector of endangered Serbs in Kosovo and, by extension, in Yugoslavia as whole.[8] By the end of that year, he had removed the head of the Serbian party (and his political mentor and one-time friend) Ivan Stambolić from office and had become the undisputable chief in Serbia.

The political setting obviously changed dramatically and Yugoslavia in 1988 was a much different political landscape, which allowed competing ideas on how to define political community or communities – in Yugoslav, republican or ethnic terms? – to flourish. In August 1988, amid an atmosphere of rising suspicion towards Milošević's political intentions and his role in the Kosovo crisis, Serbia drafted a series of amendments to the SFRY Constitution for discussion. The proposed amendments aimed at the recentralization of the Federation and the restriction of the autonomy of Vojvodina and Kosovo. Predictably, any move towards the reinforcement of Serbia's position within the Federation was perceived by other republics as detrimental to their own status and was immediately associated with Serbian nationalism. Serbia suggested the transformation of the Federal Assembly's Chamber of Republics and Provinces and the Federal Chamber into the Chamber of Republics and Provinces, the Chamber of Citizens and the Chamber of Associated Labor. The Chamber of Citizens was supposed to represent citizens proportionally (Ramet 2006: 338–339). For our analysis, centred as it is on citizenship, and from the vantage point of Yugoslavia's later disintegration, this suggestion could be interpreted as a move to reinforce a pan-Yugoslav political culture, a move which could possibly have initiated a pan-Yugoslav (as opposed to republican or ethnonationalist) politics. Nevertheless, in the context in which inter-republican balance was shaken (a balance that more often than not stood for inter-ethnic balance), the proposed amendments were accused of benefiting only one republic, Serbia, and only one group, ethnic Serbs, who were numerically the largest Yugoslav nation. Not surprisingly, all other republics, with the exception of Montenegro, rejected the idea.

Since these reforms failed to break the deadlock, the following year brought several serious attacks on the *de facto* Yugoslav confederation: first, Yugoslavia faced a unilateral attempt at recentralization by Serbia, and Slovenia made an attempt at unilateral decentralization. Belgrade's unilateral recentralization of Serbia attacked both the *de facto* Serbian federation as defined by the 1974 Constitution and, by extension, the confederal constitutional structure of Yugoslavia as a whole. By the end of 1988, massive demonstrations in Vojvodina and Montenegro – the so-called anti-bureaucratic or yogurt revolution – toppled local government officials who were later replaced with individuals loyal to Milošević (see Vladisavljević 2008). On 18 March 1989, the Serbian parliament adopted amendments to the Constitution of Serbia which abolished the large degree of autonomy enjoyed by its two provinces (Vojvodina and Kosovo). These amendments were later confirmed in a new Constitution of Serbia adopted in September 1990. Although Serbia had effectively re-centralized itself unilaterally, it kept the two seats at the SFRY

Presidency reserved for its autonomous provinces. Combined with the loyal vote from Montenegro, Serbia suddenly had four out of eight votes at the Presidency at its disposal, placing the delicate balance between the republics in jeopardy.

In September 1989, Slovenia made a unilateral attempt at decentralization when its parliament adopted amendments to the Constitution of Slovenia. The tenth amendment stated that Slovenia was part of Yugoslavia on the basis of its right to self-determination and secession. Crucially, the seventy-second amendment proclaimed that only the Slovenian parliament could determine how this right should be exercised. The Yugoslav Constitutional Court found this amendment to be in conflict with the SFRY Constitution according to which the borders of the SFRY could not be altered without the mutual consent of the republics and provinces.

Therefore, even before the Fourteenth and last Congress of the League of Communists of Yugoslavia in January 1990, the country that they had resurrected in 1945, unified under their leadership and dictatorship and progressively decentralized together with their own party, was deeply divided along republican and, increasingly, ethnic lines. After his successful recentralization of Serbia and subjugation of Montenegro, Milošević attempted to consolidate his position and impose the recentralization of both the LCY and Yugoslavia as whole. After Slovenian suggestions were rejected *en bloc* by Milošević's supporters, the Slovenian delegation left the Congress, quickly followed by the Croatian delegation. From that point on, the *League* ceased to exist as such. The republican parties hastily organized democratic elections according to their own schedule and without coordinating with other republics. It is interesting to note that the Slovenian and Croatian Parties that left the Congress were formed in 1937 as part of the Communist Party of Yugoslavia's solution to the national question. By that decision, the Party explicitly rejected unitarism – which had been tainted by association with Serbia's dominant role within Yugoslavia – in its internal organization as well as in the organization of a future socialist multinational Yugoslavia. How deeply the national question – and the solution based on the equality of constitutive units and nations – was bound up with the existence of the Party as such was demonstrated at its last Congress: as soon as unitarism threatened to dominate the Party, it dissolved. The open question was whether federal Yugoslavia could survive the Party that had created it. We know the answer today, but back then there were still many possibilities to reform and save the country, or, short of that, to avoid violence.

5

The Bridges Over the Miljacka: The Long Farewell to Yugoslav Citizenship

Yugoslav communists thought, as Sabrina Ramet summarizes, that they had found a solution to the national question in the *proportionality* in the federal organs (not present in the army), in the *ethnic quota* system (not applied in Kosovo and not always in Croatia and Bosnia), in *massive decentralization* to the point of confederalization, in the mythology of partisan struggle, in international success and in the charisma of Tito (1992: 278). As for the old wartime promise of social emancipation, the answer was the Yugoslav strain of self-managing socialism. If the partisan mythology was intensively deconstructed in the 1980s and the system of self-management did not yield much enthusiasm any more – the economic and debt crisis was increasingly seen as a crisis of self-management as a political-economic system as such – one could say that there was still a cultural-historic argument embodied in *Yugoslavism* as a narrative of identity and belonging of citizens to the common state. But, alas, by the 1980s, it had lost much of its political influence and proved incapable of yet another reincarnation that could have mobilized political spirits and imagination. From various consciously taken or unconsciously held ideological positions (ranging from anarchic sentiments, liberalism to right-wing nationalism), the whole ideological structure of the regime came under attack in the second half of the 1980s. The undermining of the anti-fascist struggle narrative went hand in hand with denouncing the inferiority of self-management as opposed to consumer-oriented liberal capitalism. The attack on historical legacy and the regime's very ideology entailed a further weakening of Yugoslavism. However, back then the relationship to Yugoslavia as identity and project varied from one republic to another, from one generation to another and heavily depended on the concrete political processes (and their perception).

One could even argue that the decentralization of the federal state and the Party would have never occurred, could have never been conceptualized and could have never gained enough political support without the simultaneous abandonment of the traditionally 'centripetal' idea of South-Slavic cultural and political unity. The practice of centrifugal federalism, the federalization of the Party, the progressive decentralization of the economy, industry, culture, media, science and education, the redefinition of Yugoslavism in less cultural, less *national* and less political terms and the perception of Yugoslavia not as a state but more and more so as a 'community', 'organization' or 'conglomerate' – all occurring in Yugoslavia from mid-1960s at a sometimes vertiginous pace – seem to be interactive parts of the same puzzle.

Nevertheless, immediately after the war it appeared that resurrected Yugoslavia and strong patriotism of the national-liberation struggle had given a new impetus to Yugoslavism – this time in a federalist form meant to dissociate the idea from the bitter experiences of pre-war unitarism. Although Yugoslavism itself went through curious re-definitions and had to compete with communist internationalism between 1945 and 1948, socialist nation-building Yugoslavism would be seen and promoted throughout the 1950s as something of uncontested worth. Having described earlier the birth and evolution of Yugoslavism between the mid-nineteenth century and the Second World War, we should recount here its last chapters.

Yugoslavism: Fading of an idea

One can summarily conclude that the idea met its *political* death much before Yugoslavia disintegrated as a country. Even after the Party abandoned it in its own ranks, the idea still had certain emotional and political value for many Yugoslavs who remained attached to it, or some parts of it, but were incapable of formulating it politically – or of formulating it in a politically successful way – at the critical junction when liberal democracy and its instruments and procedures were introduced in the Yugoslav republics. I explore this junction in depth in the next chapters. For now, let us turn to the days when (federalist) Yugoslavism meant a much better future and the only available exit from 'fratricidal war'.

The 1943 AVNOJ declaration was an ideological – not yet political let alone military – triumph of federalist Yugoslavism over both the Yugoslav unitarism of the pre-war period and separatist ethnic nationalisms. Nevertheless, the new Yugoslav leadership would soon challenge their proper Yugoslavism through its ideological commitment to communist internationalism. In other words, Yugoslavism was seen in these early post-war days as anti-nationalism (against ethnic separatism and chauvinism), as wartime patriotism and as internationalism (Djilas 1991: 165). Therefore, federalist Yugoslavism could be part of the higher ideal of communist internationalism embodied in the project of the socialist Balkan federation that, if ever realized, would have included non-Slavs as well. Yugoslavia was supposed to be the centre that would unite Bulgaria, Albania and, possibly, Greece.

The elasticity of federalist Yugoslavism was first put to the test with the project of a common Yugoslav–Bulgarian state. In 1944, Stalin pressed Tito for the creation of a Yugoslav–Bulgarian federation. The Yugoslav leadership feared that what Stalin actually had in mind was to control Yugoslavia with the help of Bulgarians. The Yugoslav counterproposal was a federation of seven republics instead of the dual Yugoslav–Bulgarian state advocated by Sofia (Banac 1988: 31–32). Although the Bulgarian leader Georgi Dimitrov and Tito signed the 1947 Bled agreement on close economic and political ties, the conflict between Moscow and Belgrade soon buried the idea of a Balkan federation. In early 1948, Stalin reiterated to Tito his command to form a federation with Bulgaria. Belgrade, now convinced that Stalin's plans were to take effective control of Yugoslavia via the Bulgarian 'Trojan horse', opposed the idea but refused to renounce Albania. The 'Yugoslavification of Albania' was under way after 1945 and Yugoslavs believed that unification was about to take place with Albania as the seventh republic within the Yugoslav federation (Banac 1988: 32–43). On 27 March 1948, Stalin sent his first letter to Yugoslavia with the intention to discipline its leadership. On 28 June 1948, the Cominform issued a declaration in which it expelled the Yugoslav Party and called for loyal forces within the country to remove Tito and 'his clique'.

Left to their own devices after 1948, Yugoslav leaders started to promote 'socialist Yugoslavism' that did not aim at merging the Yugoslav nations but at building a socialist society that would inevitably result in a strong sense of belonging to a supranational Yugoslav polity. The successful opposition to Stalin and his political and military threat boosted the popularity of Tito and the Party as well as support for socialist Yugoslavism. The practice of publishing separate textbooks, for instance, was seen as promoting ethnic nationalism and weakening the Yugoslav unity that had to be fostered and promoted in culture and education as well. Major Croatian and Serbian intellectuals signed in 1954 the Novi Sad agreement on the single language of Serbs, Croats and Montenegrins (named Serbo-Croatian or Croato-Serbian). In 1958, the Seventh party congress called for the further development of Yugoslav socialist consciousness.

Nevertheless, in the first half of the 1960s, unifying socialist Yugoslavism started to be perceived as contrary to decentralization and was soon abandoned in official policy. Significantly, Yugoslavism and relations between the republics and the federal state were openly debated in literary circles; and as usual, this anticipated the changes soon to come. In 1961, a debate between Serbian writer Dobrica Ćosić and his Slovenian colleague Dušan Pirjevec provoked a stir. It revealed the old conflict between centralist and federalist Yugoslavism that inevitably brought to the table the question of Yugoslavia's own structure. Ćosić advocated socialist Yugoslavism and the need for Yugoslav unity, whereas Pirjevec defended the idea of Yugoslavia as a federation of full-fledged nations. In the following years, the 'centripetal' period ended and the ideology of brotherhood and unity ceded place – although it did not disappear from official rhetoric – to the 'Yugoslav socialist patriotism' that promoted the more socialist and less South-Slavic features of Yugoslavia (Jović 2003b: 166). When it came to Yugoslavia as a state, more stress was put on its ideological socialist character and its multinational composition.

The Eight Congress of the LCY in 1964 championed decentralization, the necessary flip-side of which was the Party's abandonment of Yugoslavism. Tito himself repudiated the idea of the artificial creation of one single Yugoslav nation, something paramount to 'assimilation and bureaucratic centralization, to unitarism and hegemonism'. For him, 'Yugoslav socialist integration is a new kind of social community in which all nationalities have common *interests*' (partially reprinted in Kobsa et al. 1978: 354–359). Wayne Vucinich observes that 'there is a serious paradox at the core of the Communist nationality program: the attempt to encourage ethnic separateness works at cross-purpose to the desire to foster Yugoslav unity' (1969: 282). As noted above, the Eighth Party congress gave a green light to the decentralization policies that clearly won the day after the removal of their main opponent Aleksandar Ranković and his followers in 1966. It is not surprising then that the following year – indeed, 1967 can be seen as the turning point in the history of socialist Yugoslavia – brought far-reaching constitutional changes and at the same time a strong and possibly decisive blow to Yugoslavism as an idea of strong cultural and political South-Slavic unity almost a quarter of a century before the end of Yugoslavia.

In that same year, on 17 March 1967, the Zagreb-based newspaper *Telegram* published the 'Declaration Concerning the Name and the Position of the Croatian Literary Language', signed by eighteen major Croatian cultural and literary institutions such as Matica hrvatska and the Writer's Association of Croatia. The Declaration openly rejected the 1954 Novi Sad Agreement on the single Serbo-Croatian language and signalled the abandonment of cultural Yugoslavism by the Croatian cultural elite, the very elite that originally formulated and gave substance to the Yugoslav movement and provided it with numerous high-profile partisans since its nineteenth-century beginnings. The fact that Miroslav Krleža – the most important literary and intellectual figure in Croatia and an open supporter of the Communist party since its foundation – signed the Declaration represented a serious blow to any attempts at a closer linguistic unity or closer cultural unity in general.

Again, because the foundation of the Yugoslav project was linguistic unity and the proximity of the South-Slavic dialects, the declarative abandonment of a single literary language implied the abandonment of the larger cultural and political project as well (Wachtel 1998: 185). In other words, Yugoslavia could no longer be the name for a unifying nation-building and state-building project (whether of a unitarist or centralist-federalist kind), but only for a 'community' or a 'union' of fully constituted nations, characterized by linguistic and cultural independence and statehood, that should decide independently and among each other the degree of their political unity. A response to the Declaration quickly came from Serbia. Forty-two writers from the Writers' Association of Serbia drafted 'A Proposal for Consideration' requesting – if Croatian demands for linguistic autonomy were accepted – that the Serbian language should be the language of instruction in the Serb-populated areas of Croatia. The Party condemned both the Declaration and the Proposal as nationalist deviations.[1]

Over the years, the leading Yugoslav political figures, such as Kardelj and Croatia's long-term leader Vladimir Bakarić as well as Tito (although reluctantly), started to portray Yugoslavia as a purely socialist multinational union, a common political framework that did not have any particular ethnic base (although the name itself betrayed it as a state of South Slavs). Bakarić, for instance, in a book published also in 1967, interpreted the birth of socialist Yugoslavia in the following terms: 'Yugoslavia was not united on the basis of slavism, but on the basis of social progress' (in Kobsa et al. 1978: 60). Yugoslavism seemed to be understood, at best, as socialist patriotism preferably devoid of any (ethno)national content. Yugoslavia itself, unlike the republics (all but one), was supposed to be, to paraphrase a popular slogan, '*a*-national in form and socialist in content'.

Yugoslavia: Only a matter of interests?

Edvard Kardelj most influentially advocated for Yugoslavia as an ideological and non-national project, a position that, as we mentioned, Tito reluctantly accepted after the fall of Ranković and during the constitutional changes between 1967 and 1974 (Jović 2003b). For Tito, Yugoslavia as a national project was worth pursuing and he opposed the ongoing abandonment of the idea of South-Slavic unity. For him, Yugoslav socialist patriotism affirmed the multinational character of Yugoslavia and the independent nationhood of its peoples but also stressed the necessity of and preference for the common socialist state. Kardelj, however, repeatedly described Yugoslavia as a matter of the *interests* of its constituent nations: 'The unity of the peoples of Yugoslavia is not based so much on their ethnic relatedness as on joint interests deriving from a common destiny and above all on their joint struggle for socialist relations among men and nations' (in Jović 2003b: 170).

He described Yugoslavia as the 'pluralism of self-managing interests' (Rusinow 1981: 9). The *interests* for staying together in Yugoslavia were for him concentrated in only three domains: common defence, common goals of a revolutionary transformation of the country and development of a common market area (Jović 2003b: 169–170). Kardelj's introduction of interests in his definition of relations between the republics and between them and the Federation was confusing. After all, the interests change over time and Kardelj certainly did not give clear instructions about who was supposed to define these interests (after his death). For that matter, it is not obvious what Kardelj meant by 'peoples' and whether he defined them by the republics and their boundaries or by ethnic groups. Not to mention that outside his homeland of Slovenia, the republican borders did not coincide with the geographical distribution of ethnic groups; the situation that made any separation – in case there was no more *interests* to stay together – highly explosive.

What Yugoslavism came to signify in post-Tito Yugoslavia – for those who thought that it still held certain cultural and political importance, at least as an attitude in the face of intensifying inter-ethnic and inter-republican conflicts – was aptly illustrated in Predrag Matvejević's collection of essays and reflections on *Yugoslavism Today* (*Jugoslavenstvo danas*, first edition 1982). In his book, Matvejević, one of the foremost Croatian intellectuals and writers, tried to define what the substance of Yugoslavism should be in the confederated Yugoslavia that had recently lost its only strong centripetal point, embodied in Tito's person and legend. Matvejević attempted to offer multiple definitions of what Yugoslavism is or should be: Yugoslavism as preservation of the Yugoslav community, i.e. state; Yugoslavism as more than a broader nationality (understood here as a wider ethnonational identity) and more than a shared citizenship; Yugoslavism as anti-centralism in Yugoslavia and in the republics; Yugoslavism as anti-nationalism (equally against Yugoslav and ethnic nationalism); Yugoslavism as a special internationalist point of view; Yugoslavism as an individual choice based on mixed ethnicity; and, finally, Yugoslavism as a minority position in the situation of nationalistic conflicts (1984 [1982]: 13–14).

Clearly, these various definitions did not aim at formulating, and could not have formulated, any coherent or mobilizing political platform for Yugoslavia in its final decade but rather a specific intellectual and political attitude. And this attitude was far from unusual throughout Yugoslavia in the 1980s. A significant group of individuals declared their ethnicity or ethnonational belonging as *Yugoslav*. The increased number of mixed marriages as well as a general all-Yugoslav political and cultural attitude of individuals from different ethnocultural backgrounds resulted in the sharp rise of 'Yugoslavs' recorded in the 1981 census. Between 1971 and 1981 Yugoslavs grew from 273,000 to 1,219,000, or from 1.3 to 5.4 per cent of the total population. The trend that would have likely continued in the following years since the majority of those who identified as Yugoslavs came from urban centres and seemed less attentive to the sirens of ethnic nationalism. Obviously, from the nationalist point of view (shared by many party members loyal to the idea of Yugoslavia as a confederation of *nations* and not as a nation-state as such) this state of affairs openly challenged the ethnic cohesion of the constitutive nations and their respective republics as well as inter-ethnic balances (Jović 2001b: 107).

Nevertheless, from 'brotherhood and unity' to calls for 'togetherness' in the 1980s (Pavković 2003: 252), Yugoslavism went through transformations that eventually emptied it of almost any cultural and mobilizing political content. Yugoslavia seemed no longer a family house of brotherly ethnic groups but a building divided into quasi-independent apartments whose members – not as brothers or relatives bound by blood, but more as historic tenants and partners – lived under a common roof as long as this was in their *interests*, or as long as the building was able to endure their intensive, more and more aggressive interactions and disputes. 'Togetherness', however, still implied that to live *in peace* together *was* in their best interests. And to continue this metaphor, the outcome of the first democratic elections demonstrated either a wish to move out or to redefine not only the building's pillars, but its internal walls as well.

The rise and fall of Yugoslavism cannot be dissociated from writers and intellectuals. After all, it had been writers who had *imagined* Yugoslavia out of the nineteenth-century's patchwork of South-Slavic peoples, serving different masters and having diverse ideas about their collective identity and political future.

As in many other Eastern European countries, Yugoslavism, conceptualized and propagated by writers and intellectuals, arrived long before politicians joined the movement and Yugoslavia as such came into existence. No state can exist in the absence of a large majority of its citizens believing that it should exist and that they should live together under the same political-administrative structure. One could claim that Yugoslavia's political and intellectual elites abandoned Yugoslavism – in its various forms – long before its citizens did.

Knowing the influence of writers and intellectuals, one should not be surprised to learn that the political conflict between Serbia and Slovenia that arose after Milošević consolidated his power was reflected – and sometimes conceptualized – in literary circles. The Yugoslav Writer's Union was, similar to Yugoslavia itself, divided into independent republican writers' unions and, similar to the Federation, it declined in importance in the 1970s as individual republican unions began to serve as the main centres of literary life (Dragović-Soso 2003). The debates among writers – as demonstrated by the Ćosić-Pirjevec debate in early 1960s and various quarrels over the language – were highly political and even served as an arena for debating sensitive political issues, which had direct public and political effects. The SANU memorandum, or some of its nationalistic parts, became a rallying cry for Serbian nationalist writers led again by Dobrica Ćosić, a writer who went from being a socialist unitarist Yugoslavist to an ideologue of Greater Serbianism and even a short-term president of Milošević's rump Yugoslavia. He remained, until his death in 2014, influential, though sometimes grotesque 'grandfather' of the nation.

The Kosovo crisis and Milošević's policies exacerbated the conflict between Slovenian and Serbian writers, a conflict that turned on the question of the future of Yugoslavia. Serbian nationalist writers supported the repression of Albanian demands and demanded the recentralization of Yugoslavia, whereas the Slovenian Writer's Union and journal *Nova Revija* promoted a systematic change of the regime and the Slovenian national cause. They insisted on Slovenian cultural and political sovereignty vis-à-vis other Yugoslavs and Yugoslavia, and began branding Slovenia as a Central European nation, one which had more in common with even the furthest former Habsburg lands than with the rest of 'balkanic' Yugoslavia (see Jović 2003a; Wachtel 1998). Drago Jančar, a leading Slovenian novelist, in his essay entitled *Farewell to Yugoslavia* (1999 [1990]) compared the situation in Yugoslavia to a chaotic and violent 'Balkan Inn' – Miroslav Krleža's own metaphor for the history of the region. Jančar, a right-leaning advocate of an independent Slovenia, was only expressing the general tendency among many Slovenian intellectuals inclined towards secession to emphasize the urgency of leaving the Balkan 'chaos' and joining 'Europe', embodied in the then popular European Economic Community, more quickly.

In lieu of a conclusion to the long bittersweet marriage between writers and Yugoslavia, one need only refer to the telling chronology of Yugoslavia's disintegration: the Yugoslav Writers' Union was dissolved in 1989, as if symbolically paving the way for the subsequent dissolution of the Party and the state itself.

Code red: Turning citizens into enemies

Nationalist ideologues aiming at the total separation of South Slavs and a territorial reshuffle were therefore obliged to cast aside the myth of 'brotherhood and unity', a myth inextricably bound up with Tito's legacy. Carol Skalnik Leff reminds us of another important aspect in the liberalization of communist countries that involves revisions of the 'blank spots' in the historical records of multinational states (1999). Abandoning this myth served to reinforce ethnonational identification and mobilization and to undermine the supranational one. In Yugoslavia, as elsewhere in Eastern Europe, self-victimization came to the fore. Each nation claimed to be the victim of the common state's history and revived painful memories of the inter-ethnic killings carried out during the Second World War. These 'competing narratives of resentment and blame' – as a large group of international scholars[2] assembled to explain the dissolution of Yugoslavia have called them – portrayed other nations as 'enemies' who had committed genocide against them before (the Ottoman conquests, the Second World War) and were ready to do it again (Ramet 2005a). These narratives were usually constructed around a Serbs vs. non-Serbs conflict. In his book on Serbian and Croatian victim-centred propaganda, David B. MacDonald calls these narratives *Balkan holocausts* in order to show how their purpose was to portray one's own nation as a victim of genocide comparable to the Shoah (2002). As an example, one of the leading Serb nationalist historians, and a close ally of Radovan Karadžić, Milorad Ekmečić declared before the Bosnian war that:

> only the Jews have paid a higher price for their freedom than the Serbs. Because of their losses in the war, and because of massacres, the most numerous people in Yugoslavia, the Serbs, have, in Bosnia-Hercegovina, fallen to second place, and today our policy and our general behaviour carry within themselves the invisible stamp of a struggle for biological survival. (Quoted in Ramet 2005a)

Nationalist propaganda and nationalist leaders saturated the channels of mass communication with warnings of the 'dangers' that their nations supposedly faced, including their possible biological extinction by other ethnic groups. The story of 'endangered nations', coupled with demographical statistics and estimations, underlined the imminent threat to a nation's survival and the need for protection. In this situation, to be in the minority position was perceived as extremely dangerous (Jović 2001a). The urgency of the situation justified a 'pre-emptive strike' on the already demonized enemy; this logic commands that the enemy must be destroyed before he becomes capable of destroying you (see Bowman 1997).

The collapse of the communist regime and of the Yugoslav federation, together with the subsequent implementation of conflicting nationalist agendas involving inevitable struggles over the territories of new ethnic states, activated what Slavoj Žižek in a different context calls 'code red' (2009). The functioning of the 'code red' might help us to understand how in a matter of months the former 'brothers', neighbours and partners were turned into fierce competitors and cruel enemies. Žižek actually refers to a Hollywood movie, 'A Few Good Men', in which 'code red' is described as a secret military code which, though illegal, allows the torture of soldiers that break internal rules or endanger the whole group by their behaviour. This 'code red' violates both the law and common morality but reinforces the group's cohesion to the degree necessary for its supposedly endangered survival. In other words, a 'code red' situation transferred to the terrain of ethnonationalist mobilization means that law and order are suspended and that the game of survival has begun, a game that justifies massive violence, massacres and even genocide. Needless to say, the winners of the game were the ones entitled to establish ethnically homogeneous and pure new states, invent new founding myths, cover the traces of monumental crimes and re-write history.

In the last days of Yugoslavia, Yugoslavism truly became, as Matvejević would have never wanted, 'a minority position in the situation of nationalistic conflicts', the position that could not formulate a political programme for preservation of the abandoned state, but only a plea for peace. At the moment when the Bosnian war was about to break out, on 5 April 1992, demonstrators gathered in front of the Bosnian parliament in Sarajevo to protest against the nationalist frenzy of the three main ethnic parties that were clearly taking the country towards bloodletting. Their demonstration was also an act of civic courage against Bosnian Serb paramilitaries ruled by Radovan Karadžić and the remnants of the federal army, a group mostly loyal to Slobodan Milošević at that time, that deployed its troops in and around Sarajevo. The only symbols and flags they could carry in the situation of imminent ethnic conflict were the flags of socialist Yugoslavia and socialist Bosnia-Herzegovina – a red flag with a small Yugoslav flag in its upper-left corner – and, of course, portraits of Tito. The demonstrators wanted to chase away Bosnian Serb paramilitaries from their outposts around the Parliament. Serb snipers randomly fired at the crowd that gathered at a bridge across the Miljacka river. Two women were killed on the spot, a Muslim from Dubrovnik and a Croat from Sarajevo.

If Yugoslavism was one of the motives behind that finger that pulled the trigger on the Latin Bridge in Sarajevo in 1914 and thus announced the beginning of the Great War and the advent of the common Yugoslav state, it, as the final cry to stop the war among South Slavs, definitively died in 1992 at another bridge over the Miljacka, just a mile downstream. That bridge soon became a demarcation line between the Bosnian government's and Serb positions that cut the besieged city. A year later, as in some devilish *mise-en-scène*, a young couple, a Muslim girl and a Serb boy – 'Sarajevo's Romeo and Juliette' as they sadly came to be known worldwide – tried to cross the bridge and escape the war. Both were killed and their bodies lay on the bridge for days, in an embrace.

Part Three

From Nationalist Disintegration to War

6

Partners into Competitors: Divisive Democracy and Conflicting Conceptions of Citizenship

In his book *States and Power in Africa: Comparative Lessons in Authority and Control*, Jeffrey Herbst describes the conflicts between the Zulu and early Dutch settlers over their opposing conceptions of sovereignty over territory and people. The Zulu believed that their political authority extended wherever people had pledged obedience to their king regardless of the territory where they happened to be. Also, 'the Zulu believed that they could let the whites settle on land without giving up ownership', whereas for the European whites, occupation over a certain territory also meant the ownership of that territory and control of the people that happened to be there (2000: 40–41). Extrapolated from its colonial context in which the Dutch colonizers wanted to absolutely dominate the colonized and take their land, the story could be interpreted as a clash between the conception of a political community based on ethnic, cultural, hereditary or maybe also declaratory loyalty and solidarity, regardless of existing political boundaries and polities in which the members of this community live, and a political community based on loyalty to the authorities governing a territory where one lives and, ideally, on solidarity with all those who happen to be on that territory under the same authorities. Modern states in reality often combine these two principles in a particular way: they often claim that their citizens or their ethnic kin abroad are bound to their polity and thus expect a loyalty and sometimes exercise an influence on diaspora members (who, in turn, are often interested in meddling in political affairs of the 'old country'), but, internally, they always insist on undivided loyalty of the population they govern. Even further from its original South African situation, the clash between what we can generally call civic and ethnic solidarity, as well as different understandings of whom should be loyal to whom and who belonged together, turned crucial during the last years of Yugoslavia and decisive at the moment when the multi-party majority democracy was introduced in its republics.

Democracy and nationalism

In socialist multinational federations, Bunce argues, 'the very concept of citizenship [...] became dual' (1999: 49). On the one hand, according to her it implied membership in the ideological-political community attached to the 'socialist regime-state', and, on the other, membership in a national community. Nevertheless this notion of the *duality* of citizenship in socialist federations needs to be refined. This was the case in the USSR and in Czechoslovakia (before 1969). But in both Yugoslavia after 1945 and Czechoslovakia after 1969, membership in the 'ideological-political community' was *bifurcated* into federal-level and republican-level membership. Therefore, citizenship became not only formally *dual* but *triadic*: on the one hand, there was a *dual* legal citizenship – federal and republic-level citizenship – and, on the other, membership in a given ethnonational community; with no obligation, at least in the Yugoslav case, to declare ethnic belonging and with the option of even declaring Yugoslav 'ethnicity'. Since one of the crucial tasks of post-communist democratization consisted in 'identifying the community in which democratic rights and responsibilities are to be vested' (Skalnik Leff 1999: 205), democratic participation and political belonging clashed in Yugoslavia at the junction of Yugoslav citizenship, republican citizenship and ethnic membership.

One way of understanding Yugoslavia's initial democratization – a democratization that eventually exacerbated inter-ethnic conflicts which had been meticulously nurtured and controlled by those nationalist elites who were attempting to, by multi-party elections, accede to power or stay in power – is to examine furthermore the nature of Yugoslavia's confederal citizenship. As described in the preceding chapters, Yugoslav citizenship was not only *legally* ambiguous but was becoming *politically* less important owing to the progressive confederalization of Yugoslavia since the mid-1960s. Hence, given that political decision-making had been taking place at the republican level and that the federal level mostly served – since the early 1970s – as a platform for inter-republican, or almost inter-state bargaining, democracy could only have been introduced from the bottom-up, from the republics themselves as clearly identified 'communities'. In the Yugoslav case, the problem was that democratization occurred only at the 'bottom' without ever reaching the 'top'. Since Yugoslavia was *de facto* a confederation, republican citizenship was the natural answer to the question of how and where democracy should be exercised. After the break-up of the LCY, the republican elites did not hesitate to call for democratic elections *only* at the republican level in order to legitimize their power and, having attained a democratic mandate, proceeded to negotiate Yugoslavia's future.

In the confusing situation surrounding the introduction of liberal democracy in the Yugoslav republics, an ordinary citizen was obliged initially to play three mutually non-exclusive roles. First, he or she was invited to vote as a citizen and/or resident of his or her republic and to express his or her political preferences through multi-party republican elections. At the same time, nationalist elites and politicians targeted him or her as a member of their ethnic group, a group that usually stretched across republican boundaries. And, finally, during this whole period he or she was still a citizen of Yugoslavia where there were still functioning federal institutions in place, including the Yugoslav People's army and he or she was recognized in the international arena uniquely as Yugoslav. These three identities remained compatible only so long as citizens could perform all of them simultaneously, in other words, only insofar as the Federation provided a solid framework within which Yugoslavs could be at the same time members of their civic (republican) people, their ethnic nation and remain in a position of mutual loyalty, unity and solidarity within the general Yugoslav 'community of citizens'.

However, the progressive disappearance and the weakening of the federal framework immediately caused severe difficulties for those living in a republic that was not dominated numerically by their ethnic group. When it became distinctly possible that Yugoslav federal protection would be lost along with the dissolution of the supra-republican and supranational community of citizens, they realized that they would simultaneously acquire an unwanted status of ethnic minority in a new state and lose any supra-republican institutional protection and connection with their kin-state and other members of their ethnic nation. This created an atmosphere of mutual suspicion among groups as well as – in the context of Yugoslavia's imminent dissolution – an urgent need to establish new states – preferably ethnically homogeneous and territorially enlarged – that would guarantee to their future citizens their full equality and democratic rights as well as protection. It became increasingly clear that the creation of such states in the context of conflicting territorial claims could not be achieved without violence.

Consequently, the debate on the sovereignty of nations and of republics turned into a debate about membership and a given citizen's loyalty to democratic states about to be created on the basis of Yugoslavia's internal organization. Slobodan Milošević's double measure is instructive here. In a nutshell, when it comes to Serbia, only republics are sovereign and *unitary*. By contrast, when it comes to other republics, the badge of sovereignty belongs to ethnic nations. It is not surprising then that Serbia contradicted the principle of ethnic sovereignty and solidarity in its new constitution adopted in September 1990. Serbia defined itself as the 'state of its citizens', therefore as *civic* and republican – strategically a wise move if we compare it to Croatia's constitutional self-definition as an exclusively ethnic Croat state. It also meant that no internal secession is possible in a civically bound community of citizens of Serbia that as such at least rhetorically guaranteed all rights to all citizens, which also legitimized the reduction of regional autonomies. At the same time, Serbia insisted on the sovereignty of ethnic groups, portrayed itself as the protector of Serbs in Bosnia and Croatia and demanded their separation from the seceding republics and, preferably, their union with a constitutionally *civic* Serbia!

Federalism formally creates a *national demos* at the national level and *subnational demoi* at the regional level. However, in mono-national and monolingual federations this necessary product of every federal system does not entail parallel and often competing nation-building projects at the sub-federal level that could result in distinct national *demoi* living under the same federal roof. In multinational federations *nations* are usually organized territorially. The federal identity and membership is thus in constant competition with the ethnonational sub-federal identities and memberships. Centrifugal and centripetal forces continually oppose one another and the equilibrium depends, among other things, on the institutional setting in place, historical legacies and experiences, citizens' perceptions and use of the *dual* nature of their citizenship, the interaction between their multi-level citizenship status, legally codified or not, and their ethnocultural membership and also on the practical solutions to political and economic disputes and crises taken by regional and federal political elites. The socialist policies in Yugoslavia worked towards the disabling of the federal Yugoslav *demos* in favour of sub-federal *demoi* that should have had a civic component, although difficult to uphold in the context of ethnic imbalances. Only Bosnia corresponded to this ideal of civic republican citizenship that acknowledged informally its multiethnic composition as well as its high degree of inter-ethnic mixing.

Nonetheless, the introduction of liberal democracy offered, perhaps, the last opportunity for creating a Yugoslav *demos* through the means of representative democracy had the rules of the electoral game been different. Some observers believe that a majority vote at supranational level would have created such a demos (Jović 2001a: 30). Linz and Stepan (2001 [1992]) also argue that the initial democratic elections should have been organized at the federal level (see below). According to these authors, this would have legitimated the federation and reinforced federal citizenship. However, the experience of Czechoslovakia – where the first elections were organized simultaneously at both federal and republican level – demonstrates that this was not a safe bet either.

It is interesting to note that at a certain point it was Milošević who proposed nationwide elections, hoping to capitalize on his position as the leader not only of Serbia but of all the Serbs and so of Yugoslavia's most numerous nation (see Jović 2001a). He was obviously interested in profiting from the double role he played as both Serbian nationalist and the 'saviour' of a multinational Yugoslavia – rhetoric that, at least initially, had a certain appeal even for some non-Serbs and many non-nationalist Serbs as well. This initiative, however, stoked fears of the kind of ethnic imbalances characteristic of multinational polities. Obviously, the classic model of representative democracy (one citizen – one vote) at the supranational level would never have been acceptable for smaller nations (Slovenes, Croatians, Bosniaks, Albanians and Macedonians). Only Serbs and Montenegrins were interested in this kind of power sharing, but only to a certain extent. All Serbs and Montenegrins taken together were still in a minority position in Yugoslavia as a whole and thus were fearful of a potential 'anti-Serb' coalition. In the absence of an institutional counterweight that could have guaranteed separate national/republican interests, the idea eventually turned out to be unacceptable for everyone. The first democratic elections made federal citizenship politically redundant. It was *de jure* existing but only as a derivative: democratization laid bare its true confederal nature. From these elections organized between early Spring 1990 and late Autumn of 1990 to the final disintegration of Yugoslavia in 1992, federal citizenship was only relevant if citizens travelled or fled abroad and was thus limited to passports, which were themselves issued by the republics.

The moment the Yugoslav leadership decided to introduce liberal democracy and organize multi-party elections, a certain number of questions immediately arose, the answers to which would critically determine future events. Let us just enumerate the most pressing questions that anyone wishing to play the game of liberal democracy – especially if the game is played in a democratizing socialist multinational (con)federation – must tackle head on: what is the institutional and territorial framework for democracy or, in other words, where exactly, for whom and by whom, is liberal democracy to be introduced? In the Yugoslav case, is it in the Federation, in the republics or, maybe, in the ethnic groups? Democracy should be the rule of people by the people, but who is 'the people' in Yugoslavia? Is it the citizens of Yugoslavia? Citizens of Yugoslav republics? Members of constitutive nations? Or, perhaps, 'the working class and all working people', as stated in the existing Constitution? If a citizen is asked to perform his or her duty, to elect and be elected, now in multi-party elections as opposed to his or her previous socialist experience with elections at the commune level and delegate system, and to take a part at a new emerging *agora*, then where is this agora and who are his or her co-citizens? And since every agora has its limits, who will be excluded? If elections are to be called, *where* should he or she cast their vote and for *whom* can they vote? Since representative democracy usually entails majority rule, who is likely to be in the majority and who in the minority? And what relationship should be built between these two camps, the tyranny of the majority or consociational cooperation? After all, who is *sovereign* in Yugoslavia or, in other words, who is capable of making and implementing political decisions?

Indeed, the question of sovereignty was immediately posed, coupled with the unavoidable issue of the right to self-determination. Confusing definitions of Yugoslav sovereignty – contained both in its various constitutions and in the speeches of its leaders – did not make the task easy for Yugoslavs and turned the process of democratization itself into an open constitution making and thus heavily contested process. Suddenly, the previous rules were open for debate and, unsurprisingly in an atmosphere of complete liberalization, many had different, opposing and often mutually exclusive visions of the future.

The 1974 Constitution declares in its first article that Yugoslavia is 'based on the power and self-management of the working class and all working people'. The working class is complemented with 'all working people' (thus those outside the leading class as well) as the bearer of sovereign power. Since this alliance of working people is almost all-encompassing when it comes to working adults in Yugoslavia, could we read it simply as the 'people', and, furthermore, as the Yugoslav people? But, alas, this interpretation would have been contrary to the Yugoslav solution to the national question, a solution that gave all sovereignty and the right of self-determination to the constituent nations. By this reasoning, and in the context of the introduction of liberal democracy, i.e. voluntary abandonment of the socialist heritage by that very socialist elite in power and at the moment when the de-legitimization of socialist heritage was in full swing, 'the working class and all working people' and, more generally, the Yugoslav people as such were excluded as potential bearers of sovereignty. With self-management rejected and put in question as an economic and political model, it was hard to imagine how the working class and the working people could have constituted themselves as major political subjects.

Therefore, Yugoslavs essentially faced two alternatives as to who (or what) could be sovereign: ethnic nations or the republics and their citizens? Serbia and Serbia's junior partner Montenegro argued that the former was sovereign; all other republics insisted on the latter. Furthermore, the question was related to the even more explosive issue of the constitutionally guaranteed right to self-determination and secession. Into this volatile debate, Milošević launched an argument that resonated heavily among ethnic Serbs. It could be summarized as follows: if the republics have the right to secede from Yugoslavia, then ethnic Serbs as a whole have the same right to secede from everybody else (see Budding 2008: 92; also Dimitrijević 1995: 58).

Milošević used the sovereignty of ethnic nations argument against Slovenia, Croatia and Bosnia, but he insisted on it only when it concerned ethnic Serbs outside Serbia. However, at the same time Serbia expected loyalty from all of its citizens, despite the fact that up to 35 per cent of them were not ethnically Serbs. The Serbian leadership was not ready to apply the ethnic principle within Serbia and acknowledge an equivalent right of secession for ethnic Albanians in Kosovo and Magyars in Vojvodina (as 'national minorities' they were not seen as bearers of the right to self-determination), or ethnic Muslims in the Sandžak (who due to smaller number and the lack of separatism were not seen as threatening). The sovereignty of ethnic nations, regardless of actual administrative divisions, was unacceptable as a principle of Yugoslavia's disintegration both to the other republics and, later, to the international community. The general principle of the disintegration of socialist federations was – until the recent Western recognition of Kosovo's independence and Russia's recognition of Georgia's breakaway provinces – anchored in respect for their internal republican borders.

But what would the final result of the extreme application of ethnic sovereignty in Yugoslavia have been? Most probably Slovenia would have remained in its present shape alongside a series of strange state creatures: a Croatia without at least 20 per cent of its territory but with Western Herzegovina and tiny parts of Bosnia; a Greater Serbia with Serb-populated Croatian and Bosnian territories, possibly with Montenegro, but without Kosovo, Serbian and Montenegrin Sandžak and parts of Vojvodina; a Greater Albania with Kosovo and Western Macedonia attached, a smaller Macedonia; and, finally, an ethnic Muslim state comprising the patchwork of Bosnian territories and most of the Serbian and Montenegrin Sandžak. Faced with the choice of breaking up Yugoslavia along either republican or ethnic lines, nationalist politicians in Yugoslavia opted for a combination of the two in accordance with their interests at the time. Hence, Milošević's Serbia insisted on the inviolability of its own borders but demanded control over Montenegro and the Serb majority territories in

Figure 6.1 Ethnic map of Yugoslavia in 1991 (Source: Wikimedia Commons).

Bosnia and Croatia. Similarly, Tudjman's Croatia insisted on a republican form of sovereignty – though interpreted as the sovereignty of ethnic Croats – inviolability of its republican 'AVNOJ' borders, and on the right to secede from Yugoslavia, but nevertheless challenged Bosnian sovereignty in and sometimes beyond Croat-populated areas.

Citizens as voters: Democratize and divide

In socialist Yugoslavia, there was, constitutionally, no minority and no majority, but only equal nations and nationalities. The old federal framework made it, therefore, possible for any individual to move to another 'ethnic' republic without becoming a minority member in that republic; the common citizenship guaranteed equal rights throughout Yugoslavia. Nonetheless, demographic data, including ethnic group membership, competing percentages and the territorial distribution of these groups became a major concern at the end of the *ancien régime* (Stokes 2013). In a multiethnic state, the transition from self-management socialism, implying in principle widespread democratic decision-making at the workplace level and the no-majority-no-minority rule, to a liberal democracy formed exclusively around political parties and where everything hinges on the constitution of the majority and minority easily created turbulences and highlighted inter-ethnic competition. Many citizens were suddenly placed before the choice of being a member of a minority in a large state or being in the majority in a smaller one. Vladimir Gligorov's famous aphorism captures the nature of ethnic rivalry in the Balkans: 'Why should I be a minority in your country when you can be a minority in my country?' The principle of majority rule at the federal level was rejected for the above-mentioned reasons – ultimately no one would have a majority – but the majority principle was applied within the republics and that inevitably created a 'fear of becoming a minority' (Jović 2001a).

Rogers Brubaker reveals the striking historic parallels between the post-First World War context and the post-communist situation regarding the triadic relation between national minorities, nationalizing states and national homelands (1996). There was an internal triadic relation between ethnocentric republics, ethnic minorities and external homelands (republics). The federal centre was a strong guarantor of the equality of all groups and was therefore a necessary counterweight to ethnic imbalances in the republics. Nevertheless, the internal 'triadic configuration' was occasionally discussed – as testified by the debates on the position of Croatian Serbs during the Croatian Spring movement – but the federal roof and all the rights attached to federal citizenship made the question of borders, ethnic republics, national homelands and ethnic minorities politically less salient.

Early democratization in ethnically diverse societies can easily lead 'from voting to violence' (Snyder 2000). 'Naively pressuring ethnically divided authoritarian states to hold instant elections, argues Jack Snyder, can lead to disastrous results' (2000: 16). In ethnically diverse societies, democratization more often divides than unites. As Michael Mann warns in his book *The Dark Side of Democracy*, 'democracy has always carried with it a possibility that the majority might tyrannize minorities, and this possibility carries more ominous consequences in certain types of multiethnic environments' (2005: 2). This does not mean that ethnic diversity must ineluctably lead to a failed or conflictual democratization. However, it does suggest that pushing for a rapid introduction of classic democratic rules in a context where ethnic differences can be used for political mobilization – and then legitimized and reinforced through the popular vote – will more often than not contribute to and cement ethnic fragmentation. In the former socialist federations that were mostly divided into ethnonational territories, the lines of fragmentation were already clearly demarcated. Moreover, since citizens often declared their ethnic belonging in addition to their republican identity – as a rule in the USSR and less so in Yugoslavia – ethnonational lines of fragmentation were already present within republican societies as well. Katherine Verdery observes that

> Western purveyors of 'democracy' (etymologically, 'rule by the people') therefore brought it into an environment predisposed to ethnicize it. As external observers came to ratify that elections were free and fair, they failed to ask who 'the people' were who would be allowed into the social contract creating citizens and rights. (1998: 297)

As in many other post-communist countries, the first democratic elections in Yugoslavia demonstrated the 'ethno-national cartelization of opinion and electoral competition' (Skalnik Leff 1999: 214). Civic membership was soon eclipsed by ethnic belonging as the most important marker of a citizen's identity. Vojin Dimitrijević describes the mechanism of ethnic identification:

> individuals are pushed not to act primarily as citizens but as members of the ethnic group. They are induced not to recognise any social, economic, professional and other interests and to behave as if all members of the ethnic group were in the same social position. (1998: 147–154)

To illustrate the rejection of civic identity – by a great number of individuals but not by everyone! – Dimitrijević quotes Miroslav Toholj, one of the leaders of Bosnian Serbs: 'Serbs have been finally deprived of their Serb name, they have been made citizens, which they will not accept.' Toholj here basically describes a certain conception of citizenship which is based on political community brought together by 'blood' and ethnoreligious belonging as opposed to 'citizens' brought together only by neutral civic status. Thus becoming 'citizens', i.e. accepting the legal fact as the basis for political community was seen as superseding or potentially subjugating ethnic groups. Unsurprisingly, Serb nationalists in Bosnia put in practice their vision of ethnic citizenship – and even voted a law on 'Serb citizenship' to that effect – applied in ethnically cleansed territories. And they were not alone in this kind of enterprise.

I agree with Jack Snyder who dismisses explanations centred on the supposedly long-term popular nationalist rivalries that precede democratization – often a very important feature of the 'ethnic hatred' argument. Snyder claims that 'before democratization begins, nationalism is usually weak or absent among the broad masses of the population. Popular nationalism typically arises during the earliest stages of democratization, when elites use nationalist appeals to compete for popular support' (2000: 32). He argues that 'nationalist conflicts arise as a by-product of elites' efforts to persuade the people to accept divisive nationalist ideas' (32). In this sense, his position is similar to that of V. P. Gagnon who claims that the responsibility for igniting nationalism lies solely with the political elites who channel nationalist sentiments for their own political and economic benefits (2004). Skalnik Leff points out that democratization may segment rather than pluralize and liberalization may easily result in authoritarianism and intolerance (1999: 211). On the other hand, the veteran scholar of ethnic conflict Donald Horowitz notes that divisions and conflicts caused by electoral competition in ethnically diverse societies 'can often be averted by prudent planning of elections and territorial arrangements' (1985: 682).

Neither of these were present in Yugoslavia in 1990. Elections were definitely not planned prudently to avoid conflicts. They were organized hastily by the republics and with significant time gaps between them, which had serious consequences for the political dynamic in Yugoslavia's final hours. As for the territorial arrangements, the internal borders were well established. Nevertheless, they began to be openly challenged, first of all by Serbia's demands for a revision of existing 'AVNOJ' borders, judged to be 'artificial' by mostly Serb, but also many Croatian nationalists. Any eventual change of borders, naturally, was supposed to happen at the expense of others.

Similar to Horowitz, in their widely quoted 1992 article on 'political identities and electoral sequencing' Stepan and Linz diagnosed the decisive impact of the first democratic elections – their organization (at the national and/or regional level), timing and sequencing – on the survival of non-democratic multinational polities such as Spain, the Soviet Union and Yugoslavia. They claim, in short, that the 'sequence of elections *per se* can help construct or dissolve identities' (2001: 202). The very fact that democratic elections did not take place at the federal level in Yugoslavia and the Soviet Union prevented their legitimatization as states and contributed to their disintegration into democratized sub-units. The Spanish case was clearly different. The first democratic elections there were organized at the national level and this alone, by virtue of the consequent national electoral competition, consolidated all-national parties and the Spanish state in spite of its ethnonational and regional diversity. Although electoral sequencing heavily influenced the political dynamic in Yugoslavia – we will never know, however, if all-Yugoslav elections would have saved Yugoslavia as a state – one should not overlook some important differences between Stepan and Linz's various cases, especially between highly centralized and unitary post-Franco Spain[1] and federalized, to different degrees, Yugoslavia and Soviet Union where elections came after an initial period of liberalization in the 1980s that allowed republican and local elites to capture advantageous positions. It is true that 'no significant polity wide parties emerged' (Stepan 2004b: 348) in Yugoslavia. One needs to add that this happened precisely because the political space, unlike in Spain, was institutionally already fragmented. The Yugoslav communists did not *pluralize* their polity, only their own party. The League of Communists of Yugoslavia was indeed a *league* of six parties – or eight parties if we count the independent parties from Vojvodina and Kosovo – based in their republics. It easily turned regional communist elites into the representatives of their *nations* in the federal arena. The only polity-wide, all-Yugoslav and pro-Yugoslav party in Yugoslavia's history was thus a federalized 'league' that disintegrated even before the first democratic elections (January 1990). There was a dearth of politically significant actors, standing neutrally above ethnonational cleavages that could have eventually given rise to new polity-wide parties. The republican political elites decided to organize the first democratic elections separately in order to ensure their legitimacy and reinforce their positions in anticipation of future bargaining over the preservation or disintegration of the Yugoslav federation, bargaining that eventually took place in a highly volatile context.

Nevertheless, the *timing* and *sequencing* of republican democratic elections did play an important role in the electoral preferences of citizens. Slovenia held elections only three months after the failed Fourteenth Congress of the LCY. These elections brought victory to the centre-right pro-independence coalition, but Milan Kučan, a reformed communist, was elected president. Croatia completed the electoral process soon after in May 1990. Ivica Račan's reformed communists got 35 per cent of votes but lost heavily – largely due to their poor electoral calculation and poorly designed electoral rules – to Tudjman's nationalists who with 42 per cent won an absolute majority in the Parliament. The Parliament later elected Franjo Tudjman as President. Then followed a huge gap (for such turbulent times) between the elections in the northwestern republics and subsequent elections in the southeastern republics, which were finally called in late Autumn 1990. In brief, the democratically elected, mostly right-wing republican governments of Slovenia and Croatia co-existed for half a year with the old socialist governments in Bosnia, Macedonia, Montenegro and Serbia, the latter two being nationalistic as well.

Already in August 1990 local Serbs in, as it would be proclaimed later, the *Krajina* region of Croatia blocked the roads between two major Croatian cities, Zagreb and Split, in open defiance of the new Croatian authorities. A month later Serbia adopted a new Constitution confirming the abolition of Vojvodina's and Kosovo's autonomy but retaining their two seats in the Yugoslav Presidency. If Milošević's bullying clearly handed the advantage to nationalist and separatist forces in Slovenia and Croatia, inter-ethnic conflicts in Croatia, in turn, had a strong impact on the electoral preferences of Bosnian, Montenegrin and Serbian citizens. The nationalist reformed Communists won in Serbia and Montenegro, whereas in Bosnia nationalist anti-Communists (Serb, Croat and Muslim ethnic parties) formed a coalition with disastrous results for the country's future. Milošević's Socialist Party of Serbia largely won the elections and at the presidential elections Milošević won 65 per cent of the votes. Finally, in Macedonia nationalists won in November of 1990 but reformed communist Kiro Gligorov was elected president. In sum, conservative nationalist political forces triumphed almost everywhere in Yugoslavia even in the guise of 'socialist parties' such as Milošević's.

No true left-leaning pan Yugoslav party made a strong showing at the elections. In a belated attempt to fill the vacant spot left by the Yugoslav Communists as the only all-Yugoslav supranational political force, the federal Prime Minister Ante Marković founded the Alliance of Reform Forces (SRS) in July 1990. In spite of his all-Yugoslav popularity for some successful economic policies such as the introduction of the convertible dinar and stabilization of the prices in early 1990, he entered the political game too late. In addition to rampant nationalism, some social costs of his own liberal economic policies and austerity measures, as dictated by IMF, could also explain his political defeat: a huge number of the unemployed,[2] especially outside Slovenia and Croatia, and tens of thousands on strike were more likely to look for solutions in their own republic and to listen to nationalist arguments that blamed him and his federal government or other republics and other ethnic groups for their miserable conditions. His party predictably performed well only in highly mixed Bosnian urban centres and in Macedonia, two republics whose citizens were well aware that they would be the ones to pay a heavy price in the case of Yugoslavia's disintegration.

A secret handshake between nationalism and electoral democracy

In the words of Linz and Stepan, 'agreements about stateness are *prior* to agreements about democracy'. 'A "stateness" problem, they argue, may be said to exist when a significant proportion of the population does not accept the boundaries of the territorial state (whether constituted democratically or not) as a legitimate political unit to which they owe obedience' (Linz and Stepan 2001 [1992]: 200). This definition, however, needs to be amended. The stateness problem can also occur when one or more countries question a particular country's or each other's stateness and territorial shape. One can also argue that the imperative of nation-state building, as the condition for successful integration of post-communist states into the democratic family of nations, could produce extreme conflicts in states that perceive or create a perception that their stateness (in terms of their sheer existence or their borders) is disputed from within or/ and without. There is an apparent conflict between conceptions of a consolidated nation-state – which in Eastern Europe usually means an ethnically defined and homogenized nation-state – and a state that should provide equal treatment to its citizens regardless of their origins and eventually, preferably in diversified countries, promote a pluralized democracy and effective minority rights.

Messages sent from the West underscoring the importance of solid stateness for successful democratization did not pressure regional actors to redefine or reform their ethnically heterogeneous states towards greater pluralism. On the contrary, they reinforced the idea that a truly functional state could only be an ethnically homogenized nation-state. After all, it is argued, only solid nation-states successfully democratized and exited communism without violence, whereas multinational federations and countries with a significant proportion of minorities experienced serious problems, conflicts, violence and a delayed democratization. In other words – and this message resonated well among local nationalist elites – the issue of minorities could prevent the consolidation of the state and even endanger its borders and ultimately its very existence.

As Will Kymlicka points out, the West often sends contradictory demands to Eastern Europe by pushing equally hard for the adoption of state models developed in monolingual nation-states and for a series of minority rights characteristic of multilingual and multination states (Kymlicka 2001a: xiv). This ambiguous message presents local leaders with a crucial choice: either they continue to build an ethnically *consolidated* nation-state or they adopt multiple measures to reform their states on a civic and even multinational basis (which might include the 'threat' of federalization), which they do only under external pressure or when facing serious internal rebellion and almost always reluctantly. The post-communist states often argue that they need to construct themselves as solid nation-states through the process of *transition* before they can pluralize and implement high standard minority rights protections. The false belief that under communist rule nation-building was frozen and thus should be *defrosted* as part of the democratic transition is overwhelmingly accepted both on the ground and in the West. Hence, a toleration of many controversial policies by nationalist democratizing elites such as, for instance, the massive deprivation of citizenship of the former Soviet citizens on the grounds of their non-Baltic origins in Estonia and Latvia.

But the question remains as to whether *democratization* can be achieved without *pluralization*. Kymlicka sees a clear correlation between democratization and minority nationalism (2001b: 369). The Eastern and Central European countries without minorities democratized successfully, he concludes, whereas a slow and painful democratization results from the inability to accommodate minority nationalism. However, the example he cites as evidence for his claim could, contrary to his intentions, support the opposite conclusion. We have here another ambiguous message from the West because, once again, the successful democratization of an ethnically homogenous country could be perceived by other states with minority difficulties as an example to emulate in their own attempt to consolidate and democratize. Minorities, therefore, are not seen as allowing an opportunity to achieve full democratization through a joint effort, as Kymlicka advocates, but rather are considered an obstacle on this path. Since almost all countries with minorities have experienced 'difficulties' in democratization, this simply reinforces the powerful and dangerous stereotype that ethnic diversity itself is to blame for the failure. The accommodation of minorities' requests, especially if followed by consociational arrangements, veto powers and territorial autonomy, is thus seen as a threat to the functioning and even the cohesion of the state. In short, why should they bother to democratize by accommodating minorities' demands, when they can just as easily 'get rid' of them – either literally or by simply restricting access to citizenship – and thereby *democratize* successfully like the others.

Observers of democratization in countries with a high degree of ethnonational plurality often quote (often uncritically) the classic liberal authority John Stuart Mill, who claims in his *Considerations on Representative Government* (1861) that 'free institutions are next to impossible in a country made up of different nationalities' (296) and that 'it is in general a necessary condition of free institutions, that the boundaries of governments should coincide in the main with those of nationalities' (298–299). According to Philip Roeder, the post-communist experience demonstrates that 'democracy is unlikely to survive in ethnically plural societies' (1999: 855). Roeder is among those scholars worried about the 'third wave of democracy' and claims to have statistical evidence that 'successful democratic transitions are improbable when national revolutions are incomplete' (1999: 856). Democracy promoters thus very often encourage nationalist politicians – although sometimes they worry about their human rights records – through their own claims that democracy is possible only with a solid ethnic majority, or failing this, a peaceful and complacent minority. To insist on ethnic homogeneity as a pre-condition for liberal democracy in Eastern Europe is essentially to advocate a system of ethnically 'pure' and separated territories. But to achieve such ethnic 'purity', or at least to reduce ethnic plurality, as demonstrated in the former Yugoslavia and in some post-Soviet regions, requires the massive employment of *non-democratic* methods involving statelessness, discrimination, human rights violations, violence against civilians, expulsions and, ultimately, mass killings. After all, this is exactly how the countries of 'old Europe' achieved their ethnonational homogeneity and a 'democratic peace'. This 'advice', unfortunately, resonated well in post-socialist 'new Europe'. In multinational socialist federations, it promoted ethnically based political communities in opposition to the existing civic-legal political communities at the republican level as a basis for democracy. This ethnocentric vision of citizenship challenged social realities and institutional settings, put in question the existing borders and helped to open the door for violence and war.

7

Where is My State? Citizenship as a Factor in Yugoslavia's Disintegration

So, why did it happen?

The former Yugoslavia was one of those places that openly defied the 'Clinton happy years' and the superficial triumphalism of the capitalist West after 1989. Naturally, the media, politicians and the public at large required an immediate explanation for both Yugoslavia's disintegration and the ensuing violence. An enormous number of articles and books mostly focused on the period between Milošević's accession to power in Serbia in 1987 and 1988, the democratization of Yugoslavia in 1990 and the wars in Croatia, Bosnia and Kosovo. Scholars competed with journalists in providing explanations, analyses of the conflicts and predictions.[1] Naturally, journalists had the ear of the general public and, sometimes, the governments. As for scholars, they often competed with one another to provide an original thesis to explain the Yugoslav disaster and often neglected alternative approaches in order to underline the novelty of their own interpretation and position themselves securely in the scholarly debate (for critical reviews of the literature on Yugoslavia's disintegration and wars, see Dragović-Soso 2008; Jović 2001b; Ramet 2005b).

I fully agree with Dejan Jović (2001b) and Sabrina Ramet (2005b) on the necessity of a multifactor analysis in order to understand Yugoslavia's 'disintegrative synergies' (Cohen 2008). Obviously, only a multifactor analysis or a combination of approaches could yield satisfactory results in explaining such a complex process that involved changes in the international order, the disintegration of a state, the creation of new states and dramatic political, social and economic mutations which were often followed by large-scale violence. In this chapter, I do not present an exhaustive literature review but concentrate instead on describing, commenting and criticizing some of the most important arguments, and especially those related to my own research on citizenship in Yugoslavia and its successor states. I therefore pay special attention to studies dealing with institutional design, constitutional redefinitions of Yugoslav republics, socio-economic processes and the role of political elites. Finally, I present my own addition of the thus far neglected factor of citizenship to the list of multiple causes of Yugoslavia's disintegration.

However, it is important first to highlight the argument that should be rejected entirely. The famous 'ethnic hatred' argument, coupled with the now infamous 'clash of civilizations' that influenced the media, the general (and generally uninformed) public but also officials in international organizations and national governments, is generally dismissed as academically irrelevant and intellectually shallow. Nonetheless, it was probably, like in so many other cases, the most influential argument in the media and the favourite explanation of all those unfamiliar with the history of Yugoslavia but still determined to have a stance. It is said that one book in particular – *Balkan Ghosts* by journalist Robert D. Kaplan published in 1994 – had wide appeal and even convinced Bill Clinton not to intervene during the first phase of the Yugoslav war. The argument is simple: the Balkan peoples have hated each other throughout history but large empires and Tito's dictatorship kept these sentiments in check. Upon Tito's death these ethnic hatreds came to the surface. Moreover, the argument continues, the outcome is not surprising since this is a region of constant 'clashes' between Roman Catholicism, Orthodoxy and Islam. Furthermore, there is something embedded in the character and the behaviour patterns of these peoples that cause them to cut each other's throats whenever they can.

Scholars spilled a lot of ink in rebuking this argument and in some instances the media's oversimplification of the Balkan conflict served as the primary motivation for them to write their studies (see, for instance, Gagnon 2004). In short, the 'ethnic hatred' argument only blurs the real causes of the conflict and more often than not serves the participants in the conflict by providing a justification or rationale for their violence. If ethnic hatred really governs these peoples' minds and actions, then everything is a matter of survival; if the war is just one episode in the centuries-long game of survival, then no one can be blamed for pulling the trigger first (after all, in history the 'other side' did the same).

One has to mention here that nationalists used one more argument that found many receptive ears in the West or created an even bigger confusion. During the 1990s the recognition of collective identities and of communities' rights to preserve their cultural specificity and self-govern themselves was understood as a basic human right. Mix it with democratization after the years of 'totalitarianism' in the East that allegedly was not allowing for full expression of ethnocultural identities and you can be sure to gain some sympathies in the West (after all the 'West' is the only audience to which you actually speak and from which you expect recognition). I would suggest that nationalist arguments centred on identity politics played quite well with the proliferation of multiculturalist discourses and a general shift towards policies of recognition of specific cultural identities and their subsequent empowerment through various forms of autonomy. Add territorial claim to this in an ethnically mixed environment and you will soon have conflict and violence. In this regard, as Valerie Bunce observes, the exit from socialism was not only a matter of regime change or state rejection but also of national liberation (1999: 132). Democracy itself thus turned out to be one of the crucial tools for mobilizing ethnic populations around an agenda of final national emancipation.

Relevant factors of Yugoslavia's disintegration

It's the economy, stupid!

Putting Yugoslavia in the perspective of global economic changes since the late 1970s seems necessary. The economic argument, coupled with an argument emphasizing the role of the international community, was strongly presented by Susan Woodward in her widely quoted book *Balkan Tragedy* (1995a). For Woodward the violent disintegration of Yugoslavia was 'the result of the politics of transforming a socialist society into a market economy and democracy' (1995a: 15). Woodward locates the causes in the economy in general and in the foreign-debt crisis in particular. For her, 'a critical element of this failure was economic decline, caused largely by a program intended to resolve a foreign debt crisis' (1995a: 15). John Allcock similarly sees a failure of Yugoslavia as a failure of a modernization process (2000). For Woodward, the conflict was only exacerbated by an inadequate Western response to the crisis and the general international context (1995a: 379).

By highlighting economic factors, Woodward and Allcock underline an important element in understanding Yugoslavia's disintegration. Although this was one of the crucial elements that affected the general political and social crisis in Yugoslavia in the late 1980s, it is not, in my opinion, the direct cause of the state's disintegration and violence. Woodward's insistence on the role of the international community, particularly Germany, in igniting the war is less convincing but consistent with her interpretation of Yugoslavia's disintegration as mostly managed by foreign actors (little surprise then that her argument was widely praised by nationalists, especially in Serbia, since it shifted the culpability towards the international arena or at least to other actors such as economically 'egoistical' Slovenes). Concentrating only on the international community simply fails to grasp how local elites, those in power or eager to grab it, responded to the profound socio-economic changes and the announced incorporation into the global capitalist order. In other words, how existing elites attempted to use their political capital inherited from socialism for gaining the economic rewards and how rising elites understood the democratic process as political empowerment that could be easily translated into economic gains as well.

Although both the changes in international order and inadequate and incoherent Western responses influenced and sometimes exacerbated the conflict, they could not have put Yugoslavia on the road to war. Nor could they explain the course of the war itself or the extreme violence against the civilian population employed for control of the territory and its resources. A bad economy, induced by foreign debt and inadequate austerity measures championed by the IMF, as Woodward rightly argues, coupled with tectonic changes in the international order, and conflicting signals coming from world powers would shake any country, especially one like Yugoslavia, but they would not be sufficient to bring it to the brink of collapse and, a step further, into a bloody war. For that, people had to make concrete decisions and prepare a civil war by heavy employment of organized violence.

... but also the federal institutions

There *was* also something in Yugoslavia's socialist institutions themselves that made it difficult, though not impossible, to guarantee Yugoslavia's political existence after socialism. Valerie Bunce in *Subversive Institutions* (1999) describes their 'design and destruction' in the Soviet Union, Czechoslovakia and Yugoslavia. As for the last, Yugoslavia's centrifugal federalism produced a confederal system of quasi-independent states that was hardly suitable for liberal democratic procedures for the reasons I enumerated in the previous chapter. Bunce sees a clear correlation between the collapse of regime (socialism) and the subsequent disappearance of the state in the USSR, the CSSR and the SFRY (1999: 5). But in this regard it must be said that the subtitle of her book – 'the design and the destruction of socialism and the state' – is misleading. What was actually destroyed was not the *state* – a strong unitary model of nation-state actually triumphed – but the *federations* of these states. The political space of 'really existing socialism' was fragmented according to nation-states that were intentionally created as such by socialist regimes. States that were already there got rid of the federal system they had been part of and through which they had been consolidated as states. The collapse of the regime was followed by the *national* unification of two Germanys, the democratization of mono-national unitary states and the disintegration – between 1991 and 1993 – of multinational federations into mostly unitary national states dominated by their ethnic majorities. We can thus conclude that the acceptable model for post-socialist democratic times was the unitary mono-national state. It is exactly what the former Yugoslavs tried and mostly succeeded in achieving in the 1990s and early 2000s. There where we can still find multinational states such as Bosnia-Herzegovina, the ethnocentric model has been transferred to the sub-state level.

There is also an important difference between, on one hand, the Soviet Union – whose very name designated it as an a-national ideological union of ethnonational states – and, on the other, Yugoslavia and Czechoslovakia that were – as their names suggest – created as the 'national homes' of the culturally related South Slavs and Czechs and Slovaks respectively. The disintegration of Czechoslovakia and Yugoslavia could also be seen as a failure of bi-national and multinational integration respectively. But were these really failures? Were citizens completely disenchanted with these federations at the moment of the regime's collapse? Democratizing a (con)federal system entailed the empowerment of the republican elites who were to negotiate the end of these federations often in spite of popular will. The Czechoslovak 'peaceful divorce' was staged by political elites in spite of the fact that a huge number of Czechs and Slovaks were in favour of maintaining a common state. One could say the same for Yugoslavia before 1990 (not anymore after that year), although Yugoslavs were divided as to what form their union should take. However, they did not have a political platform from which to express this shared desire to live in a common state and this possibility definitely vanished with the first violent clashes breaking out, organized and instigated by republican or local political elites (for a graphic illustration of organized violence see the BBC documentary *The Death of Yugoslavia* from 1995).

The federal institutions already in place were another critical element. Stepan claims that the 'activation of federalist structures in a context where they had previously been *latent* rapidly creates "political opportunity structures" and new forms of "resources mobilization" possibilities' (2004b: 347). However, by putting all of these federations into the same category, Stepan overlooks the fact that in Yugoslavia republics were not autonomous only 'on paper', but were already experienced 'institutional veto players'. One could even adopt Stepan's expression 'moribund federal institutions' (2004b: 348) to describe, not facade federalism but a centrifugal federal system that empowered constituent units to the point where it began losing its own autonomy.

When it comes to the differences between these three federations one also needs to state the obvious: the Soviet Union was composed of fifteen republics with the Russian Federation being territorially, politically, economically and culturally dominant within a largely centralized federation; Czechoslovakia was after 1969 a bi-national federation of a senior partner (Czechs) and a junior partner (Slovaks); Yugoslavia, on the other hand, was composed of six institutionally equal units. This created completely different internal political dynamics. It is not surprising then that the Soviet republics united against the federal centre and got rid of it. Yugoslavia's republics turned against each other or formed opposing coalitions between the republics, whereas Czechoslovakia's survival was played out in negotiations between two partners.

Yugoslavia's internal structure and the relations among the republics as defined by its system of centrifugal federalism, as well as its position outside the Soviet bloc, made it a unique case among socialist federations. As mentioned before, Sabrina Ramet described socialist Yugoslavia as a balance of power system (1992: 4). The fundamental principle of the balance of power system is that no single actor has sufficient power to dictate terms unilaterally to the others and that no unit, regardless of its size, is deprived of equal status. This theory is compatible with Henry Hale's claim that the absence of a 'core ethnic region' guarantees equilibrium, equality and stability of ethnofederations (2004: 165–193). Hale argues that the collapse of a multinational polity is more likely if it has a 'core ethnic region' and less likely if the dominant group is territorially divided. According to Hale's criteria of what constitutes a core ethnic region – in which either the unit constitutes a majority of the whole population or it makes up at least 20 per cent more of the whole population than the second largest group – the USSR (Russia), Czechoslovakia (Czech Republic) and Yugoslavia (Serbia) also had core ethnic regions (2004: 169–170).

However, until 1989, Yugoslavia was, in my view, a country without a 'core ethnic region' capable of precipitating 'ethnofederal state collapse' since the only region capable of acting as a core ethnic region (Serbia) was *de iure* divided internally into Serbia proper (which could not qualify as a core ethnic region), autonomous Vojvodina and autonomous Kosovo. However, it was divided *de facto* after the constitutional reforms carried out between 1967 and 1974. Serbia was *re-unified* under Slobodan Milošević after the abolition of the provincial autonomies in 1989, and this is what transformed Serbia into the core ethnic region in Yugoslavia during the crucial 1989-1991 period. Re-centralisation of Serbia consequently radically altered the existing balance of power. In addition, the dependence of Montenegrin elites on Belgrade reinforced Serbia's position as the core ethnic region of Yugoslavia.[2] When he consolidated Serbia's position within Yugoslavia, Milošević was attempting to re-centralize Yugoslavia as well. Faced with resistance from other republics, the core (ethnic) region abandoned the project of re-centralizing Yugoslavia altogether and focused instead on the ethnonational unification of Serbia, Montenegro and ethnic Serbs in neighbouring republics. This, in turn, gave a strong impetus to secessionist movements in Slovenia and Croatia. Nevertheless, the core ethnic region would have never had the same leverage over the others without the tacit and later overt support of the federal army (JNA), the majority of whose personnel had an ethnic Serb background or was originally from Serbia itself.

...with a help of constitutional engineering

Even before the final disintegration of the federation, the Yugoslav republics rushed to reinforce their statehood by introducing significant constitutional changes. This sometimes involved the constitutional redefinition of the republics as the national states of their ethnic majority, a practice that Robert Hayden called 'constitutional nationalism' (1992). In fact, all of them with the exception of Bosnia had already been defined as the national states of their titular nation. However, there were some important qualifications. Croatia, for example, was defined as the state of the Croatian people and the state of the Serbian people in Croatia. Constitutional changes emphasized the ownership of the state by the titular nation, except in the curious case of the Serbian new constitution. 'A system of constitutional nationalism thus institutionalizes a division between those who are of the sovereign nation, ethnically defined, and those who are not. The latter may hold citizenship but cannot aspire to equality' (Hayden 1999:15). Hayden also sees 'constitutions as configurative of conflict' (1999: 11). New citizenship policies are inseparable from 'constitutional nationalism', which had been the prominent feature of democratization in post-communist Europe.

Hayden claims that Slovenian constitutional amendments from November 1989 'destroyed the federal structure of Yugoslavia'. I agree that Slovenia's 'unilateral' (as I called it above) attempt at decentralization was a blow to Yugoslavia as defined by the 1974 Constitution. However, to claim that this 'destroyed' the Yugoslav federation is an exaggeration. It ignores the fact that Serbia's earlier unilateral abolition of the autonomy of Vojvodina and Kosovo in March 1989 was an equally serious attack on the SFRY constitution and, moreover, Tito's legacy, and that Slovenian attempts at reinforcing their sovereignty were directly related to Milošević's aggressive attempts at re-centralizing Yugoslavia. A number of constitutional amendments had limited the autonomy of Vojvodina and Kosovo resulting in a centralized Serbia. By the same token, the Serbian government challenged the federal system by appointing its own foreign minister (Malešević 2000: 157).

Interestingly, Hayden sees Serbia's new 1990 constitution as an example of constitutional nationalism but reduces it to a platform for the one-man rule of Slobodan Milošević (Hayden 1999: 73) rather than seeing it as an attempt to consolidate an ethnocentric Serbian nation-state. Even if we grant that the new constitution helped Milošević strengthen his power, this was hardly the only reason behind the constitutional re-design of Serbia. The most important feature of the new constitution was the confirmation of the abolition of the provincial autonomy of Vojvodina and Kosovo. This move suited the political goals of nascent Serbian political parties – no major party would ever oppose Milošević's re-centralization of Serbia – at the very moment Serb nationalism was reaching its peak. Belgrade's intention to abolish the autonomy of these provinces, to codify this change in the new constitution and to suppress any opposition, primarily in Kosovo, by the massive deployment of the police and army was also perceived by ethnic Serbs and non-Serbs alike as a first step towards realizing the nationalist objective of bringing 'all Serbs into one state'. If we take into account the general political context and subsequent events within Yugoslavia at the time, as well as the suppression of the provincial autonomies which had guaranteed equality within Serbia to ethnic Albanians in Kosovo and to the multiethnic population of Vojvodina, the very wording of the constitution could be seen as a move to enhance the position of the Serb majority within a unified and ethnically heterogeneous Serbia and by doing so strengthen Serbia's own position within a failing Yugoslavia.

... and under the control of political elites

The constitutions are important but the scrutiny of concrete events shows that politicians were the primary players in the Yugoslav drama. Among them, Slobodan Milošević reserved the central part for himself with supporting (though crucial roles) played by, in order of importance, Franjo Tudjman, Milan Kučan and Alija Izetbegović. In this respect, it is not surprising that Milošević is the subject of the majority of journalistic and scholarly works dealing with Yugoslav political elites (see Gordy 2008). After the first democratic elections, these elites firmly established a monopoly over the political arena, the economy, the media and the security apparatus of their republics and, in the case of Milošević, over the federal army as well. The future of Yugoslavia was to be decided thereafter among the leaders of the republics. The Yugoslav public watched helplessly as the leaders were meeting at various places throughout Yugoslavia in 1990–1991, failing each time to reach an agreement. In the meantime, violence broke out, very often orchestrated by those same political elites as a tool in the power struggles between them and within their republics. That the political leaders undoubtedly held the political destiny of Yugoslavia in their hands was later confirmed by reports on several secret agreements that were made at this time (see Little and Silber 1995). In January 1991, for example, Milan Kučan met Slobodan Milošević at his presidential villa in Karadjordjevo (Vojvodina). At this meeting, Milošević allegedly agreed that Slovenes had the right to an independent state, while in turn Kučan agreed that Serbs too had the right to live in one state. Two months later, Tudjman joined Milošević again at Karadjordjevo. There, they supposedly agreed on the partition of Bosnia, a deal that was never officially confirmed, unless we count what happened on the ground in Bosnia subsequently as proof.

V. P. Gagnon claims that conservative elites in Croatia and Serbia employed violence and images of a threatening enemy in order to *demobilize* those pushing for political, economic and structural changes that would have endangered the elites' position and power. By creating political homogeneity in their republics, these elites also managed to keep control over the existing structures and to convert by various means previously socially owned property into private wealth that was to serve as the basis of their power within a newly introduced free market economy. Gagnon further argues that war and violence were not the expression of a population's sentiments. Rather they were imposed from outside on plural communities by political and military forces (Gagnon 2004: xv).

Although I do agree with Gagnon's general argument concerning the crucial role played by elites in managing Yugoslavia's disintegration and violent ethnic conflicts, I find the demobilization argument more problematic. Gagnon, in my opinion, does not pay sufficient attention to the strategies of both mobilization and demobilization. It was important to *mobilize* the population around an ethnonationalist agenda; strategies that had been employed by elites in Croatia in 1990 and 1991 and in Serbia between 1987 and 1991, but also to *demobilize* the political opposition in Croatia and in Serbia starting already in 1991. In

Gagnon's analysis, there is a tendency to mirror the events in Milošević's Serbia (1987–2000) against those in Tudjman's Croatia (1990–1999) and to blur some important differences both in the sequence of events and in their respective elites' strategies within their particular context.

Furthermore, these strategies cannot be understood without bringing into the picture other interconnected players in the Yugoslav drama, namely the Slovenian leadership, the JNA, the federal Prime Minister Ante Marković and the separate nationalist elites in Bosnia. Gagnon thus overlooks the fact that even before the first democratic elections that legitimized Milošević's power and brought Franjo Tudjman to office, both the incumbent elites and up and coming nationalist elites used nationalist rhetoric to effectively *mobilize* their populations.

In the case of Croatia, they continued to do so both prior to and during the war in order to secure strong support for Croatian independence and national unity. A large political *demobilization* of the population in Croatia was carried out successfully during the war years and Tudjman's party managed to consolidate power and used similar methods of demobilization again when opposition to his reign started to show signs of political recovery after the war in 1996. In Milošević's case, it could be said that he played the ethnonationalist card before the outbreak of war to *mobilize* Serbs around his programme for the recentralization of both Serbia and Yugoslavia and to portray himself as the only one capable of building a Greater Serbia on the ruins of Yugoslavia. By doing so, he effectively tried to *demobilize* a strong nationalist opposition that seriously threatened his power in March 1991. Being a symbol of the old communist regime, the conservative nationalist opposition perceived Milošević as, at best, a tool to be used for implementing the nationalist agenda. In 1996 and 1997, massive anti-Milošević protests erupted at which he was accused, not only of being authoritarian and 'communist' but also of losing wars fought for the unification of Serbs. In other words, at that point Milošević had become an obstacle rather than an asset for the achievement of nationalist goals.

The citizenship factor

In the previous passages, I have underlined the factors I consider crucial to Yugoslavia's disintegration. The socio-economic situation in the second half of the 1980s is the key to understand why the Yugoslav self-managing socialism faced a rapid and widespread delegimitization as both a political and socio-economic model. Foreign debt, inflation, IMF standby arrangements, austerity measures applied to unprofitable industries and public sector resulting in rising unemployment and massive workers' strikes in the 1980s (see Lowinger 2009; Woodward 1995a, 1995b), all contributing to open conflicts among republics over economic issues (culminating in mutually imposed economic sanctions between Serbia and Slovenia in late 1989), were among elements that corroded the Yugoslav socialist system and openly put in question the two precious wartime promises: national and social emancipation that were conditional upon one another. The economic crisis of socialism that was incapable of providing a certain socio-economic standard inevitably meant not only that a different economic model was needed but that such a model might need another political framework as well, a view strengthened by the paralysis of the federal institutions. The economic crisis itself was translated into inter-republican and inter-ethnic competition and growing mutually exclusive demands were undermining further Yugoslav self-management as a system incapable of delivering both higher standards of living and a solution to national aspirations acceptable for all. The existing institutions of centrifugal federalism were crucial in this process of both republican leaderships' internal quest for legitimacy and the inter-republican relations reassembling inter-state relations even before the first elections. In 1989 and 1990, the major republics (Slovenia, Croatia and Serbia) engaged in constitutional engineering to secure the internal legitimacy and a more independent position within the federation (even when this went against its Constitution). The democratization process was further entirely manipulated by these political elites, composed of either old or, mostly, a mixture of old and new political actors.

In this situation, competing visions of citizenship, I would argue, were one of the crucial factors that pushed the country towards disintegration and conflict. By late 1989 and definitely in 1990, it became clear that the republican centres had abandoned the Yugoslav federal citizenship as the framework of existing political community. However, they did not clearly opt, like in the Soviet sub-units, for the republican political communities. Instead, they positioned themselves as representatives of both their ethnic communities regardless of the republican borders and at the same time as representatives of their civic communities within their borders (that would not tolerate the disloyalty that they encouraged their ethnic kin to display in other republics). In other words, they acted as both the Zulu kings and the Dutch settlers and required the control of both their territory and of all members of the community that they saw themselves entitled to represent and to whom, often, these external members pledged loyalty. However, if the Zulu kings were more interested in governing people than the territory, in Yugoslavia controlling external members meant aspiring to control the territory they inhabited as well. A glance over the ethnic map of the former Yugoslavia in 1991 is enough to understand that that was a recipe for an open conflict.

Therefore, the citizenship factor must be added to the multifactor synergy that sealed the fate of Yugoslavia. I claim that the fundamental questions of citizenship related to the very definition of membership in a political community as well as to citizenship contract by which a citizen exchanges his or her loyalty and duties for the rights and protection by his or her political community and its institutions (state) influenced critically the democratization process and Yugoslavia's disintegration. At the crucial junction, in the context of imminent redefinition and possible collapse of federal Yugoslavia, between early 1990 and early 1992, citizens were asking themselves these basic questions: *To what political community do I belong?*, or, *to whom do I owe my loyalty?* And, finally, *who (what state?) guarantees, or promises to guarantee my rights – starting with human, civic and political rights, employment and property... – and, last but not the least, protection?* If Yugoslav citizens were asking these basic citizenship questions, the answers to which determined the collective political outcomes and their personal destinies as well, one has to ask: how did they come to the answers to these questions? Did they ever have a choice, or did they have to deal with suggested answers (as during the various referendum and plebiscite practices) and, finally, *faits accomplis*? How did they make themselves heard or how they were silenced? To whom were political channels open and to whom were they closed? Citizenship thus turns into an explanatory prism through which we can understand an enormous political, social and economic transformation that wiped out Yugoslavia.

Generally, the democratization of Yugoslavia reinforced the factor of ethnicity, i.e. the citizen's identification with his or her ethnic group. The democratic elections confirmed the conflict (in case of minorities) or complementarity (in case of majorities) between the citizens' civic/republican and ethnic identities. The very fact that almost all republics were defined as the 'national homes' of their core ethnic group only underlined the primacy of ethnic identity even when the citizens themselves, regardless of their ethnic origins, rejected ethnonationalism and expressed a purely *civic* patriotism or loyalty to the institutions of their republics and of the Federation. These two political identities could only be easily reconciled if a citizen resided in his or her own ethnic republic and therefore belonged to its ethnic majority. However, this was not the case for the considerable number of individuals who lived outside the 'national homes' of their ethnic groups, in republics to which they had historically belonged *civically* (as republican citizens), or simply as long-term residents, but not *ethnically*.

With the disintegration of Yugoslavia looming after the break-up of the LCY in January 1990, citizens began to wonder *how*, if at all, Yugoslavia would disintegrate. The obvious lines of separation were the republican borders, but the signal sent from the republican leaders and nationalist politicians suggested ethnic separation was the aim: the break-up of Yugoslavia presented an opportunity to redraw 'artificial' republican borders. In this context, constant communication via the republican-controlled media between the nationalist leaders and their ethnic bodies is essential for understanding the political dynamic of Yugoslavia's dissolution. The first democratic elections took place in an atmosphere of conflicting nationalist aspirations. It is not surprising, then, that the elections revealed strong backing for ethnic leaders and their parties whose message of ethnic solidarity traversed republican borders. They promised to 'protect' and guard the interests of their ethnically defined electorate[3] in the inter-republic and inter-ethnic conflicts and in the case of Yugoslavia's disappearance.

I argue that the ethnonational conception of citizenship finally prevailed and fuelled conflicts over the redefinition of borders within which the ethnonational states were to be formed on the basis of absolute majorities of the core ethnonational groups. Democracy, on this view, was seen as workable only if it was essentially ethnonational. In other words, majority rule should not entail a division between an ethnic majority and an ethnic minority but rather should be practiced *within* the core ethnonational group with the majority/minority division formed on the basis of ideological preferences. In this sense, a projected ethnonational state, territorially expanded in order to include most if not all members of the ethnic group, could be truly democratic *only* if the core ethnic group had an absolute majority and ethnic minorities were reduced to an insignificant percentage of the population. This conception of citizenship, coupled with the new democratic order, in the context of the rapid delegimitization of the Yugoslav socialist heritage, only gave boost to extreme nationalism as well as to revisionist rehabilitation of right-wing nationalist and fascist political programmes from the period of the Second World War.

Needless to say, not every Yugoslav succumbed to a programme of ethnic homogenization and territorial redefinition of Yugoslavia's successor states. However, those who did oppose it – and who advocated instead either the continued existence of the federation or its peaceful dissolution into civic and ethnically heterogeneous states – did not have a political platform from which they could articulate their views and discontent or engage in concrete political action.

With the progressive disappearance of the federal state, citizens were left with only their republican citizenship. In the context of the federation's immanent dissolution, many simply refused to be loyal to their republics, which they perceived as another ethnic group's national home. On the other hand, in these republics, the ethnic majority often succumbed to the temptation to re-define the republic as being exclusively its own state. (The multinational character of the Bosnian state was, in a similar fashion, rejected in favour of ethnic partition.) In both cases, citizens simply switched their loyalties to whatever they considered their ethnic 'state in the making'; a state that would ideally also include their homes within its new borders. If this scenario failed to materialize, an individual was faced with an alternative: either a forced or a (to varying degrees) voluntary migration to their ethnic homeland and, in so many cases, abroad, or the acceptance of minority 'second-class citizen' status.

Nationalist elites attempted to reduce ethnic heterogeneity and to create 'pure' ethnonational states, the territorial shape of which was to be decided either militarily or by mutual agreements between these elites. This was confirmed through the practice of constitutional nationalism and through citizenship legislation (see Chapter 9). This process was intimately related to electoral democracy itself and to the fact that only citizens would be invited to participate in the political arena and, ultimately, allowed to vote. Therefore, the inclusion of the core ethnic group's members, regardless of their places of residence (inside or outside state borders), and the parallel exclusion – as much as possible – of members of other ethnic groups was one of the strategies most crucial to the transformation of Yugoslavia's multinational space into a series of ethnically homogenized democratic states and sub-state territories. The citizenship factor thus played one of the pivotal roles in bringing Yugoslavia, upon its democratization, to the brink of political collapse. Moreover, it was one of the triggers of violence that would seal its fate.

8

Enemies: Citizenship as a Trigger of Violence

One could safely conclude that there is an intimate historic affinity between citizenship and war. From the antique city-states where full citizenship status was acquired by serving in war (Anderson 1996: 28, 33; Pocock 1998), via the traditional military draft for men (and in some places for women) to contemporary practices that enable immigrants and foreigners serving in the armed forces, such as the US army or in the *Légion étrangère*, an easier access to citizenship. There is a historic relationship between 'blood', either inherited or spilled (one's own or of other people), and citizenship. However, violence related to citizenship is not only physical but often invisible. It is the violence of administrative decisions, hierarchy of different statuses, 'wrong' passports and 'papers' or deprivations of citizenship. In the following chapter, I will also tackle the issue of physically invisible but nonetheless effective violence caused by the post-Yugoslav citizenship regimes. In this chapter though, I will turn to the outbreak of that 'visible' violence that spread across almost all corners of the former Yugoslavia. To examine why and how this violence happened, and what was the role of citizenship, we need to cast the net more widely all over post-socialist post-partition European states.

The dark side of 1989: Violence in post-socialist Europe

The two decades after 1989 in Central and Eastern Europe might be branded *les années 89*. Here I paraphrase what is in France nowadays called *les années 68*, the years of 1968, to underline the long-lasting effect of a historic turning point. The fall of the Berlin Wall heralded sweeping changes in the 'other Europe'. These included the end of decaying state socialist regimes between

1989 and 1991, the end of the Cold War, the re-unification of Germany, the introduction of liberal democracy, the beginning of a hasty 'transition' to a free market economy and, eventually, the unification of most of the European East and West under the administrative umbrella of the European Union. However, from this vantage point, perceptions on the years of 1989 depend on diverse political, social and economic consequences of these profound changes that affected in different ways different parts of the former socialist Eurasia. When the real, political and symbolic walls started to crumble in 1989, it was difficult to predict – nor would the euphoria of those days allow this kind of pessimism – that the change would also bring many unwanted consequences. Not only did these unwanted consequences involve economic hardships, travesties of a new democratic order and painful social shocks, but also – at the moment of Western European unification – disintegrative political trends which swept away three former socialist federations during 1991 and 1992. This process was followed by the outbreaks of violence, destructive and bloody wars, the return of concentration camps in Europe, massacres and ethnic cleansing which culminated with the Srebrenica genocide in 1995, as well as the brutal destruction of cities such as Vukovar, Sarajevo, Mostar and Grozny. This dark side of 1989 found one of its most horrifying manifestations in the almost four-year-long siege of Sarajevo. When asked about the fall of the Berlin Wall, a citizen of besieged Sarajevo allegedly said that, on the one hand, it had been a good thing, but, on the other, the Wall had unfortunately 'crumbled down upon our heads'.

The question of why these federations disintegrated so soon after the collapse of the socialist regimes is followed by more puzzles. Why did violence occur in some places and not in others? Where, under what circumstances, and when was violence most likely to happen? Finally, why was the disintegration of Yugoslavia so uniquely brutal? I start my analysis by asking two crucial questions. The possible answers to these determined the fate of many citizens of the former socialist federations in the context of their imminent disintegration: *Did the federal centre and the incipient states (republics) accept the separation and the existing borders? Did all groups and all regions accept independence and the authorities of the new states?* The analysis of the possible answers to these questions will bring us to what I call three decisive *triggers of violence*: first citizenship, then borders and territories, and, finally in the early 1990s, the role of the military apparatus of defunct federations.

The possible combinations of the answers to the two questions above produce four scenarios:

		Did the federal centre and other incipient states (republics) accept separation and existing borders?	
		YES	NO
Did all groups and all regions accept independence and the authorities of the new states?	YES	Czech Republic, Slovakia (*no violence*)	Slovenia, Lithuania (*limited violence*)
	NO	Georgia (Abkhazia, South Ossetia), Russia (Chechnya), Moldova (Transnistria), Serbia (Kosovo) (*high likelihood of violence*)	Croatia/Bosnia/Serbia/Montenegro; Armenia/Azerbaijan (*inevitable violence*)

If the answer to both questions is positive, then clearly there is little room for conflict, as in the case of Czechoslovakia. The Czechoslovak Federation dissolved by the mutual agreement of the Czech and Slovak political elites on 1 January 1993. There was no interference from the federal centre. Although many citizens were sympathetic to the former federation, there was no significant opposition to the disintegration coming from groups of citizens, regions or ethnic groups. A small percentage of Czechs living in Slovakia and Slovaks living in the Czech Republic – and there were no concentrations in any particular region – did not pose a problem in mutual relations. Slovakia is, however, home to a sizable Magyar minority but the Czech–Slovak divorce was not a concern for them nor did it change much their relationship with the Slovak majority.

The second possible scenario in our matrix can also generate violence, but on a smaller scale. This situation arises when citizens largely obey the authorities of the new state and agree with independence and the borders of the new state. In such a situation, there are no regional or ethnic protests, or, if a minority is not content with independence (as was the case in the Baltic states), it does not act to prevent it or rebel against the new authorities. The federal centre's institutions do however question the decision to separate. The Yugoslav army's (JNA) one-week intervention in Slovenia and the Soviet army's intervention in Lithuania in 1991 are examples. Since both federal centres were politically weak at that point and since other republics did not directly oppose independence of the republics in question, the violence was ultimately short-lived and resulted in withdrawal of the federal troops.

However, if the answer to both questions is negative, then violence is almost inevitable, as in the former Yugoslavia where war broke out among the republics with Serbia and Montenegro on one side and Croatia and Bosnia on the other from 1991 until 1995. From 1993 to 1994, Croatia was also militarily engaged against the Bosnian government. Violence also erupted between two republics in the former USSR, Armenia and Azerbaijan.

The majority of Croatian and Bosnian Serbs did not accept the independence of Croatia and Bosnia and refused loyalty to the authorities. It is important to note that they did not have any regional autonomy, unlike Nagorno-Karabakh, and were dispersed over Croatian and Bosnian territory. Their rebellion meant conquering territories which they claimed as belonging to Serbs, or which they managed to conquer with their at that time overwhelming military power, with the idea of attaching them to Serbia or the Serbian-Montenegrin state in the making. They were backed by Serbia, Montenegro and the Serb-dominated JNA, who did not accept the independence and existing borders of the neighbouring republics.

Although the war between Armenia and Azerbaijan over Nagorno-Karabakh resembles the conflicts in the former Yugoslavia insofar as it involved direct violence between the former republics over borders and territories, there is a significant difference. Nagorno-Karabakh is an Armenian-populated former autonomous region within Azerbaijan. It opted for independence from Azerbaijan with the obvious intention of joining the Armenian state, a goal supported by Armenia itself. The only problem was how to attach the region surrounded by ethnic Azeri territories that Armenia eventually 'solved' by simply occupying these territories. In this case, we can see both an autonomous region populated by an ethnically different group than the rest of the republic rebelling against the republican centre, and the neighbouring republic demanding a change of borders and claiming the region for itself.

If the former republics mostly agree among themselves on their territorial shape but (ethnic) groups and/or regions within the republics either disobey the newly independent authorities or express discontent with independence or with their position within the new state – or even attempt secession, with or without the intention of joining another state – there is a high likelihood of violence occurring. This was the case with Georgia (Abkhazia and South Ossetia), Moldova (Transnistria), Russia (Chechnya), and Serbia (Kosovo). In Georgia and Moldova, the new authorities were unable to quell the rebellion, whereas Russia succeeded after almost a decade to crush the Chechen uprising after a horrible price was paid in human lives and material destruction. Special attention should be paid to the case of Serbia. In an open expansionist campaign, Serbia militarily questioned the territorial shape of the western neighbouring republics (Croatia and especially Bosnia), but no other republic challenged its own administrative borders. The case of Kosovo appears different from the other cases in this category since Serbia *initially* managed to suppress Albanian demands for autonomy and even independence after Kosovo's autonomy was revoked in 1989. Kosovo Albanians opted for a peaceful rebellion against the Serbian state and built their own parallel institutions until 1998 when the conflict erupted between the Serbian authorities and the Albanian guerrillas. It ended with the NATO intervention and withdrawal of Serbian troops from Kosovo in 1999.

Macedonia deserves a special status in our analysis and therefore it does not find a place in our matrix. It exemplifies a situation in which the ethnic Macedonian majority and the ethnic Albanian minority *initially* – at the moment of Yugoslavia's break-up in 1991 – accepted independence. The state was thus not threatened with external intervention and it secured the loyalty of its ethnic minority. However, over the years – ten years later and under different circumstances – the Albanians' discontent with their position in Macedonia, coupled with political demands and secessionist threats, resulted in an armed rebellion, backed by armed groups from Kosovo, and open defiance of the Macedonian state authorities in 2001.

Although it was not part of the initial implosion of the Yugoslav Federation and it took place fifteen years later, it is necessary to mention here Montenegro's independence from the State Union of Serbia and Montenegro in 2006 as well as Kosovo's independence from Serbia in 2008. Many expected and perceived Montenegro's independence as a final stage of fragmentation along the republican lines of what had been Yugoslavia. First steps towards independence had already been taken in the late 1990s when the Montenegrin leadership – comprising many people such as Montenegrin current Prime Minister Milo Đukanović who enthusiastically supported Milošević and his war campaigns in early 1990s – turned their back on Belgrade (Džankić 2010: 10). By 2003, when the Federal Republic of Yugoslavia was replaced by a malfunctioning State Union, Montenegro was already a semi-independent country. Although it opposed Montenegrin independence, Serbia did not dispute the territorial shape of Montenegro and furthermore decided to respect the outcome of the referendum on independence in 2006. As for the Serbs in Montenegro, they expressed their discontent with independence rather peacefully, and did not rebel against the authorities. However, many Montenegrin Serbs continue to press for special status and special relations with Serbia. Once again, the case of Montenegro's independence in 2006 must be placed in the context of an entirely different political setting than the one that dominated Yugoslavia's disintegration in the early 1990s. Finally, in February 2008 Kosovo declared independence from Serbia and acquired only partial but significant international recognition: the move was opposed by both Serbia and the ethnic Serb minority. Since Kosovo has been completely separated from Serbia for almost a decade and governed by international bodies (UN), with their strong international military and police presence (NATO, EU, UN), and, since Serbia renounced the use of violence, violence has been limited to an ethnic Serb enclave in North Kosovo.

Only one case does not fit this matrix at all because of the entirely different nature of the conflict. From 1992 to 1997, the Central Asian republic of Tajikistan was plunged into a conflict between the government and an opposition that ranged from liberal-democrats to Islamists. All sides accepted independence and there were no challenges to Tajikistan's borders or the state. Although the war was in some aspects characterized by mostly regional and some ethnic rivalries, Tajikistan clearly constitutes a separate case of civil ideological war for political power.

It is important to add here that in the post-1989 international arena, the international community generally accepted only the former republics as independent states that were therefore entitled to join international organizations such as the United Nations. The only major exception to this unwritten rule came seventeen years later with Kosovo's independence. Both the US and the EU members who recognized Kosovo insisted that it was an *exceptional* case. The move was opposed by some EU members (such as Spain, Slovakia and Romania) and, most staunchly, by Russia. In response, and coming to the conclusion that the rule was irretrievably broken, Russia recognized the independence of the Georgian provinces of Abkhazia and South Ossetia after the war with Georgia in August 2008. The NATO deployment in Kosovo in 1999 was used as justification for Russia's own takeover of the Crimea in 2014.

Triggers of violence: Citizenship, borders and territories, and the role of the federal military

Trigger 1: Citizenship

The first question – *did the incipient states (republics) and the federal centre accept the separation and the existing borders?* – is intimately related to future territorial shapes and thus borders of incipient states and, inevitably, to the role of the federal military in the initial phase of the break-up. The second question – *did all groups and all regions accept the independence and the authorities of the new states?* In other words, *did they attempt rebellion, secession or even integration with another state?* – is intrinsically bound with citizenship or, generally, with the relationship between state and individuals and/or groups involving, among other things, political inclusion or exclusion, citizens' loyalty, duties and rights, and personal security.

Another perspective on violence in the post-1989 post-communist space opens up if we look at it through the lenses of citizenship, the struggle over borders and territories, and the role of the federal military that I define as main, though not the sole *triggers of violence*. By the triggers of violence I understand stakes (in this case disagreements on the citizenship issue and the territorial shape of the new states) and actors (in our analysis we focus on partial or full engagement of the federal military during the period of disintegration) that could facilitate or initiate the use of violence by the parties in conflict having opposing political agendas. The role of the federal forces as the major military formation and their active involvement in the events, or their non-involvement, certainly determines the level of violence, although the federal army competed – collaborated or confronted – with less powerful police forces, territorial defence forces in Yugoslav republics and diverse paramilitaries often related to political parties or mafia gangs.

Needless to say, if all three triggers of violence are *pulled*, large-scale violence occurs. An example of this is the war in which five of the six Yugoslav republics participated together with the disintegrating federal army which sided with Serbia and Montenegro and ethnic Serbs' paramilitaries in Croatia and Bosnia in 1991–1992. The war was finally brought to an end by the general peace agreement in 1995 sponsored by the United States and the EU and signed by Croatia, Bosnia-Herzegovina and the Federal Republic of Yugoslavia (Serbia and Montenegro). The Serb rebellion in Croatia failed, but Bosnia was internally divided into the Serb republic and the Croat-Bosniak Federation, which was further divided into mixed and ethnic cantons. Regardless of widespread destruction and the serious loss of human life (as many as 100,000 in Bosnia and around 20,000 in Croatia),[1] the former republican borders were not changed.

The conflict over Nagorno-Karabakh, on the other hand, involved two triggers of violence: citizenship (the rebellion of ethnic Armenian citizens against Azerbaijan as a state) and conflict over disputed territories and new borders among states (the intervention of Armenia with the intention to annex the Azeri territory). Although initially the Soviet army was militarily involved in the conflict – that started already in 1988! – it was played out among two neighbouring republics and an autonomous province. The final result was a frozen conflict which lasts until this very day: a *de facto* annexation of Nagorno-Karabakh by Armenia together with Armenian control over the regions outside Nagorno-Karabakh linking the region to Armenia.

If you pull the trigger of citizenship involving refusal of loyalty to a new state and if you couple it with the secessionist demands, this inevitably means pulling also the trigger of control over territories and borders, then the result is internal conflicts between the new states and one or more rebellious regions. The outcome is likely to be, as in the case of Nagorno-Karabakh, a frozen conflict. Only internationally supervised Kosovo managed to achieve a partial but significant international recognition. This recognition is not the case for some of the rebellious regions in the former USSR, such as Transnistria, Nagorno-Karabakh, Abkhazia and South Ossetia (the latter two indeed recognized by only Russia, Nicaragua, Venezuela and Nauru), which are *de facto* self-ruled statelets or, for that matter, Chechnya which has been brought under Moscow's control again. In many of these regions, the federal military or its remnants and the Russian army as its successor played a highly controversial role. For example, the former Fourteenth Soviet army generously helped the rebellion in Transnistria, the Soviet army was implicated in the first phase of the Armenian-Azerbaijani war and Russia militarily backed Abkhaz and South Ossetian secessionism.

Macedonia is a special case for the reasons discussed above. It escaped initial violence, but faced an Albanian rebellion in 2001 that pulled *only* the trigger of citizenship and played with the prospect of secession. Albanians perceived themselves as 'second-class' citizens in the state constitutionally defined as ethnic Macedonian state, complained about the discriminatory citizenship law and demanded more autonomy for municipalities with an Albanian majority and some important cultural rights such as higher education in the Albanian language. The uprising started in the area inhabited mostly by Albanians who did not have a previous autonomous region within Macedonia. In this regard, their armed rebellion was similar in some respects to that of Croatian and Bosnian Serbs, or to the one in Transnistria where the Slavic speakers (Ukrainians and Russians) unilaterally declared autonomy and secession from Moldova in the municipalities of the Dniester region. With Albania not interested and Kosovo not a state, and without international sympathies, the armed insurgency was welcomed only in Albanian nationalist circles. The Macedonian case ended in settlement. For their acceptance of citizenship and loyalty, the Macedonian state offered Albanians concessions in citizenship matters, linguistic and educational policy, and internal administrative divisions which consolidated the Albanian majority in the Western Macedonia. Also included were significant political concessions such as re-definition of the constitution and the larger participation of Albanians in government.

Trigger 2: Territory and borders

The previous paragraphs clearly show how the questions of citizenship, the control of territory and the territorial shape, i.e. the borders of new states, are closely related. The conflict over territories and borders is an infallible trigger for violence both in cases where a region or a group inhabiting a certain territory refuses loyalty to the authorities of a new state and furthermore declares secession, and in cases when the (usually) neighbouring country questions the existing borders claiming more often than not that its minority in neighbouring country should join the 'homeland'. As mentioned above, the arguments for re-arranging political borders are often centred on the argument about the 'artificiality' of the existing territorial divisions. These socialist 'solutions' did not correspond, it was claimed, to 'natural' ethnic territories. Once the communist regimes had imploded the legitimacy of political and territorial arrangements made under their rule was also called into question. However, any separation according to the ethnic lines had to solve the 'problem' of many ethnically mixed regions. Therefore, the physical separation of ethnic communities was to be created in these zones by the use of mass violence, executions, expulsions and 'ethnic cleansing'.

Although the post-Soviet states, except in the case of Armenia and Azerbaijan, recognized the existing republican borders as new borders between independent states,[2] the internal borders became the blueprint for fragmentation where autonomous regions rebelled against the republican centre. However, in the former Yugoslavia one witnessed conflicts where there were no previous intra-republican administrative borders, except in the case of Kosovo, and some republics (Serbia and Montenegro) openly challenged the existing inter-republican divisions. In all cases, the project of creating ethnically homogenized independent states on a territory inhabited by co-members of an ethnicity put in question the inherited political geography.

The wars between the Yugoslav republics over territories and borders were the most intensive and destructive ones. Therefore, a closer look is needed to explain the logic behind the wars for territories. Initially, in Yugoslavia, the motivation for the conflict over territory was the position of Serbs outside Serbia (in Croatia and Bosnia). On the other hand, Serbia itself had the largest proportion of minorities on its soil in Kosovo and Vojvodina. But both Albania and Hungary renounced any claims to Serbian territory inhabited by ethnic Albanians and Magyars, whereas ethnic Muslims from the Sandžak region (divided between Serbia and Montenegro) lacked a kin state in the conventional sense and never formed a political platform to advocate secession or integration with their ethnic kin in Bosnia. As for the Macedonian Albanians, they struggled in the 1990s to have their minority rights and equal position alongside the Slav majority recognized.

In other words, the possibility of violent conflict opened up in the former Yugoslavia when a kin-state supported or engineered the irredentist ambitions of its kin-minority in neighbouring republics with the more or less explicit intention of annexing a certain portion of their territories. In the context of Serbia's expansionist policies, the conflict in Croatia was facilitated, as explained by Rogers Brubaker, by a nationalizing Croatian state that threatened and reduced the political, social and economic rights of local Serbs (downgrading them from a constituent people of Croatia to a minority), and which itself refused to shun its own expansionist policies in neighbouring Bosnia. The war 'was a contingent outcome of the interplay of mutually suspicious, mutually monitoring, mutually misrepresenting political elites in the incipient Croatian nationalizing state, the incipient Serb national minority in that state, and the incipient Serbian "homeland" state' (Brubaker 1996: 76).

But if Croatia represents a textbook example of Brubaker's triadic relationship between a 'nationalizing state', a 'national minority' and a 'national homeland', the devastating war in Bosnia-Herzegovina, as the only true multiethnic country with no titular nationality, defies the model. Indeed, Brubaker admits in his above-mentioned study that he does not intend to deal with the conflict in Bosnia. Nonetheless, since the triadic relationship – though in the case of Bosnia it was more of an *imagined* triadic relationship – is considered a hotbed of ethnic conflicts in Eastern Europe, it is necessary to explain the Bosnian situation in exactly these terms.

Bosnia was not a 'nationalizing state' to start with nor could it later qualify as one. Bosnian Serbs and Croats were not 'national minorities' in this truly multinational country with, regardless of actual percentages, no majorities and no minorities. So far as Brubaker's triangle is concerned, only Serbia and Croatia were perceived as 'external homelands' by nationalist Bosnian Serbs and Croats. The mobilization of Bosnian Serbs for war was mostly motivated by the Greater Serbia project that had already begun in Croatia in 1991 and was territorially inconceivable without the acquisition of Bosnian territories. However, Bosnian

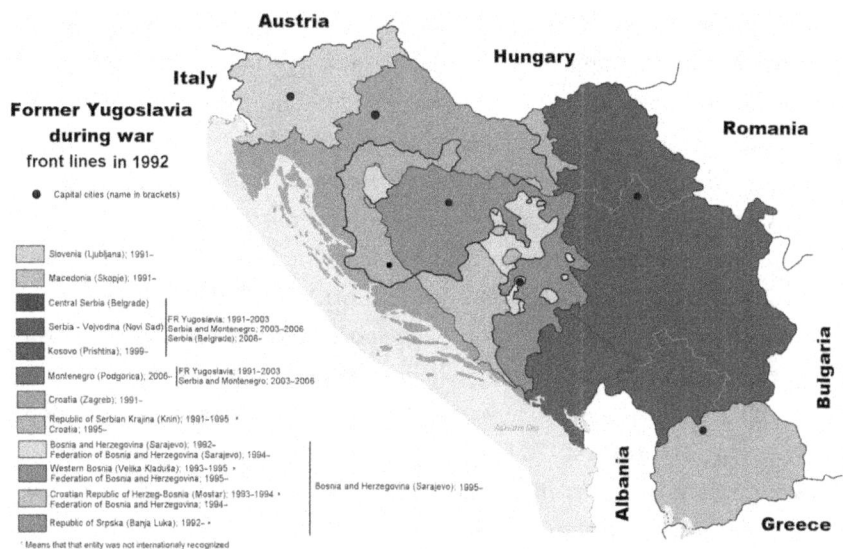

Figure 8.1 The post-Yugoslav States in 1992 (Source: Wikimedia Commons, transferred from en.wikipedia, author: Paweł Goleniowski, SwPawel).

Serbs could have not claimed to be in the same position as the Croatian Serbs, that is to say, a 'national minority' whose rights were threatened by a 'nationalizing' state. Moreover, their representatives shared power with Croat and Muslim ethnonationalist parties. Serb nationalistic propaganda therefore concentrated on portraying Bosnia as an incipient Muslim nationalizing state and in portraying Bosnian Muslim leaders as 'fundamentalist' plotters who wanted to subjugate or eliminate Serbs in a future Islamic state. Eventually, the main political party of Bosnian Serbs, led by Radovan Karadžić and supported by the federal army and Serbia, rejected Bosnia as an independent multinational state, formed 'Serb autonomous regions' brought together into a 'Serb republic' and decided to join Serbia, taking with them as much Bosnian territory as they could conquer.

As for Bosnian Croats, their tactic, in 1991 and 1992, was initially to support Bosnia's statehood. During this period, the reinforcement of Bosnian statehood also entailed the reinforcement of Croatia's bid for independence from Belgrade. However, as the war progressed, in 1993, Bosnian Croats – under direct influence and control from Tudjman's government in Zagreb – adopted a position similar to that of the Bosnian Serbs. They rejected Bosnia as a state, portrayed Bosnian Muslims as fundamentalists, entered into an open conflict with Sarajevo and tried to get as much territory as possible with the intention of attaching it to Croatia. Again, it is impossible to speak about a *real* triadic relationship. It is only possible to speak of how the triad was *simulated* in order to legitimize Serbs' and Croats' ambitions to join their 'national homelands'.

Finally, what were the results of these devastating wars over territories and borders? The internationally recognized borders are still those that separated the republics within the former socialist federations, except in the case of Kosovo. When it comes to the contested territories the situation on the ground is quite different: Serbs in Croatia lost their short-lived republic, Serbs in Bosnia obtained an autonomous Serb Republic but failed to join Serbia, the Chechen rebellion failed, Kosovo eventually separated from Serbia thanks to international intervention, Transnistria, Abkhazia and South Ossetia are internationally unrecognized quasi-independent territories, as well as Nagorno-Karabakh which is *de facto* attached to Armenia.

Trigger 3: The role of the federal military

Finally, it is necessary to return to the role of the federal military as discussed above. The federal armies, by the simple fact of their 'monopoly on violence', played one of the crucial roles in the violent clashes that occurred during the progressive disappearance of the socialist federations. The federal army stayed in the barracks in Czechoslovakia and, unlike the Yugoslav federal army, was not interested in any kind of intervention into political affairs (Rupnik 2000). Valerie Bunce argues that the bloc provides the answer and that violence was likely to occur in countries such as Yugoslavia, Romania and Albania whose military apparatus was not controlled by Moscow (1999: 71). Although Moscow decided not to use its huge army to keep the Soviet Union together and Russia later accepted the independence of other republics and the often unfavourable position of Russians living outside Russia, the Soviet army was implicated in violent events occurring in the former Soviet space. It *did* intervene in Lithuania in 1991, some of its generals staged a coup against Gorbachev in 1991, it was implicated initially in the conflict in Azerbaijan and its remnants in Moldova helped the rebellion in Transnistria. In addition, Russia, as the sole successor of the Soviet army later on played an important role in the conflicts in Georgia.

I concur with Bunce that an independent and powerful military in Yugoslavia, Albania and Romania succumbed to the temptation to enter into an already volatile political arena in order to defend their own privileges.

However, violence in Albania and Romania resulted from short-term conflicts that ended in democratic changes demanded by citizens themselves. This did not endanger the existence of the state as such. Whereas the intervention of the Soviet army was relatively limited, the Yugoslav People's Army (JNA) fully participated in the inter-republican and inter-ethnic conflicts by choosing not to defend the Yugoslav federation (although in Slovenia it intervened to protect the federation's borders and it portrayed its role there and in Croatia as a defence of Yugoslavia). Instead, its leadership decided to support the Serb nationalist programme of creating – on the ruins of Yugoslavia once it became clear it was about to collapse – a greater Serbian state out of Serbia, Montenegro and the Serb-populated areas of Croatia and Bosnia.

The Serbian member of the Yugoslav Presidency Borisav Jović writes in his memoir about the plan 'to attack Yugoslavia' which was discussed among Serbian leaders as early as March 1990 after the failure of the Fourteenth Congress of the League of Communists of Yugoslavia (LCY). The plan involved a change of internal borders if Slovenia and Croatia decided to defect from the federation (Gordy 2008: 285). The JNA confirmed its close ties with Milošević after the army, on his orders, crushed the Belgrade demonstrations of 9 March 1991. 'At this moment, the JNA ceased to function as the defence force of the Yugoslav federation, and transformed itself into the military wing of a political faction' (Gordy 2008: 285). Numerous reports and testimonies confirm the JNA's submission to Milošević and to the close and secret collaboration and planning of the war between the army's chiefs and Serbian and Montenegrin leaders. Belgrade's lawyer Srđa Popović draws on an enormous number of documents (memoirs, transcripts and testimonies) to show that this was – according to the Yugoslav Constitution and laws still in force at that time – an anti-constitutional conspiracy of the above-mentioned leaders which had as its goal the creation of a Serbia-dominated state on the ruins of the Yugoslav federation (2008).

The JNA and Milošević himself often claimed that they were actually defending Yugoslavia against separatists whether they were Albanian, Croatian or Slovenian. The fact that their 'defence' of Yugoslavia went hand in hand with Serbian nationalist expansion progressively alienated non-Serbs from any idea of a common South-Slavic state. The JNA, therefore, became a key player in the inter-republic strife, not as an independent actor, but rather as 'an army without a state' as it was dubbed by its last military commander Veljko Kadijević in the subtitle of his 1993 memoir 'My View of the Break-up'. Indeed, 'an army without a state' – in search of a state.

Conclusion: The price of war

The consequences of the wide-scale violence that occurred in the former Yugoslavia and USSR are still felt. Croatia ended the Serb rebellion in 1995 with a military takeover that left large portions of Croatia empty of its Serb minority. Bosnia-Herzegovina is internally divided and supervised by international bodies. Although local nationalist leaders often invoke partition of the country, there has been no significant inter-ethnic violence since 1995. Serbia is still a country with no consensus on its borders and is still fighting its nationalist ghosts, the consequences of its engagement in Croatia and Bosnia and the loss of Kosovo as well as Montenegro's departure. The recent fragmentation turned it into a landlocked country much smaller in size than it was before its expansionist campaigns. In the post-Soviet world, meanwhile, one finds a series of self-governed entities and frozen conflicts that erupt from time to time, such as that in Georgia in summer 2008. There is no strong will by local actors or by the international community – which is unprepared to tackle the issues in Russia's immediate zone of interests and engagement – to solve the conflicts in Transnistria, Abkhazia, South Ossetia and Nagorno-Karabakh. Chechnya seems to be forgotten and the brutal Russian governance of the region forgiven in a post-September 11 world. The Ukrainian crisis, the *de facto* annexation of the Crimea by Russia and a conflict in Eastern Ukraine come as a delayed replay of what was already seen elsewhere after the dissolution of socialist multinational federations.

In this chapter, I have suggested that the eruption of violence and its intensity largely depend on questions related to citizenship and individual's citizenship status, his or her rights and security, conflicting interpretations about who should 'own' certain territories and where inter-state borders should be drawn, and, finally, the role of the federal military, its successors or remnants, as the only force possessing the overwhelming means of warfare during the period of dissolution. Obviously, other factors that are closely related to the proposed analysis should be taken into consideration. Any multifactor analysis of each individual case needs to include regional particularities, historical experience, economic concerns, relations between democratic procedures and violence, functioning and forming of political elites, their manipulation of the above-mentioned issues, their armament of loyal formations and paramilitaries, as well as general international context and involvement.

More than twenty years on from that *annus mirabilis*, this analysis has tried to tackle the darker side of the fall of the Wall that has involved the mass destruction of human lives as a consequence of profound changes in the post-socialist world. Finally, a very general lesson from that gloomy side is very simple: when the walls crumble down, no matter where and when, they tend to crumble down on somebody's head. Ironically, the walls sometimes fall down on the heads of the very people who dreamed of tearing them down.

Part Four

From Ethnic Engineering to European Re-Integration?

9

From Equal Citizens to Unequal Groups: The Post-Yugoslav Citizenship Regimes

The break-up of Yugoslavia and its two-tier citizenship regime opened a period of continuous experimentation with defining and re-defining political communities through citizenship laws and citizenship-related practices. New citizenship regimes, in various ways, effectively turned equal citizens into members of unequal groups. In the words of Pierre Bourdieu, 'legal discourse is a creative speech that brings into existence that which it utters' (1991: 42). The main 'creative' role of citizenship laws was to bring into existence new political communities, within which the dominance of the major ethnic group would be undisputable. This group would be consolidated, often across borders, by uniting all of its members, regardless of where they resided, by the bonds of citizenship. Almost all of the successor states of the former Yugoslav federation – with some variations according to their specific contexts – have used their respective citizenship laws as an effective tool for ethnic engineering. This practice was widespread in the 1990s but, in various forms, continues until this very day. By ethnic engineering I mean an intentional policy of governments and lawmakers to influence, by legal means and related administrative practices, the ethnic composition of their populations in favour of their core ethnic group (Štiks 2006). Similar intentions have influenced the writing of most of the new constitutions. The laws on citizenship and their administrative implementation are obviously closely related and even inseparable from the practice of 'constitutional nationalism' (Hayden 1992), that is, the constitutional re-definition of new states as, in broad terms, the *national* states of their core ethnic group. Thus, ethnic engineering, in constitutional and citizenship matters, paved the way for the establishment of a series of ethnic democracies either at the state or at the sub-state level (see below).

Citizenship laws played a key role in determining the citizenry of the new states, as well as the rights guaranteed to citizens by the new state. New legislation in various ways in almost all post-Yugoslav states offered a privileged status to members of the majority or core ethnic group regardless of their place of residence (inside or outside their borders). On the other hand, they substantially complicated the process of naturalization for those outside the ethnonational core group, especially for ethnically different citizens from other former Yugoslav republics who were permanent residents on their territory when the new citizenship regime came into effect. In their extreme manifestation, citizenship laws and practices have also been used as a subtle, but nonetheless powerful tool for ethnic cleansing. The deprivation of citizenship, and the subsequent loss of basic social and economic rights, has been quite effective in forcing a sizable number of individuals to leave their habitual places of residence and move either to 'their' kin states or abroad. The break-up of Yugoslavia and the other two multinational federations meant that millions literally went to bed as full-fledged citizens and woke up as individuals with questionable status.

The citizenship conundrum in post-socialist Europe

Between 1989 and 1993 some former socialist countries recovered their full sovereignty by exiting the Soviet bloc, whereas the others achieved full independence – some of them for the first time in history! – and all of them found it necessary to wipe out the traces of the *ancien régime* and establish themselves constitutionally as nation-states representing their ethnic majorities, despite the ethnic diversity within their borders. Many of these states frequently fell back upon the 'legal fiction of uninterrupted statehood' and on 'state-reinforcing overcompensation' (Liebich 2007: 18). Usually, the new constitutions' preambles traced the historical foundation of the state back to medieval kingdoms. The first few articles frequently confirmed the country in question as unitary, indivisible, independent and sovereign (Culic 2003). Such an eagerness to reassert its own statehood – this desire could be explained by a historic and/or current weakness and vulnerability – was also translated into the political organization of post-communist states. For instance, all new EU member states from East, Central and Southeast Europe are unitary states (Liebich 2007). In the post-communist world the only real exceptions to unitarism are Bosnia-Herzegovina (organized under the Dayton Peace Agreement as a federal union of two entities, one of which is itself a federation of cantons!) and the much more centralized Russian federation.

Constitutional re-definitions had direct impact on the citizenship legislation and practices in these countries as well. Katherine Verdery observes that 'socialist-era constitutions had placed all socialist citizens on formally equal footing, guaranteeing the rights of co-resident nationalities and providing for proportional representation of national minorities in Party organs. The collapse of socialism and of several socialist states ended these constitutional protections. In both new (post-Yugoslav and post-Soviet) states and ongoing ones (such as Albania, Romania and Hungary), the process of writing new constitutions enabled ambitious politicians to manipulate the very definition of citizenship' (1998: 294). Although post-communist constitutions usually offer all of the standard democratic rights to minorities, those minorities are generally portrayed as 'historic guests' on the territory belonging to the 'autochthonous' ethnic group that, as a rule, gives its own ethnic name to the country in question, or the dominant group adopts the regional name as its own ethnic name. The 'post-communist nation-state is, at its mildest, a state of latent discrimination. Even when official differentiation is rare, the "spirit" of the constitutions and laws signals to members of all minorities that they are inferior citizens, submitted to frequent tests of loyalty' (Dimitrijević 1998: 166–167). In other words, they 'may hold citizenship but cannot aspire to equality' (Hayden 1999: 15).

By the same token, the post-communist nation-state offers a privileged relationship to its ethnic kin abroad. In many constitutions (see, e.g., those of Hungary, Croatia and Albania) or in special laws and acts (e.g. special acts or laws on ethnic kin in Hungary in 2001, Slovakia in 2005, Slovenia in 2006, Serbia in 2009 and Croatia in 2011), one can find declarations of responsibility and duty towards ethnic co-nationals, whether abroad, overseas or in the 'near abroad' just across the border. Almost all post-communist countries provided their ethnic diaspora (including descendants up to the third generation in some cases) with access to their citizenship. These constitutional re-definitions of the state and enactments of new citizenship laws thus often created the situation in which yesterday's citizens – such as in the former multinational federations – were turned into today's aliens or second-class citizens, and yesterday's aliens (actually national minorities in neighbouring countries or descendants of those residing abroad for economic or political reasons) into lawful citizens with more rights than those living within the state's jurisdiction. Citizenship laws in some post-communist countries were also written with the intention of repairing 'past wrongs' (Liebich 2007: 27). The laws targeted ethnic diaspora members to whom citizenship rights, often for ideological reasons, had been denied during socialism. However, we must add that this belated justice was often ethnically exclusive. Fixing 'past wrongs' done to those now abroad went hand in hand with committing 'new wrongs' to those who were at home.

This outcome was especially dramatic in the former USSR and Yugoslavia. The ethnic diaspora politics, this 'long-distance nationalism' or 'politics without accountability' (Anderson 1992), amounted to the opposite of the American revolution's famous slogan, namely to 'representation without taxation' and to 'taxation without representation' in the case where the defunct socialist federations' citizens found themselves without the citizenship of the newly independent states – a blatant example being numerous ethnic Russians in the Baltic countries, but many former Yugoslavs as well.

Citizenship – access to it and exclusion from it – became an important political battlefield in the former multinational socialist federations. The consequences of the new citizenship laws and the determination of the initial citizenry were less dramatic in the former Czechoslovakia (Barsova 2007; Gyarfasova 1995; Kusa 2007; Palous 1995) than in the former USSR and in the former Yugoslavia. Determination of initial citizenries in the Czech Republic and Slovakia was primarily made on the basis of legal continuity with the republic-level citizenships of two Czechoslovak republics that legally came into existence in 1969. The Constitutional Act of October 1968 transformed the largely unitary Czechoslovakia into a bi-national federation and each Czechoslovak citizen acquired, alongside his or her Czechoslovak federal citizenship, the citizenship of his or her republic. Following the 'divorce', the option of taking either citizenship was extended to persons having the citizenship of one republic but who resided in the other. The Czech law made this conditional upon two years of residency and of having five years with no criminal record. The latter condition targeted many Roma who held Slovak citizenship but who resided in the Czech Republic (see Iordachi 2004: 118–119; Palous 1995: 158). Initially, having dual citizenship – probably the most satisfactory solution following the dissolution of a bi-national federation – was not permitted. Later, it became possible to hold both citizenships at once, with Slovakia proving to be more flexible on the matter than the Czech Republic which generally forbids dual citizenship. In 1999 and in 2003, the Czech law on citizenship was amended to allow dual Czech and Slovak citizenship for various groups of former Czechoslovak citizens (Barasova 2007: 167–168). Eventually, in 2004 both countries joined the EU, thus making citizens of both countries European citizens, and thereby rendering the question of dual citizenship less significant.

The situation in the former USSR was quite different. In his early analysis of the 'citizenship struggles' in the former Soviet republics,[1] Rogers Brubaker (1992) distinguished between three models of citizenship policy adopted by the new successor states: the 'new state model', or a zero option model, whereby a new state defines the initial body of citizens simply by including all residents on its territory (the large majority of the former Soviet republics); the 'restored state model', by which citizenship is granted only to the lawful citizens of the inter-war independent republics and their descendants, whereas the other residents are excluded (Estonia and Latvia); and, finally, the third model as a combination of the two: both restored citizenship and inclusiveness that should satisfy general democratic standards (adopted only by Lithuania). Lithuania was also the first Soviet Republic to adopt its own republic-level law on citizenship in November 1989 (and later as an independent state in December 1991) by which it restored or reaffirmed citizenship to those who had Lithuanian citizenship prior to 1940 and to their descendants, and adopted an inclusive policy towards the non-Lithuanians then residing on its soil, namely the large Russophone population. The latter Brubaker explains by timing (the laws were adopted while Lithuania was still part of a still powerful USSR) but also because ethnic Lithuanians never feared that they would become a 'minority in their own country'.

This prospect produced great anxiety in Estonia and Latvia. The newly independent Baltic States claimed to be the successors of the inter-war independent states and not of the republics formed under the Soviet occupation. The lawful citizens were thus those who held citizenship during the inter-war period and their descendants (including those living abroad who were invited to 'return' as citizens), whereas other individuals who happened to find themselves on these territories in the interim were simply considered aliens and excluded from citizenship (Brubaker 1992: 278).[2]

The 'new state' model, on the other hand, was implemented in all other republics, although, as Oxana Shevel observes (2009), there is a clear difference between those that actually added various favourable provisions for coethnics (Armenia, Belarus, Kazakhstan, Kyrgyzstan and Turkmenistan) and those that, due to internal diversity and political contestation opted for a 'civic' model (Ukraine, Russia, Azerbaijan, Georgia, Moldova, Tajikistan and Uzbekistan).

None of Brubaker's post-Soviet models can be applied to the former Yugoslav republics. The crucial difference lies in the fact that the Yugoslav republics had had their own citizenship laws and their registers of citizens since 1947–48. Therefore, they were able to claim at the moment of independence that their citizenries already existed and comprised those listed in the republican registers. The dissolution of federal Yugoslavia and Czechoslovakia thus clearly shows the third model (the 'federal dissolution model')[3] for the initial determination of citizenship after the collapse of multinational federations. It involves the automatic acquisition of citizenship of new states by all previously registered republic-level citizens, although some states additionally used residence as a basis for citizenship acquisition.

Ethnic engineering after Yugoslavia: The included, the invited, the excluded and the self-excluded

The creation of post-Yugoslav citizenries was based on four legal pillars: initial legal continuity with republican citizenship, ethnicity or facilitated naturalization for kin members abroad, naturalization of residents, i.e. citizens of other republics, and regular naturalization procedure for aliens (with a defined period of residence). Ethnic engineering was obvious in the cases of facilitated naturalization and in the naturalization process for residents (either favouring again ethnic kin already residing in the state or excluding residents of different ethnicity). The policies of ethnic engineering, including new citizenship legislation and related administrative practices, together with political activities and conflicts based on ethnic solidarity, resulted eventually in four different groups of individuals in Yugoslavia's five initial successor states (Slovenia, Croatia, Bosnia-Herzegovina, Federal Republic of Yugoslavia (FRY) and Macedonia). Previously equal Yugoslav citizens were now replaced with the included, the invited, the excluded and the self-excluded.

The included

All former republican citizens, regardless of their ethnic backgrounds, who were registered in the citizens' republican registers, were automatically transferred into new registers. Those were *the included* by a simple operation of law. Possessing the citizenship of the new state was essential when individuals requested new documents such as IDs and passports but also for maintaining previously held jobs, access to health care and property rights. The problem with the civic registers was their occasional incompleteness.

The principle of legal continuity would not have been problematic had it not left a considerable number of people in a legal limbo, among which those Yugoslav citizens who resided outside the republic whose citizenship they possessed, whether they knew it or not, those whose parents had different republican citizenship, families where different members had different republican citizenships and, finally, those who could not establish their exact republican citizenship. An alternative approach would have been collective naturalization for these categories respecting their residence and family circumstances.

The invited

Finding themselves in a demiurgic situation to define the exact boundaries of their new political communities, and convinced that old communist republican citizenships (too civic for their taste) were not entirely responding to the ongoing ethnocentric re-definition of their states, new polities often sent an open invitation to certain individuals – ethnic kin in the 'near abroad', i.e. neighbouring republics and ethnic diaspora in Europe or overseas – to join their newly formed citizenry and political communities. This invitation to ethnic brethren abroad was probably inspired by the practice of some European states such as Germany, Italy or Greece. The implicit or explicit 'right to return' for those abroad and oversees could have been inspired by the Israeli example.

A very open invitation to citizenship was included in the new law on Croatian citizenship in 1991 (see Ragazzi and Štiks 2009) and, in view of the policies many states have adopted since the early 1990s, Croatia can be considered a Balkan pioneer in ethnocentric citizenship practices. Among those who were invited to acquire Croatian citizenship on the grounds of their Croat ethnicity, one must distinguish between three sub-categories: those ethnic Croats who resided in Croatia but who did not have its republican citizenship; those residing in the 'near abroad', mainly in Bosnia-Herzegovina – as the main target of the invitation – and finally, those members of the ethnic Croat diaspora in Europe or overseas (pre-Second World War, economic or post-1945 political diaspora and Croat guest workers). Since the grounds for granting citizenship to these individuals were their ethnicity, the question immediately arose as to what proves one's Croat ethnicity. In a number of documents such as school certificates or university certificates or some other administrative forms – but not IDs and passports – citizens were asked to declare their ethnicity. Yet, Roman Catholic Church certificates were also accepted by the Ministry of the Interior as proof of someone's 'Croatness'. Furthermore, article 16 of the law on citizenship even provided a facilitated naturalization procedure for Croats not residing in Croatia, mostly those in Bosnia-Herzegovina. According to some estimates, more than 1.15 million people have become naturalized Croatian citizens since 1991; up to 800,000 of these are from Bosnia-Herzegovina or previously held citizenship of Bosnia-Herzegovina, around 100,000 from Serbia and Montenegro combined and some 10,000 from Macedonia (these numbers also include a considerable number of non-Croats who somehow managed to get Croatian passports for practical purposes such as visa-free travel).[4]

Bosnia-Herzegovina, a multinational country without a core ethnic group, also issued an invitation to citizenship in the 1993 amendments to its 1992 decree on citizenship, but only to certain individuals inside its borders. It provided that all SFRY citizens residing on the territory of Bosnia-Herzegovina on 6 April 1992 – the day of its international recognition and the beginning of the war – should be automatically considered citizens of Bosnia-Herzegovina, which, coupled with the legal continuity, basically corresponded to the new state model. However, some other more problematic 'invitations to citizenship' were issued during the war as well. The same amendments facilitated the naturalization of those who had been actively involved in the defence forces (Muminović 1998: 79). Bosnian citizenship was granted on this basis to a limited number of foreigners (up to 2,000), mostly from Islamic countries who had fought on the Bosniak side. These problematic naturalizations also involved a certain number of Serbs from Serbia and Croatia who had acquired citizenship from the Serb entity (that had its own extremely ethnocentric citizenship regime during the war), and ethnic Bosniaks from the Sandžak region who were naturalized in the Bosniak-Croat entity (see Sarajlić 2010: 20). The Dayton Peace Agreement annulled all wartime legislation. It introduced, following a pattern familiar from socialist Yugoslavia, a two-level citizenship regime composed of the state and the entity citizenships. Unsurprisingly, similar to Yugoslavia, the debate is open as to what citizenship actually has primacy or, in other words, which political community is actually sovereign.

The FRY, formed by Serbia and Montenegro in 1992, adopted its own law on citizenship only in 1996[5] after the wars ended in Croatia and Bosnia-Herzegovina. Individuals entitled to FRY citizenship were those in possession of the republican citizenships of Serbia and of Montenegro on 27 April 1992. A clearly problematic dimension of this law was its retroactive application (Pejić 1998). Those who were invited to hold FRY citizenship were permanent residents from other republics living in the FRY on that very day, if they did not have a foreign citizenship. In other words, when it comes to this category, the FRY retroactively applied the 'new state model'. The apparent liberal approach of the FRY authorities towards this group must be explained by two factors.

The FRY unsuccessfully tried to portray itself as the sole legal successor of the SFRY – therefore accepting all SFRY citizens permanently residing on its territory as its citizens – but one also has to take into account that a majority of these individuals were also of Serb ethnicity. Ethnocentric migrations within Yugoslavia were a recurrent phenomenon: Zagreb attracted many Croats outside Croatia, Belgrade many Serbs outside Serbia and Montenegrins, Pristina (especially after 1974) Albanians from Macedonia and Montenegro and Sarajevo many ethnic Muslims from the Sandžak region.

However, in spite of the positioning of Belgrade as the political centre of ethnic Serbs, and not only of the FRY, the law offered to thousands of Serb refugees settled in the FRY a narrow possibility for acquisition of its citizenship. One might assume that this mistreatment of Serb refugees in Serbia and Montenegro – by contrast with the Croatian approach in treating ethnic Croats from Bosnia-Herzegovina, for instance – contradicts my claim about the general use of citizenship legislation for ethnic engineering. However, this is not entirely the case. The deliberate manipulation of the refugee problem was part of Milošević's political strategy. Without the citizenship of their republics of origin, and without the real possibility of acquiring that of the FRY, Serb refugees became the true hostages to Milošević's wartime policies and their failure in both neighbouring countries and within Serbia. Many refugees were re-directed to the multiethnic region of Vojvodina, and to a lesser degree to Kosovo and Montenegro, where they influenced to a certain degree the ethnodemographic balances (see Rava 2010). In addition to that, offering citizenship for half a million refugees from Bosnia and Croatia would have entailed voting rights for this group that by the mid-1990s mostly blamed Milošević for their sufferings and found the nationalistic rhetoric of other political parties much more appealing. Many of them, however, found ways (some less than legitimate) to obtain the citizenship of the FRY (Svilanović 1998: 244). In 2001, new amendments to the law made it easier for this group to finally acquire citizenship status.

Lastly, in Slovenia and Macedonia, which are countries with a small number of ethnic Slovene or Macedonian kin in neighbouring countries, the law also included a special provision for facilitated naturalization of ethnic Slovene and ethnic Macedonian political or economic diaspora members.

The excluded

Since legal continuity with republican citizenship was established as the rule, the group that was immediately excluded were those Yugoslav citizens residing in republics other than their own. Their situation was often even more complicated if they were of different ethnicity to the core ethnic group of the republic where they lived. Once Yugoslavia had disappeared, these lawful citizens were, overnight, turned into aliens and, in many cases, the stateless. For the most part, they were required to follow naturalization processes reserved for aliens, requiring a certain number of years of continuous residence and certain additional tests. The Ministries of the Interior that were in charge of deciding on the validity of the applications often had no obligation to state the reasons for refusal; many reports testify to widespread discrimination against members of ethnic minorities (see Dika et al. 1998; Imeri 2006; UNHCR 1997).

The most drastic case of administrative exclusion happened in Slovenia, an ethnically homogenous country barely affected by violent conflicts. The only former Yugoslav republic to become an EU member state in 2004, Slovenia, with its functioning state apparatus, its respect for the rule of law and its successful adoption of EU legislation, has often been upheld as exemplary in protecting human rights. This image would probably remain unquestioned were it not for the case of the so-called erased. The citizenship law adopted in June 1991 provided that individuals from other republics who had had lawful residence in Slovenia on 23 December 1990 – the day of the referendum on Slovenian independence, not the day of actual independence and a year before international recognition – could become Slovenian citizens upon request within six months.[6] The law itself becomes quite controversial when we consider that it enabled policies of ethnic engineering. One such measure was taken on 23 February 1992. On that day, according to official sources, 18,305 lawful residents – according to the European Court of Human Rights the number amounts to 25,671 – from other republics were literally erased from the civic registries in Slovenia. In the months to come, their documents (e.g. passports, driver's licenses and IDs) were invalidated. They lost all civic and social rights, jobs, health care and social benefits, and became 'dead' from an administrative point of view – they were *izbrisani*, i.e. erased. This was facilitated by a short application period of six months, confusing procedures, numerous difficulties in obtaining all necessary documents at the moment of Yugoslavia's break-up and subsequent escalation of violence, and finally by the overall political confusion since Slovenia was still legally part of the SFRY and was not internationally recognized until January 1992 (Deželan 2013; Medved 2007).[7]

In war-affected Croatia, together with residents from other republics (non-Croats, mostly ethnic Serbs) who were struggling to resolve their citizenship status in new Croatia, the most significant problems concerned the status of Serbs living in the breakaway Krajina region. Serb militias, acting in concert with the disintegrating federal army, took control of one-third of Croatia's territory during 1991. Their rebellion or self-exclusion (see below) from the Croatian legal framework was followed by exclusionary practices after the Croatian government retook control of these areas during two blitzkrieg operations in Western Slavonia and Krajina in 1995 (Eastern Slavonia was peacefully reintegrated into Croatia in January 1998). The majority of Croatian Serbs from these regions left or were forced to leave their homes and their property was damaged or occupied by Croat refugees or local Croats. The Tudjman government did everything to prevent their return to Croatia. They were all still legally Croatian citizens, but – since so many of them were refugees outside Croatia, in Serbia and Bosnia-Herzegovina and could not re-enter Croatia – they could not obtain the certificate of Croatian citizenship (*domovnica*) and therefore could not re-claim full citizenship rights (see the report on Croatia in Imeri 2006: 129–131; also Koska 2013). However, after Tudjman's death and subsequent political changes in 2000, and during Croatia's bid for EU membership, this group of Croatian Serbs for the most part regained their citizenship status.

In Macedonia, one provision of the first law on citizenship from 1992 considering residents from other Yugoslav republics proved that Macedonian legislators at the time were also preoccupied with ethnic engineering. The provision affirms that a permanent resident must live continuously in Macedonia for no less than fifteen years. This affected all residents from other republics, but it was clear that one particular group had been targeted: ethnic Albanians who had moved to Macedonia during socialist Yugoslavia and were thus numerically reinforcing the relative size of the Albanian minority. Albanians complained that the new Constitution rendered them second-class citizens and that the law on citizenship purposefully excluded a considerable number of ethnic Albanians (see Spaskovska 2013).

In the FRY, or more precisely in Serbia, the politics of exclusion took on a different, political and not legal shape, and were mostly concentrated in one particular region, Kosovo. Although ethnic Albanians continued to be Serbian and thus FRY citizens, the province of Kosovo, in the period between Serbia's revocation of Kosovo's autonomous status in 1989 and the expulsion of Albanians from state institutions, to the 1999 NATO intervention, was a place of continuous violations of their citizenship rights (see Krasniqi 2013a). Under Serbian administrative, military and police rule, this group of Yugoslav citizens was deprived of political and many civil rights. Ethnic Albanians often had problems not only with registering in the citizens' register, but also with obtaining travel documents and re-entering the country.

The self-excluded

Self-exclusion from existing citizenship status (of one's own republic) – with the idea of forming one's own ethnically based state and/or joining the kin state and its citizenship – was, as I showed in the previous chapters, part and parcel of the Serb rebellions in Croatia and Bosnia-Herzegovina and the Bosnian Croats' political strategy in 1993 and 1994. Already in August 1990 – three months after Tudjman's nationalist party took power in Croatia – the roads leading from Zagreb to the Dalmatian coast were blocked in the Serb-populated area and Serb police officers refused to commit their loyalty to the Croatian Ministry of the Interior as well as to wear new uniforms decorated with Croatian insignia. In October of the same year, the Serb autonomous region of Krajina was declared; local Serb leaders openly advocated that, in case of Yugoslavia's disintegration, Yugoslav Serbs should unite in a greater Serbian state regardless of the actual republican borders. In March 1991, what would become known as Krajina declared independence from Croatia.

A similar scenario occurred in Bosnia-Herzegovina. The mobilization of Bosnian Serbs for war was also motivated by the prospect of changing internal Yugoslav borders and joining a new, larger Serb entity. With the Dayton Peace agreement the territories under their control as well as the population in these territories would be re-integrated into the Bosnian citizenry. In a similar fashion, nationalist Croats in Bosnia-Herzegovina established their own statelet, the Croatian Republic of Herzeg-Bosna. In 1994, after the signing of the Washington agreement with the Bosnian government, they re-joined the state institutions.

One needs to mention another self-exclusionary practice, namely peaceful rebellion – until the emergence of the Kosovo Liberation Army in 1997 – of Albanians in Kosovo against the Serbian authorities.[8] Local Albanians judged Serbia's presence in Kosovo to be illegitimate after the unilateral revocation of Kosovo's autonomy and the waves of political repression against Albanians. Albanians opted for a boycott of the Serbian state and the construction of parallel political community, society and institutions. Eventually, the self-exclusionary practices failed in all but the case of the Kosovo Albanians. Thanks to the international intervention, they got rid of Serbian rule, formed their own institutions and established an independent citizenship regime in Kosovo and, after 2008, gained partial international recognition.

Epilogue: The citizens, the metics and the aliens

One could safely conclude that the implementation of the new citizenship laws in the former Yugoslav states was marked by 'confusion and arbitrariness' (Pejić 1998: 173). Nevertheless, this confusion was only partly the product of an unstable political context. In the majority of cases, the governments involved in the conflict created confusion intentionally. Arbitrariness could be found in many of the legal prescriptions and actual administrative practices, and was clearly part of a general strategy of creating ethnically re-designed states – a strategy that often called existing borders into question – in favour of a given ethnic majority.

The citizenship laws and the procedures for acquiring new citizenship proved to be the main weapon of administrative ethnic engineering. The targeted populations were usually comprised of individuals living in republics other than their 'own', especially if they numerically reinforced a domestic ethnic minority (perceived as not sufficiently 'loyal' to the new state), or were simply of a different ethnic origin. Citizenship laws provided an opportunity to eliminate a certain number of citizens from the political, social and economic life of the new states. They were useful tools for the modification of ethnic balances and social and ethnic structures. The new aliens saw their rights reduced and their residency threatened, which proved to be a powerful means of forcing them out of their homes and usually out of the country, without employing physical violence and thus avoiding condemnation by international bodies or human rights agencies.

In general, we could conclude that the dissolution of a multinational federation and the common efforts by successor states to define their citizenry deprived a huge number of individuals of their previous status as lawful citizens. Rogers Brubaker's description of the internal Soviet migrants in the post-Soviet period is equally valid for many former Yugoslavs: 'The breakup of the Soviet Union has transformed yesterday's internal migrants, secure in their Soviet citizenship, into today's international migrants of contested legitimacy and uncertain membership' (1992: 269). When this break-up was followed by a violent conflict, it also resulted in massive migrations and in millions of refugees and internally displaced persons. Citizens *à part entière* are thus transformed into *metics*, authorized residents with limited rights or illegal aliens. Of relevance here is Michael Walzer's analysis of the status of *metics* in Western Europe and in North America as residents who, like *metics* from ancient Greece, are not citizens: 'They are ruled, like the Athenian Metics, by a band of citizens-tyrants' (1983: 58). In post-Yugoslav states, the major difference is that, unlike the *metics* in the ancient Greek *polis* that had never had the privileged position of citizens or immigrants today, the post-Yugoslav *metics* and *aliens* used to be *citizens* enjoying full citizenship rights in their places of residence. The former citizens became either legal alien residents or obtained only temporary visas, without a clear indication of whether they would ever regain the status of citizens, and lived with a potential threat of deportation, or they were simply transformed into illegal aliens such as the erased in Slovenia and thus subject to immediate expulsion.

Classical citizenship entails a bipolar relationship between citizens and aliens, whereas citizenship in a federation is characterized by a triangular relationship between citizens of the member states, citizens of the federation and aliens (Béaud 2002: 317–318). This triangular relationship might be called the *federal citizenship contract*. It consists of offering equal rights to all federal citizens over the whole federation's territory, regardless of their sub-state citizenship (the citizenship of a constitutive part, if legally provided). In the case of the dissolution of the Yugoslav federation and in some ex-Soviet countries, the successor states broke the existing federal citizenship contract and adopted the classical citizenship contract that distinguishes only between nationals and aliens, a direct consequence of which was the transformation of vast numbers of lawful citizens into *metics* or aliens – legal or illegal residents with no right to the status of citizen or subject to overly complicated procedures for acquiring it – as if the previous federal citizenship contract had never existed.

To a huge number of individuals in the former Yugoslavia that experienced the fate of *metics* and *aliens*, we should add refugees as well. After fleeing from their republic of origin, they often found themselves in the territory of another republic with, in most cases, no right to its citizenship (even after several years) and with no possibility to renew their citizenship status in their republic of origin. To make the whole situation even more complicated, their republic of origin was more often than not in open conflict with the republic in which they found shelter. It was not until the late 1990s and after 2000 that the situation generally began to improve, with many aliens being turned into *metics* and *metics* slowly reacquiring their *droit de cité*, and with yesterday's enemies gradually being transformed into neighbours.

Enemies into neighbours: Unconsolidated and overlapping citizenship regimes

Since 2000, multiple changes and reforms of the citizenship policies and citizenship-related administrative practices – both improvements and regressions – have been introduced in post-Yugoslav states. The matter is even more complicated by the fact that we have since seen another disintegration (of Serbia and Montenegro in 2006) and secession (of Kosovo from Serbia in 2008), the result being three new states with three new independent citizenship regimes. Some problems similar to those from the 1990s thus arose again.

In the former northwestern Yugoslav republics of Slovenia and Croatia (that already joined the EU), citizenship laws and regulations have not been profoundly modified since independence. It took more than twenty years for Slovenia to face the problems of the 'erased' and to accept full responsibility for such an act. In Croatia, one of the most important conditions for joining the EU was the return of Serb refugees and the full restitution of their civil status and the reparation of their material goods. The actual practice of managing citizenship has demonstrated a greater degree of inclusiveness due mostly to the change in political climate. To sum up, inclusiveness and generally fair treatment of minorities are here combined with the preservation of a trans-border ethnic Croat community tied together by the bonds of citizenship (Ragazzi, Štiks and Koska 2013).[9]

On the other hand, considerable changes in legislation and administrative practices have occurred in the former southeastern Yugoslav republics, post-conflict Macedonia and in the newly independent states of Serbia, Montenegro and Kosovo. By signing the Ohrid Framework Agreement in August 2001, ethnic Macedonian and Albanian parties committed themselves to a multiethnic Macedonia in order to end the Albanian rebellion. Albanian demands for a reform of both the Constitution (in 2001) and, subsequently, the Citizenship Law (in 2004) were also met. Macedonia was re-defined as a '*civic* and democratic state' [emphasis added] (Constitution of the Republic of Macedonia 2001). The Albanian language was recognized as an official language in the majority Albanian areas, and the greater representation of ethnic Albanians in the state sector was affirmed. Finally, in early 2004, Parliament adopted a new law on citizenship that reduced the controversial residence requirement from fifteen to eight years.

In 2004, the Serbian National Assembly also adopted a new law on Serbian citizenship that annulled both the old one (1979/1983) and the law on FRY citizenship. The main characteristic of the 2004 law is the invitation to acquire Serbian citizenship given to ethnic Serbs and members of the Serb diaspora. After Montenegro's declaration of independence, Serbia automatically and unwillingly became an independent state as well. This provided a good opportunity for a new exercise in 'constitutional nationalism'. The new Constitution re-defines Serbia as 'the state of the Serbian people and of all citizens living in it' (Constitution of the Republic of Serbia 2006). This ethnocentric definition – again similar to the Croatian constitution – directly affected the law on Serbian citizenship that was further amended in September 2007 (see Vasiljević 2013). It confirmed that the road was open for ethnic Serbs from the former SFRY and abroad to acquire Serbian citizenship without the residency requirement, provided they sign a written declaration that they 'consider Serbia to be their country'. The 2007 law has also smoothed the way for Montenegrin citizens living in Serbia to acquire Serbian citizenship.

This move provoked an angry reaction from Montenegro, which feared Serbia's influence on a large number of its citizens. Montenegro reiterated that it would not allow its citizens to hold dual citizenship and that those citizens violating the law would be stripped of their Montenegrin citizenship. As early as 1999, in preparation for eventual independence, Montenegro adopted its own law on citizenship, in which primacy over (and an open defiance of) the existing federal citizenship was clearly stated. Montenegro as a now sovereign and again internationally recognized state adopted a new Constitution on 19 October 2007. Its first article defines Montenegro as a '*civic*, democratic, and *ecological* country' (Constitution of Montenegro 2007, emphasis added). After many debates and delays, the Montenegrin parliament adopted a new law on Montenegrin citizenship in early 2008. The law, as with the Constitution, states in its first article that Montenegrin citizenship is 'the legal tie between a person and the Republic of Montenegro and *does not imply national or ethnic origin*' [emphasis added]. The law forbids dual citizenship, which, given the size of the Serb minority (28 per cent according to the 2011 census) as well as many Montenegrins residing in Serbia, has been a source of continuous tension between these states (see Džankić 2013).

In Serbia and Montenegro, the laws on citizenship were once more used as a way to sustain and promote the demographic superiority of a core ethnic group and – in contexts where ethnic origin often determines one's political preferences as well such as in Montenegro – as a means of reinforcing a particular political position. In the Montenegrin case, we see, however, a novel approach. Since ethnic Montenegrins are numerically the largest (45 per cent) but not

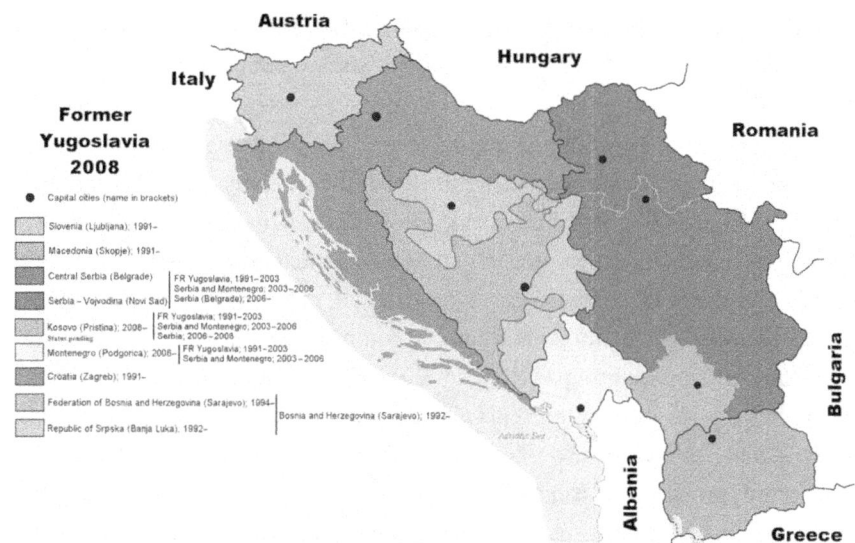

Figure 9.1 The post-Yugoslav states since 2008 (Source: Wikimedia Commons)[10].

the majority group in Montenegro, insistence on the civic nature of the state and its citizenship could be interpreted as a measure to reinforce Montenegro's independent statehood – narrowly achieved in the referendum in 2006 – which still deeply polarizes its citizens along ethnic lines.

'Newborn' Kosovo declared independence in February 2008, and its new Constitution came into effect on 15 June 2008 following the basic lines of the Ahtisaari plan for Kosovo's 'supervised independence'. Its first article defines Kosovo as 'a state of its citizens' that 'shall have no territorial claims against and shall seek no union with, any State or part of any State' (Constitution of the Republic of Kosovo 2008). On the same date the law on Kosovo citizenship came into effect. The law extended Kosovo citizenship to all citizens of FRY who had 'habitual residence' in Kosovo on 1 January 1998. However, a new example of self-exclusion immediately appeared. Kosovo Serbs largely refused to accept Kosovo as an independent state with its own authorities and they have been building their own 'parallel institutions' in Serb-majority zones in North Kosovo that has been, after the 2013 agreement between Serbia and Kosovo, slowly becoming part of the new state, although under a special political and citizenship regime (see Krasniqi 2013a, 2013b).

Since 2000, we have generally witnessed greater inclusiveness and less discrimination on ethnic grounds, as well as increased sensitivity to the political aspirations of ethnic minorities (e.g. in Macedonia and Croatia). Montenegro, on the other hand, shows how even the civic definition of citizenship, although favoured by the EU, can be deeply divisive when combined with intolerance towards dual citizenship, which in the particular Montenegrin context has the effect of reinforcing the core ethnic group even though it does not have a majority of the population. The Kosovo case shows that the carefully worded citizenship law, with a high degree of inclusiveness, does not help if one community (namely, Kosovo Serbs) wishes to remain part of the Serbian citizenship regime and rejects, together with Serbia, Kosovo's secession. After all, calling your state *civic*, and at the same time insisting on its multiethnic composition and representation and protection of smaller groups (Krasniqi 2013b), becomes practically irrelevant when the majority group represents almost 90 per cent of the entire population.

This brief overview also shows something else: one could see that the citizenship practices of Yugoslavia's successor states within the context of eventual EU enlargement are used both as tools of reconciliation and of fostering divisions among neighbours. More inclusive citizenship policies, coupled with political inclusiveness, definitely play a role in the reconciliation process in Croatia and Macedonia and are intended to promote reconciliation in Kosovo. In Bosnia-Herzegovina, the two-tier system of citizenship at least provides common ground for equality of all citizens. On the other hand, one can see that ethnocentric practices of granting citizenship to ethnic kin in neighbouring countries (practiced by Croatia and Serbia) are sources of new divisions and blurred loyalties in Bosnia-Herzegovina and Montenegro. Serbia considers citizens in Kosovo to be Serbian citizens (although its activities in reality are mostly directed towards the Serb minority and effectively ignore Albanians), whereas Kosovo and the international institutions try to get as many Kosovo Serbs to accept and take part in Kosovo citizenship as well.

Obviously, 'citizenship struggles' continue in what used to be Yugoslavia and what is today a landscape of increasingly overlapping citizenship regimes and their political communities. The picture gets even more complex with the division of this region between *the included* in and the *excluded* from the supranational membership of the EU.

Concluding remarks: From ethnic engineering to ethnic democracies

Democratization in Eastern Europe, and especially in the former socialist multinational federations, demonstrates that the rules of democracy including, among other elements, a solidified state, a defined territory and majority rule, are understood more often than not in ethnic terms. This in itself is unsurprising given that the majority of these states were formed as the ethnic homelands of their core ethnic groups and, in the post-socialist period, had free rein to impose their dominance over minority groups and individuals not fitting the criteria of ethnic membership.

At the end of the communist era, these states perceived themselves as 'nationalizing states'; that is states in the process of becoming full-fledged nation-states (Brubaker 1996: 63). Liberal democracy was considered crucial in their attempts at national liberation from foreign tutelage or multinational unions. Democracy itself legitimized the dominance of the core ethnic groups and created, in almost all of these states, multiple memberships within a single citizenship regime: citizenship as membership is overshadowed by ethnic membership or dominance by the core ethnic group that, constitutionally codified or not, 'owns' the state. These dominant groups therefore set about completing the revolution for national self-determination by aiming to create a nation-state of a given majority ethnicity or, failing to secure numerical dominance, a state with the given ethnicity as the core ethnic group. Constitutions and citizenship laws were critical tools for their success. They championed divisions among citizens along ethnic lines as the primary category of identification. These strategies inevitably created favourable conditions for conflict in the context of ethnic diversity and competing claims over territory.

This chapter shows how crucial citizenship policies and ethnic engineering were for creating, after socialism, a series of state-level or sub-state-level ethnic democracies. Sammy Smooha defines ethnic democracy as a democratic political system that combines the extension of civil and political rights to permanent residents who wish to be citizens with the bestowal of a favoured status on the majority group. This is democracy that contains the non-democratic institutionalization of dominance of one ethnic group. The founding rule of this regime is an inherent contradiction between two principles – civil and political rights for all and structural subordination of the minority to the majority. The 'democratic principle' provides equality between all citizens and members of society, while the 'ethnic principle' establishes explicit ethnic inequality, preference and dominance (Smooha 2005a: 21).

Smooha based his model on the case of Israel in its internationally recognized pre-1967 borders and compares ethnic democracy with the classic liberal model and consociational democracy. Confronted with the experience of the post-communist period Smooha offered a revised model of ethnic democracy (see 2005b). Some of the features of ethnic democracy according to this revised model are therefore ethnic ascendancy, perceived threats and diminished democracy. The only reasons for introducing democracy at all, Smooha argues, lie in the ethnonationalist drive of the majority and its belief in democratic values, political considerations both domestic and international, its quest for legitimacy and its calculation of democracy's utility. A strong state, a stable numerical and political majority and a small and manageable minority assure the viability of an ethnic democracy. It is crucial for the viability of this type of democracy that the majority continues to perceive threats and that the external homeland and international community do not intervene. Ethnic democracy entails a privileged position for the ethnic majority; this majority uses the state for its own political, social, cultural and economic benefits. However to qualify as an ethnic *democracy*, Smooha warns, a state must guarantee minimal minority rights as well as the rule of law.

Many post-communist countries obviously only half-implemented the model. They found the ethnic dominance of the core group an attractive proposition in addition to liberal democracy but often failed to fulfil the democratic criteria when dealing with their minorities. This led to widespread discrimination, restrictions in citizenship rights and in some instances violence. For Smooha, many post-communist countries failed to establish ethnic democracy 'because they lacked a strong state and a good measure of democracy', and did not provide benefits for their minorities to guarantee the acceptance of ethnic democracy (2005b: 257). Although I acknowledge the applicability of the ethnic democracy model in Eastern Europe, it does not help us to understand the link between ethnic democracy and the attempts at territorial expansion. Smooha's model presupposes defined borders, hence his insistence on Israel in its pre-1967 boundaries. Israel's expansion here differs from the situation in Eastern Europe: it was meant to conquer territories – understood as being part of a Biblical Jewish state – in order to settle Jewish migrants there, whereas in many Eastern European cases, ethnic democratic state was seen as incomplete if it did not include the territories already inhabited by co-ethnics in neighbouring countries. The stateness, on the other hand, was seen as threatened if ethnic minority was not 'small and manageable'.

When it comes to the post-Yugoslav states, this was certainly the case in the 1990s. However, after the conflicts and in the 2000s, it seems that these states satisfy the general criteria suggested by Smooha, while the use of internal and external 'threats' varies according to a given context. This happens even if they define themselves as being civic, which often hides the dominance of the core ethnic group, or multiethnic. In the situation of recognized multiethnic composition followed by the introduction of consociational rules, ethnic democracy is mostly practised at the sub-state level as in Bosnia-Herzegovina (entities and cantons), Kosovo (special statuses for Serb municipalities) and Macedonia (municipal level). Furthermore, ethnic democracies are complemented by ethnocentric citizenship policies in the majority of states in Southeast Europe. In the absence of the classic territorial expansion, expansion of citizenship succeeds in bringing under the same citizenship regime ethnic kin abroad and in the near abroad and thus further empowers ethnic membership and solidarity.

10

Partners Again? The European Union and the Post-Yugoslav Citizens

The final chapter in the story of one hundred years of citizenship in and after Yugoslavia brings to the scene another powerful player whose influence in shaping the post-Yugoslav citizenship regimes and influencing the lives of their citizens is far from insignificant. The EU has been the most powerful political and economic agent in this region that has effectively divided it into the EU members and the potential candidates for membership. The former Yugoslav space overlaps with the so-called Western Balkans, a changing geopolitical construct forged in Brussels, composed of those former Yugoslav republics that have not joined the EU so far *plus* Albania. The 'Western Balkans' approach as an umbrella term for the countries outside the EU but completely encircled by the EU, though the Schengen border moves much slower, hides the fact that, regardless of the EU membership, Slovenia is still deeply involved with its southern neighbours and Croatia remains one of the most important actors in the former Yugoslav space. One could say that 'Yugoslavia' in this respect has disappeared as a political entity but not as a geopolitical space.

The EU does not only directly influence its members (Slovenia and Croatia), supervises the Western Balkan candidates – 'negotiations' being a euphemism for a one-way communication amounting to the huge translation operation of the *acquis communautaire* – but it actually maintains there two semi-protectorates (Bosnia and Kosovo). It has developed varied approaches: bilaterally negotiating membership (Croatia before 2013, Serbia, Montenegro and Albania), punishing and rewarding (Serbia, Bosnia, Kosovo and Albania), managing (Bosnia), governing (Kosovo) and, finally, ignoring (Macedonia blocked in the name dispute with Greece). The EU in the Balkans is therefore not only a club that tests its candidates. It is an active player in transforming them, politically, socially and economically. David Chandler concludes that 'the EU's discourse of governance enables it to exercise a regulatory power over the candidate member states of Southeastern Europe while evading any reflection on the EU's own management processes, which are depoliticized in the framing of the technocratic or administrative conditions of enlargement' (2010: 69). If the EU basically builds future or potential member states, then we have to ask how the EU manages both citizenship regimes of the post-Yugoslav states and their citizens.

The EU's direct and limited influences

The EU's role in influencing, shaping, defining and re-defining the citizenship regimes in the post-Yugoslav region often, alongside obvious improvements, appear problematic, counterproductive or fruitless. It must first be noted that the EU frequently acts in this region in cooperation with or in parallel to other international organizations such as the UN or OSCE (Organization for Security and Co-operation in Europe). There is also a myriad of international norms (conventions, adopted or not, and regulations) and bodies that influence citizenship regimes in these countries such as the Council of Europe and its Venice Commission, and, quite significantly, the European Court of Human Rights (see Shaw 2010). In this respect, 'Europeanisation' of the citizenship regimes in place cannot be identified only with the 'EU-isation' of the region, even though the two are generally conflated. Nonetheless, the actual membership of some states and the overall orientation of the Western Balkans towards political, legal and economic integration into the EU give the Union the major role in actively transforming not just these countries as such but also their citizenship regimes and the political communities these regimes define.

After stating that it does exercise a considerable influence, we have to ask if the EU has a coherent policy or a particular norm in the vital domain of citizenship, which is, clearly, crucial for the functioning of 'new democracies'. It appears, however, that there is no consistent citizenship policy towards actual or future members. This comes as no surprise since the previous enlargements showed limited EU influence on national citizenship regimes of the candidate countries, as exemplified by the EU's tolerance of statelessness in the Baltic countries and the case of the 'erased' in Slovenia. And yet, in sharp contrast to Central and Eastern Europe, the EU appears to be quite actively involved in managing post-Yugoslav citizens.

Broadly speaking, the EU's influence on citizenship regimes in the post-Yugoslav region could be defined as either *direct* or *limited*. When it comes to *direct* influence this is doubtless strongest in Kosovo, strong in Bosnia and, finally, significant in Macedonia. Those are the countries where the EU actually intervened militarily and administratively (in Kosovo and Bosnia) or where it influenced considerably constitutional and political changes that directly affected citizenship regimes as well (as in Macedonia after the 2001 conflict and the EU-sponsored Ohrid Framework Agreement). In these countries, the citizenship legislation was either proposed to local actors or imposed ready-made by the internationals themselves (with the EU in the driver's seat) or else changes in legislation affecting citizenship were introduced according to the EU's stated preferences (as in Macedonia).

In contrast, the EU's *limited* influence can be observed in Montenegro, Croatia and Slovenia. In Montenegro the governing structures are keen to please the EU but are also very careful to preserve, via the country's citizenship regime, fragile ethnic (and therefore electoral) balances. The case of Croatia surely deserves a different kind of attention for being the first post-socialist, post-partition and post-conflict country to enter the EU with a legacy of war (not experienced by Slovenia) that significantly complicated its accession process. Finally, both Croatia and Slovenia as EU member states need special treatment, since joining a new supranational union also entailed introducing another supranational layer to their citizenships.

Serbia seems to stand between the direct influence group and the limited influence group depending on how one perceives the EU's role in the territory of that country, i.e. how one perceives what *is* actually its territory. On the one hand, the EU has a limited influence on Serbia's citizenship legislation and practices, mostly through the visa liberalization process, but, on the other, the EU's role in Kosovo, where a new separate citizenship regime has been created with the direct assistance of the EU (and also other international bodies), could be equally seen as having a direct and major influence on the Serbian citizenship regime and the Serbian citizenry as a whole.

In the previous chapter, I concentrated on how the political elites in the new states (mis)manage their citizenship regimes. This final chapter focuses on what I see as five major ways whereby the EU itself (mis)manages these citizenship regimes and their citizens: (a) direct intervention and supervision; (b) the visa liberalization process; (c) the pre-accession influence; (d) the post-accession influence and, finally, (e) the influence exerted by individual EU member states.

Five ways to (mis)manage the post-Yugoslav citizenship regimes

Direct intervention and supervision

The EU's actions with regard to citizenship are, as underlined above, most direct in Kosovo. After the North Atlantic Treaty Organization (NATO) bombings in 1999 Kosovo was turned into a *de facto* protectorate under the UN mission (UNMIK, UN Interim Administration Mission) and with a heavy NATO and EU presence. The EU took complete control when EU Rule of Law Mission (EULEX) replaced UNMIK in 2008. However, in spite of the complete separation from Serbia, Kosovans remained *de jure* citizens of Serbia and the Federal Republic of Yugoslavia (FRY) and, between 2003 and 2006, citizens of the State Union of Serbia and Montenegro. After the disintegration of the State Union in 2006, Kosovans were technically transformed into citizens of the Republic of Serbia exclusively. Following Kosovo's declaration of independence in February 2008, a new Constitution based on the Ahtisaari plan was adopted defining Kosovo as 'a state of its citizens'. On the same date, the new law on Kosovo citizenship came into effect as well. The main aim was to establish the body of Kosovo citizens by using a highly inclusive and liberal 'new state' model that grants citizenship to all permanent residents on the territory of the new state (in this case, the former FRY citizens residing in Kosovo back in 1998 and/or holders of UNMIK documents).[1] Although the first Kosovo passports were issued in summer 2008, the Serb-majority municipalities, especially in northern Kosovo around the town of Mitrovica, refused to accept the jurisdiction of the Kosovan authorities. In the context of Serbia's EU bid, the situation in the North changed in 2013. Both Serbia and Kosovo have been awarded (one with the candidate status and the other with the Stabilisation and Association Agreement) for reaching a 'deal' which foresees progressive inclusion of the North into the Kosovo institutions with a certain degree of autonomy and political position between two states (for Serbia between itself and its province) confirmed by dual citizenship. The international bodies also induced a redrawing of Kosovo's internal map and the creation of new autonomous Serb municipalities.

As with the Constitution itself, the Kosovo citizenship law was drafted by the international bodies supervising Kosovo, namely the International Civilian Mission whose head was also the EU representative. The local politicians promptly accepted the documents with little local debate or initiative. State building in Kosovo is thus designed and supervised by the international community and, since the EULEX mission started to operate, directly by the EU itself. This oxymoronic 'supervised independence', as it was known until 2013, amounts to a neocolonial situation without a clear roadmap towards total local control and EU membership. Conflicting signals therefore have been sent out: the EU is heavily present in Kosovo but the country's eventual EU accession process is not expected to start anytime soon. At the same time, the EU mostly runs the place but cannot speak or act unanimously since five EU member states still refused to recognize an independent Kosovo. Without a clear prospect of joining the EU, which in itself would have to result from an EU-led effort, without a prospect of breaking the visa deadlock, and without solving some of the pressing issues between Kosovo and Serbia (such as economic normalization, border issues and management of the Mitrovica region), the Kosovan citizenship regime remains highly unstable.

Another state under direct EU intervention is Bosnia-Herzegovina. It has been a theatre of major EU external involvement for two decades. As in Kosovo, a gradual transfer of competences from the international bodies towards the EU has taken place. The Office of High Representative (OHR), endowed by the extensive so-called Bonn powers with the authority to basically rule Bosnia, was headed since the beginning by EU member state politicians and since 2002 the High Representative also serves as the EU Special Representative. Since the Dayton Peace Agreement and an ensuing peacekeeping operation in which both the United States and the EU played a major role, Bosnia has been under direct supervision, making it effectively a semi-protectorate. The new Dayton law on citizenship was introduced, or rather imposed, much later in 1997 by the High Representative.

If the citizenship situation was quite chaotic during the war, the citizenship landscape after the war remained highly complex. The 'Dayton' Constitution of Bosnia and Herzegovina (annex IV of the Peace treaty) defined citizenship of the country, similarly to socialist Yugoslav citizenship, as *dual* or two tiered. Citizens thus possess both state citizenship and citizenship of one of the two entities. There is also the curious case of citizens from the self-governing district of Brčko (under international supervision until 2012), functioning *de facto* as Bosnia's third entity. Brčko is 'shared' by the entities, although under direct state-level sovereignty, and its citizens may choose which entity citizenship they wish to have. Bosnia's citizenship could be defined as *multiethnic* insofar as almost all political participation of citizens is based on their ethnic affiliation. Bosnia's Dayton-enshrined *ethnopolitics* not only consolidated ethnic division and led to permanent institutional paralysis but also provoked widespread discrimination against so-called others, i.e. those not belonging to any of the three ethnic groups or not wishing to state their ethnic background (Mujkić 2007; Sarajlić 2013; Štiks 2011). Due to this apparent discrimination among citizens, the European Court of Human Rights in the Finci–Sejdić case ordered Bosnia-Herzegovina in December 2009 to change the laws forbidding anyone who do not belong to three constitutive peoples (Serbs, Bosniaks and Croats) to run for the state presidency and the House of Peoples of the Parliament. In other words, if you are Jewish or Roma, as Mr Finci and Mr Sejdić happen to be, or if you simply decline to declare your ethnicity, you cannot enjoy full political rights in the country. Even four years after the ruling, the political elites failed to implement this binding decision that would remove discriminatory provisions of the Dayton peace constitution.

The reason that Macedonia ranks among the group of countries where the EU has a direct influence is the aftermath of the short-lived conflict between the Macedonian government and Albanian rebels in 2001. The EU backed the Ohrid Framework Agreement and sent a military and police mission to the country. The agreement transformed Macedonia from a nation-state dominated by its ethnic majority into a state functioning on consociational principles designed to guarantee a balance between the Macedonian majority and the 25 per cent-strong Albanian minority. The EU played a major part in these constitutional transformations that directly affected the Macedonian citizenship regime (Spaskovska 2013). Albanian demands for a reform of both the Constitution and, subsequently, the citizenship law were met as well. The agreement also included the country's decentralization, administrative reorganization and a change of linguistic policies. Although Macedonia is not a country under EU supervision like Bosnia or Kosovo, its relationship to the EU is seen as crucial for the country's future. However, the EU's intervention in order to ensure stability and Greece's blocking of Macedonia's accession, despite the fact that it has been officially recognized as a candidate for EU membership since 2005, provoked even further instability. The inter-ethnic balance as defined by the Ohrid Agreement (the subject of a lot of grievances on both sides) is seen as fragile, the relationship between the two communities, without any unifying supraethnic political platform, is far from perfect, and the perspective of EU accession, regarded as the only guarantor of future peace and the country's consolidation, remains unclear.

The visa liberalization process

The EU successfully applied visa liberalization as a tool of legal and administrative engineering in Serbia, Montenegro, Macedonia, Bosnia and Albania (see Kacarska 2012). Not only was visa liberalization used to consolidate civic registers and to introduce new security measures via biometric passports, but was also used to alter existing legal provisions related to criminal law and the functioning of the police, customs and border control. However, the process itself was followed by many unintended political and practical consequences.

It could be said that the visa liberalization process constitutes the most visible and tangible example of the EU's influence for citizens of the Western Balkans, unlike a distant membership prospect offered in return for an undertaking to implement often painful reforms. The EU used the visa liberalization process as a way of applying leverage. To fulfil the conditions, the countries on the Schengen 'blacklist' (to which they could be relegated again) had to revise parts of their legislation concerning their citizenship regimes (laws on foreigners and asylum), including the penal code in some cases, as well as to implement significant police and administrative reforms. The process itself, especially the evaluation of the benchmarks as well as the decision to allow visa-free travel to holders of Macedonian, Serbian and Montenegrin passports at the end of 2009 – but not to citizens and residents of Kosovo, even those possessing Serbian citizenship and passports! – or Albanian and Bosnian citizens included at the end of 2010, became mired in controversy and reinforced the bitter sense of isolation among those who were left behind.

Not only is Kosovo excluded from visa liberalization but, furthermore, at the EU's insistence, Serbia agreed to exclude from the benefits of visa liberalization those Serbian citizens, regardless of ethnicity, who reside on the territory of Kosovo. Serbia was thus forced by the EU to discriminate against one group of its citizens (not only Serbs but many Albanians still have Serbian identity documents and passports). One of the stated reasons is that since 1999 Serbia has not exerted control over the territory and individuals in Kosovo. Regardless of this fact, the policy breaches the right of every citizen to possess valid travel documents of his or her state and to be treated equally by that state – the right that Serbia, under EU pressure, denied to people it claims are its citizens in its own province. It seems, however, that the EU was primarily concerned with a possible influx of asylum seekers or illegal migrants from impoverished Kosovo and the readmission process.[2] In addition, Kosovans were left with no alternative, thus further devaluing the attractiveness of Kosovo citizenship (especially for Kosovo Serbs) and rendering Kosovo's new symbols of independence (such as the Kosovan passport) practically useless. In sum, the EU attempts to reinforce Kosovo statehood and to win the allegiance of Kosovo minorities (namely, the Serbs) to the new state and its institutions on the one hand and, on the other, undertakes initiatives that undermine these efforts and, in addition, effectively force people to search for less legitimate ways to acquire useful travel documents.[3]

It was not until November 2010 that the EU Council of Ministers gave the green light for visa liberalization for Bosnia and Albania after they had completed all necessary reforms. The visa liberalization strategy proved to be highly effective in forcing local politicians to adopt certain administrative reforms following their dismay when in December 2009 Bosnia was left out of the visa liberalization scheme. The majority of the Bosniaks were hit hardest by this decision. Croatian passports already permitted those (almost all ethnic Croats but some members of other groups too) holding these documents to travel without visas and it was assumed that many Serbs either already possessed or would try to acquire visa-free Serbian passports. Again the EU's bureaucratic insensitivity proved problematic on the ground and created even deeper divisions in Bosnia. On the other hand, during the election year, Bosnian politicians were ready to accept also the reforms that were not necessarily related to citizenship issues or administrative practices. The EU thus pressed for effective police coordination, harmonization of the criminal codes in both entities and in Brčko district with the state criminal code as well as for additional measures in fighting corruption and organized crime.

Montenegro also readily satisfied all the conditions for visa-free travel, including amending its law on foreigners. Here again it was clear that the EU's policies could lead to some problematic outcomes. Insistence on satisfying strict criteria for visa liberalization in the context of recent conflict and disintegration and the restrictive citizenship policies such as those in Montenegro resulted in the marginalization of the Roma refugees from Kosovo and their *de facto* statelessness. With their FRY documents invalidated and with no financial and practical means of acquiring new Serbian or rather travel-restrictive Kosovo identity documents, with no prospects of returning home and in a situation where they cannot hope to acquire Montenegrin citizenship (due to the criterion of ten-year permanent residence that the majority of them do not have or cannot prove), they linger in an administrative limbo, which results in complete socio-economic marginalization and, in many cases, extreme poverty (Džankić 2010).

Although the majority of post-Yugoslav citizens cannot afford to travel to the Schengen zone, having a visa-free passport, similar to the visa-free Yugoslav 'red passport', has a strong symbolic resonance. The bottom-up pressure thus had certain results. However, some EU member states are worried about the asylum seekers whose numbers, especially those from impoverished parts of Bosnia, Serbia and Macedonia, have sharply risen. To combat false asylum seekers the EU pressured the states not only to sign readmission agreements but also to engage in control of their exiting citizens. Besides checking return tickets and sufficient funds, this also includes a practice of ethnic profiling focused on the Roma mainly. This example shows that security concerns not only top a long-term political investment in the Balkans but also human rights issues as well (Kacarska 2012). The visa liberalization process demonstrates how the EU has influence on the value of someone's citizenship. A hierarchy of citizenship in the Balkans necessarily designs some passports as 'better' than the others and naturally induces people to try to belong to more beneficial citizenship regime. The political consequences of widespread dual and multiple citizenships are yet to be seen, but one thing is clear: a 'useless' passport disengages citizens from their already weak states, a trend that can be clearly observed in Bosnia and Kosovo.

The pre-accession and post-accession influence

The general pre-accession influence of the EU on the candidate countries, when the EU dictates the tone of negotiations, is obvious. So far only Slovenia and Croatia have gone through the whole process. Macedonia is still blocked; Serbia, Montenegro and Albania are at the early stages of negotiations, whereas Bosnia and Kosovo are still not official candidates. It remains to be seen if the negotiation process will bring further changes to the citizenship regimes of these countries. However, the experience shows that the EU's influence on the candidate countries' citizenship regimes, although indeed potentially considerable, does not necessarily result in profound reforms being initiated. Two Baltic states, Latvia and Estonia, managed to enter the EU despite the widespread statelessness of their substantial Russophone minority populations. Slovenia also practised human rights abuses and social and political discrimination and exclusion, though on a much smaller scale than in the Baltics. It did not solve the issue of 'the erased' before entering the EU but only after the decision of the ECHR (European Court of Human Rights). On the other hand, during the accession period Croatia showed much more inclusiveness, both administrative and political, towards the Serb minority. It also showed that the EU influence was acceptable but not in all areas (keeping its 1991 citizenship law mostly intact and not adopting the European Convention on Nationality) and that there was more willingness to change legislation in politically less sensitive areas (e.g. the asylum law). Nonetheless, this administrative and political inclusiveness, constituting perhaps one of the EU's most important legacies in the context of the Croatian accession process, did not alter the ethnocentric character of the state and its citizenship regime (ethnic preference has been 'moderated' by minority inclusion). The 'EU-isation' of Croatian citizenship demonstrated how candidate countries could 'satisfy' general EU criteria without actually reforming the fundamental substance of their polities.

Regardless of the changes in citizenship laws that remain under the sovereign jurisdiction of member states, joining the EU itself entails a significant change in the new member's citizenship regime. It automatically introduces another, supranational level to state citizenship with rights and duties attached to the institution of European citizenship. Slovenia and Croatia as the two post-Yugoslav states that joined the EU have therefore a similar two-tier citizenship regime to that which operated in socialist Yugoslavia. The advent of European citizenship in Slovenia and Croatia introduced changes when it comes to EU citizens residing in the country with regard to their participation in local (involving also third-country nationals) and European elections, rights that are also shared by Slovenian and Croatian citizens residing in other EU countries. It is interesting to notice in this context that Croatia used a linguistic opportunity, namely the distinction between citizenship as *državljanstvo* and citizenship as *građanstvo*, to introduce a significant difference and accentuate the primacy of national citizenship: Croatian citizenship is thus *državljanstvo* (something related to state, *država*), whereas European citizenship is *građanstvo* (something related to citizens, *građani*, and their activities but not necessarily to a state).

On the other hand, both Slovenia and Croatia demonstrate that EU membership does not seriously call into question the ethnocentric conception of citizenship and, moreover, that the EU has failed to convince its members to adopt more inclusive citizenship policies, if indeed it ever seriously tried to do so. It is hard to expect the other Western Balkan states to act differently and to re-define their citizenship policies allowing for ever-greater inclusiveness and non-discrimination on an ethnic basis unless there is a targeted pre-accession pressure (as in the case of Croatia) or some form of direct intervention.

The EU member states' influence

The picture of how the EU (mis)manages the post-Yugoslav citizenship regimes and citizens would be incomplete without describing a rather new phenomenon. Some EU member states have recently started, unilaterally, to influence these citizenship regimes by offering citizenship to 'co-ethnics' in the near abroad. Bulgaria interferes directly with the Macedonian citizenship regime by granting Bulgarian citizenship to those claiming 'Bulgarian descent' (at least 40,000 people in Macedonia have acquired Bulgarian citizenship in this way so far, probably much more).[4] A new Hungarian law on citizenship has already provoked fierce reactions (especially in Slovakia) but the real effects are felt in Serbia. It is already expected that up to 100,000 Serbian citizens of Magyar descent have acquired Hungarian citizenship.[5]

However, Croatian accession to the EU has had a major impact on its surroundings. If it is true to say that the EU's influence has certainly been felt in pre-accession Croatia, it is equally certain that two decades of Croatia's citizenship policies will affect the EU itself. At the moment of its adhesion Croatia brought to the EU a great number of EU citizens living in the neighbouring post-Yugoslav but non-EU countries such as Bosnia (estimates put the number of people actually having Croatian citizenship and living in Bosnia at around 500,000), Serbia and Montenegro combined (around 100,000), but also thousands in Macedonia and Kosovo. Is having a European passport in a non-EU state only a matter of additional security for these individuals or might its advantages be effectively used, i.e. by moving within the EU itself? Only time will tell.

Partners, or just neighbours?

From a larger historical perspective, it is interesting to see how citizens of a former multinational federation with a two-level citizenship regime become part of another multinational union of states with a similar citizenship structure that will, once in place, restore to them some of the basic privileges they enjoyed during the Yugoslav era. Moreover, many of those that were united by the bonds of Yugoslav federal citizenship – including those who wanted to break them – found or will find each other united again in another, though different, supranational citizenship regime. It is hard to miss here a certain historical irony.

However, whatever is generally seen as ironic is often tragic on the ground. The long process of more than two decades took the form of numerous partitions, secessions, social fragmentations and widespread political and material violence that turned the citizenship status of many former Yugoslav citizens into a highly complex and in some instances nightmarish one. The results of economic devastation, war and general insecurity sent millions into exile. Today, the process of gradually turning the former Yugoslav citizens into European citizens is clearly under way. Slovenians have been EU citizens since 2004; with Croatia's entry another 4.5 million people together with those living abroad will follow suit; tens of thousands possess already Bulgarian and Hungarian passports. Mention should also be made here of refugees and economic migrants living today within the EU member states and enjoying EU citizenship. Some of them returned to the Balkans and some are circulating between their EU residence and their places of origin. The EU will thus continue to shape the destiny of many post-Yugoslav citizens and their seven citizenship regimes currently existing, where in 1991 there was only one. It remains to be seen if turning all former Yugoslavs into tomorrow's Europeans will turn today's neighbours into partners one more time.

Could European citizenship serve as a tool of new cooperation among post-Yugoslav states? Notwithstanding some additional rights it provides, European citizenship is not federal and it has been cautiously defined – it is derived from the national citizenship of the member states and does not replace it – in order to displace any discussion on primacy. However, one is tempted to ask what the practice of European citizenship would be in the countries that constituted the former Yugoslavia. Above all, this additional citizenship layer would provide the right to circulate freely and to settle in other member states. In spite of the negative experiences of the recent past, we should not neglect the importance of the shared language and of personal and family ties for future migration within the region. It is hard to predict the scale of such migrations, but the fact is that today – following the general democratization of citizenship policies that favour more inclusive civic solidarity but also the existing ethnocentrism of many citizenship laws favouring ethnic solidarity – many individuals hold the citizenships of two and, in some rare instances, three post-Yugoslav states, a fact that has already had a certain political and social impact.

Furthermore, European citizenship would provide important economic, social and political rights. Participation and eligibility at the local and the European level (the national level will, for the time being, remain inaccessible for non-nationals in almost every state across the world) will certainly add new dynamic elements to the relations between the former Yugoslav states. Doubtless, the supranational roof of the EU, if it stretches far enough to embrace all former Yugoslavs, would indeed provide a new legal and political framework for yet another experiment in the Balkan laboratory of citizenship.

Epilogue: The Citizenship Argument – Why Are We in This Together?

'Who is in and who is out? – these are the first questions that any political community must answer about itself' (Walzer 1993: 55). We can agree with Michael Walzer on this point, but there is one important question that precedes asking who is in and who is out and that is, why are we in *this* together in the first place? How did a concrete political community come into being, and why does it still exist? How does a person find himself or herself in a particular community whose members are then recognized as co-citizens? And, are we all satisfied with the existing legal, political and social arrangements within the shared polity? Maybe we want our political community to be organized differently, or we want to belong to an entirely different community, one that exists or the one that is yet to be? In short, every political community is confronted with the *why* of its existence, having to convince its members – or at least a good portion of them – that they do belong together. This is what I call *the citizenship argument* of a political community.

Every polity exists and reproduces itself through a mutually solidifying interplay between the citizenship argument on which a political community is based and its legal codifications, including the laws on citizenship that clearly define who is in and who is out. The mutually reinforcing or opposing tensions between the citizenship argument (a widely shared narrative of the 'why are we in this together') and the legal provisions defining and reproducing citizenship and citizenry are the fundaments on which every modern state citizenship is based. Rarely can we find communities without contestations and struggles over the citizenship argument, i.e. definition of political community, its borders, its nature and the organization of social, economic and political life. In this respect, the definition and internal organization of every political community at any given moment is the outcome of the hegemonic citizenship argument that remains in constant polemic with counterhegemonic (alternative, radically different or even historic) ones. Thus, no community is stable, although some are more so than others. The collision of different citizenship arguments might lead to a *crisis* that, in turn, can lead to a *change* (redefinition of political communities, both as entities and internally) or to a *reversal* of hegemonic positions. This Gramscian perspective on citizenship allows us, in these final pages, to take another perspective on what was presented in the preceding chapters and to examine how hegemonic struggles (dominant narratives, counternarratives, crises, changes or reversals of positions) over the main citizenship arguments and their counterarguments were played out in Yugoslavia and the post-Yugoslav states over the last century.

Wars usually open up space for the flourishing of political ideas on *what* ought to come 'after the war'. The Yugoslav unification in December 1918 annulled all other political options that might have been thinkable such as a reformed Austria-Hungary, separate South Slavic states or a greater Serbia. It confronted two main visions of how the unified country should be organized internally. Two citizenship arguments clashed: the unitary and the federal vision of the new state. This conflict came to dominate the twenty-two years of the existence of the first Yugoslavia and to determine the political alignments of the main political forces, with Serbian parties generally favouring unitarism, Croat and Slovene nationalists as well as communists mostly advocating federalization of Yugoslavia, and some also calling for its disintegration (e.g. radical Croat and Macedonian nationalists but also, for different reasons, the communists during the period 1924–1934). The end of the Second World War and the victory of the communist-led resistance movement brought the triumph of federalism over both the unitarist vision of Yugoslavia and nationalist (and mostly fascist) ideas about ethnonational and ethnically cleansed national states (the Ustashas' Independent State of Croatia and visions of a Greater Serbia, within or without Yugoslavia, promoted by the Chetnik leaders).

Socialist Yugoslavia (1945–1990) introduced the two-tier citizenship, comprising the federal supranational citizenship and the republic-level citizenship that had a civic nature. This meant that one would claim his/her republican citizenship based on place of birth, residence or parents' republican citizenship and not on his or her ethnonational belonging. However, the federal citizenship regime went through important transformations that were themselves a product of the conflict between centralist and decentralist visions of the Yugoslav socialist state. We can say that the federal centralizing citizenship argument dominated between 1945 and 1967 and that it was, with the constitutional changes between 1967 and the last Yugoslav constitution in 1974, replaced by the confederal argument that politically empowered the units over the federal centre. The federal and confederal citizenship regimes had two main enemies: unitarism, usually coupled with Serb nationalism, and separatism, usually associated with nationalism of smaller nations.

The return of multi-party electoral competition (at the level of the republics) in 1990 was coupled with almost complete delegitimization of the main arguments on which socialist Yugoslavia existed: federal/confederal arrangements that in the view of Yugoslav communists solved the national question and socialist self-management as political and social ideology of the entire community of citizens. The delegitimization process resulted in the reversal of positions: ethnic nationalism became hegemonic ideology. The nationalist reversal basically opened the doors for the argument claiming that true political communities, in which liberal democracy can be practiced, were neither to be found in the republics nor at the level of the Yugoslav federation but in the existing ethnonational communities. In other words, the ethnonational argument started to undermine the idea of civically constituted political communities at the republican level and eventually invalidated the idea that there was a political community at the Yugoslav supranational level.

However, the conflict between civic and ethnocentric arguments, the former advocated by the liberal or the left-leaning forces and the latter by the conservative and the nationalist forces, has continued to unfold in all post-Yugoslav political communities until this very day. In addition, in some states, we also witnessed the emergence of the multiethnic argument as the basis for internal organization, promoted by the international community as part of the peace and post-conflict processes. Although the emphasis here is also placed on the ethnic groups, it underlines their plurality and seeks solutions that will manage their relationship. Thus, the history of the last twenty-five years in the post-Yugoslav states can be told based on which one of these arguments was hegemonic at what point and what were its main counterhegemonic competitors. However, the political outcomes of these ideological struggles are never straightforward. Although the ethnocentric argument might dominate the political scene and society, the constitutional arrangements or citizenship laws often combine both ethnocentric and civic elements, mostly due to internal contestations but also international pressures. In other words, a state is often defined as 'belonging' to a majority ethnic group but with minorities also accepted into citizenship; the ethnocentric principle dominates the public life and state symbols but civic loyalty towards the state is expected from all citizens, including minorities; ethnocentric states often claim that they do not discriminate between majority and minorities and that they fully conform to international human rights norms.

The ethnocentric argument is dominant in Slovenia, Croatia and Macedonia (until the 2001 Ohrid Peace Framework) and in Serbia (even constitutionally after 2006). This prevalence of ethnocentrism in constitutions, citizenship laws and political life (resulting in what we termed, following Sammy Smooha, ethnic democracies; see Chapter 9), and at times formal or informal discrimination of those not belonging to the core ethnic group, is countered by the civic argument demanding legal and formal equality of all citizens. Another counterhegemonic argument to be found in these states is the *multiethnic* argument. Usually advocated by minorities, it can encompass demands ranging from better representation mechanisms (other South Slavic minorities in Slovenia) and even more territorial autonomy (Albanian parties in Macedonia) to open separatism (e.g. the Serb rebellion in Croatia between 1991 and 1995; present as well in the Albanian rebellion in Macedonia in 2001). In this group, Serbia represents a special case. Although ethnocentrism has been dominating Serbia's political life since the late 1980s, it was not enshrined in legislation until the 2004 citizenship law and the new 2006 Constitution. Before that, Serbia was part of the Federal Republic of Yugoslavia and was nominally a civic state. Serbia abolished Kosovo's autonomy in 1989; a 90 per cent strong Albanian majority in this region opted for secession and independence and countered the Serbian state with the creation of a parallel society, and later with armed rebellion. Today, Serbia is defined in ethnocentric terms. Other citizenship arguments in this country include civic, multiethnic (more autonomy for minorities, for which there is a constitutional basis as well) but also an autonomist one (more autonomy for the region of Vojvodina).

The civic argument seems to dominate only in Montenegro. In the 1990s, the Montenegrin civic principle went hand in hand with political unionism with Serbia, based on the then widely shared belief that Montenegrins are *ethnonationally* Serbs. However, not everyone agreed so the counterarguments asked for the equal position for Montenegrins as a nation (bi-national union) or even advocated independence. The independentist argument won the day at the Montenegrin referendum on independence in 2006. Montenegro today is defined strictly as a civic state with no ethnic majority (ethnic Montenegrins make up 45 per cent of the population), which is opposed by those who either advocate multiethnic redefinition (Serbs, but some other minorities as well) or closer ties with Serbia.

Wartime Bosnia-Herzegovina was also defined as a civic republic of all its citizens, but that was only in legislation; the reality on the ground echoed the military victories of ethnocentrist and separatist forces. However, the country survived the war and avoided partition. The Dayton Peace agreement abolished the civic constitution and introduced multiethnic division at all levels, dominated by three major groups in often-paralysing consociational settlement. This Dayton argument has its opponents; on the one hand, we can hear demands for further ethnofederalism (the Serb Republic and Croat-dominated cantons) or even secession (the Serb Republic) and, on the other, for re-centralization and territorial unification coming mostly from the Bosniak-dominated areas.

The multiethnic argument seems to be on offer as a 'solution' to all post-conflict societies. For example, in Macedonia after the 2001 conflict, the country was redefined from ethnocentric to multiethnic, which resulted in stronger minority representation and political influence, but also in more autonomy at the municipal level. That peace agreement seems to be to no one's liking: the civil society sector calls for a civic solution, Macedonian nationalists for domination of their majority and Albanian nationalists oscillate between ethnofederalist and secessionist options. Finally, internationally supervised Kosovo, after its declaration of independence, is imagined (and managed) as both a civic – residence-based citizenship and formal equality of all citizens – and multiethnic polity (separate communities have special rights to representation, whereas the Serb minority can aspire to a broader municipal autonomy). Opposing visions abound. Many Kosovar Albanians believe that the 90 per cent Albanian majority makes Kosovo in reality the second ethnic Albanian polity, which is a position often coupled with proposals for unity with Albania. As for the Serb minority, apart from re-integration with Serbia, their representatives either ask for multiethnic arrangements similar to those in Bosnia or for the secession of the Serb area in North Kosovo and its reincorporation into Serbia.

Out of this brief tour, we can distil four major arguments about the limits and forms of political community present in Yugoslavia and the post-Yugoslav states between 1914 and 2014. The *civic* argument implies equality and unity of all citizens. It neglects ethnonational identities, the primary identity markers in this region, thus running a risk of (unintentionally or not) promoting, under the cover of citizens' unity, the domination of one group over the other(s). The *ethnocentric* argument implies a distinction between an ethnic majority and minorities and thus the political, social and cultural domination of the core group. Usually it entails legal guarantees for minority members and sometimes even extensive cultural and political rights, but the 'ownership' of the state is in the hands of the majority group. This argument often results in conflicts, violent or not, over the relationship between majority and minority (or minorities). Since the state is defined as being owned by an ethnonational group, which often includes even those members not living within the state boundaries, this might lead to inter-state tensions, especially if designated co-ethnics live just across the border. The *multiethnic* argument, on the contrary, is based on the recognition of dominant ethnic groups as primary political communities in a common state. Politics is then posited on consociational rules and often assumes some kind of ethnofederal territorial arrangements. It does not leave much space for non-ethnic and purely civic identities and, moreover, it does not alleviate the risk of conflicts or disintegration. Finally, the fourth argument is *supranational*. We can see it at work in socialist Yugoslavia and to a certain extent in the EU integration process. It means that political communities at the level of subunits are recognized as autonomous and even primary sovereign bodies but a common framework offers a possibility for a higher supranational political identity. Socialist Yugoslavia in this respect was an example of a relatively functional supranational political community. In the EU – which Slovenia and Croatia have joined and into which all other post-Yugoslav states aspire to integrate as well – the role of its institutions, including European citizenship, does not seriously challenge the primacy of national member states.

In this epilogue, I have presented the dominant arguments in the Yugoslav and the post-Yugoslav political entities and how their hegemonic struggles resulted in various constitutional arrangements and political practices. The three states named *Yugoslavia* clearly testify to the sometimes productive and sometimes conflicting co-existence of various citizenship arguments. The Kingdom of Yugoslavia was a unitary state, with a civic citizenship regime, that at the same time insisted on national unity but progressively recognized various independent group identities. The second socialist Yugoslavia was *supranational* at the federal level and *civic* at the level of republics, whilst its *multiethnic* composition was promoted, recognized and respected. Finally, the third *rump* Yugoslavia in the 1990s, with the exclusion and self-exclusion of Kosovo Albanians, was dominated by Serb ethnocentrism that not only reduced the official supranational element of its federal citizenship but also corroded the civic definition of the republican citizenships of Serbia and Montenegro.

Finally, one has to add to the arguments about the definition, organization and limits of a political community the ideological conflict over its social composition and economic functioning, i.e. in this case, between socialist and capitalist visions. Socialist Yugoslavia designated working class and working people as equal bearers of sovereignty alongside with the republics, their citizens and the Yugoslav nations. Its socialist character supported the supranational citizenship argument and, in addition, an internationalist worldview. Since 1990 homogenous ethnonational communities have been held to be the main sites of liberal democratic politics coupled with the neoliberal engineering of a socially hierarchical society.

The liberal vision of legal equality and the respect for human rights sees the completion of the post-socialist 'transition' of the post-Yugoslav states in their integration into the EU. In this respect, this liberal argument insists on civic values, preferably within a supranational EU framework. However, we can detect today an emerging argument that is not only putting in question the predominant ethnonational character of the new states (as discriminatory), and liberal democracy (as not sufficiently democratic and inclusive), but also, increasingly, the neoliberal capitalist restructuring of these societies (due to social injustices and widening inequalities). This new citizenship argument, brought about by growing progressive and left-wing social and political movements (see Horvat and Štiks 2015), accepts the given boundaries of the political communities (while looking beyond them in a wider regional and internationalist perspective), but insists that every political community must be a community of self-governing and politically and socially equal citizens.

Future studies will surely trace the continuing transformations of political communities inhabiting the post-Yugoslav space, where the rich and contested heritage of the last one hundred years of citizenship will continue to resonate.

Notes

Introduction

1 Some authors suggest different analytical understandings of citizenship and its various dimensions. Christian Joppke (2007) sees citizenship as status, as rights and as identity. Rainer Bauböck (2001) understands it as membership, rights and practices, whereas Richard Bellamy defines citizenship as rights, belonging and participation (2004). Finally, Seyla Benhabib (1999) segments citizenship into collective identity, political membership and social rights and claims.
2 For detailed histories of pre-modern citizenship, see, for instance, Pocock (1998) and Shafir (1998).
3 Here I am drawing upon the understanding of citizenship regime that I developed together with Jo Shaw (in Shaw and Štiks 2010, 2012, 2013b).
4 Many papers and studies are available on the website of the project, www.citsee.law.ed.ac.uk and the project's web magazine 'Citizenship in Southeast Europe', www.citsee.eu.

Chapter 1

1 Writers continued to enjoy this dubious privilege during the communist period too, albeit under a different ideological arrangement: they became in Stalin's famous words 'engineers of human souls', whether they were loyal to the regime or its dissidents. For more on this and the serious challenges to the writers' traditional societal role in post-communism and the various strategies they deploy to 'remain relevant' under new circumstances, see Wachtel (2006).
2 One should not forget another important political actor in late nineteenth-century Croatia, namely a very strong pro-Hungarian current in favour of closer political unity between Hungary and Croatia within the Dual Monarchy.
3 One should not forget to mention here Matija Ban, a writer and diplomat from Dubrovnik, who was a partisan of the Yugoslav cause and had strong ties with nascent Serbian state. He worked closely with Garašanin and lived in Belgrade where a part of the city is still called after him – *Banovo brdo* or Ban's Hill.
4 For more details on the first years of the political life in the Kingdom of Serbs, Croats and Slovenes, see Banac (1984), and for an analysis of political developments until 1941, see Djokić (2007).

5   The most important treaties are the Peace Treaty of St.-Germain-en-Laye with the Republic of Austria signed on 10 September 1919; the Peace Treaty of Trianon with Hungary signed on 4 June 1920; and the Peace Treaty with Bulgaria signed on 27 November 1919 in Neuilly-sur-Seine. The treaty between the Kingdom of Serbs, Croats and Slovenes and the Kingdom of Italy was signed in Rapallo on 12 November 1920.
6   Interestingly, when the law on Croatian domicile or *zavičajnost* was introduced in 1880 within the Hungarian kingdom, it was already interpreted by some politicians and jurists as a form of Croatian citizenship since it involved electoral rights and the right to exercise public functions which was not possible for those not having *zavičajnost* in Croatia (Čepulo 1999).
7   Official Gazette 254/1928. The full text of the Law also available in Tepić and Bašić (1969: 105–130).

Chapter 2

1   There has been a surge of interest in Austro-Marxism and the theory of non-territorial national cultural autonomy within the fields of nationalism, multiculturalism, transnationalism and diaspora studies. Somewhat belated proof of this trend is the long overdue first English translation of Otto Bauer's *The Question of Nationalities and Social Democracy* (2000).
2   It is hard not to notice again a certain similarity with the federalization of the Communist Party of Yugoslavia and the future *League* of Communists of Yugoslavia.
3   The Resolution and many other documents to which I refer in this and subsequent chapters are published partially or entirely in Kobsa, Koprivnjak and Šaškor (1978). For the Tivoli Resolution, see Kobsa et al. (1978: 173–174).
4   For detailed accounts and analysis of the debates on the national question within the CPY, see Perović for the period until 1923 (1984), Vlajčić for the period until 1927 (1984) and Haug for the inter-war years (2012: 17–57). For original documents, see Vlajčić for the period between 1919 and 1945 (1974) and the above-mentioned anthology (Kobsa et al. 1978).
5   It is hard to know whether it was this theoretical confrontation with Stalin, or simply the fact that he found himself as an international communist in Moscow at the end of the 1930s, that sealed his fate. Marković disappeared in Stalin's purges in 1939. He was posthumously rehabilitated in 1958 (see Lazitch and Drachkovitch 1986: 303).
6   Parts of Tito's speech are quoted in Connor (1984: 146–147). Connor, in his turn, refers to Stephen Clissold's book *Whirlwind: An Account of Marshall's Tito's Rise to Power* (1949) which fails to cite the source.

7   This was the fate of several hundred Yugoslav communists who found themselves in the USSR at that time. Miroslav Krleža would later refer to the shadows of his comrades and friends as 'my Siberian graves'. Tito not only survived the purges but Moscow appointed him in 1937 secretary general of the CPY. The fact that the majority of Yugoslav communists perished in the USSR while Tito was sent by Stalin to take over the Party leadership cast a shadow of doubt on Tito's true role during the purges (see Djilas 1980: 28–29). However, Milovan Djilas' personal opinion is 'that Tito's participation in the purges was limited'.
8   Connor does not miss an irony of history in Tito's speech: 'Had the purged Marković been present, he would have undoubtedly found it a bit droll to hear himself criticized in a speech denigrating separatism and extolling autonomy' (Connor 1984: 146).
9   The anti-fascist council for this region was abolished in March 1945 and the territory of Sandžak (predominantly populated by Muslims) was divided between Serbia and Montenegro.
10 At that time the list did not include the Slavic Muslim population of Yugoslavia as a separate nation. Muslims were seen as a specific ethnoreligious group that belonged to the Serbian, Montenegrin and Croatian nations. This view would change in the 1960s.

Chapter 3

1   Pijade also chaired the committee that prepared the Constitutional Law of 1953.
2   *Službeni list DFJ* (Official Gazette of Democratic Federal Yugoslavia 64/1945). The law was confirmed and amended on 5 July 1946, *Službeni list FNRJ* (Official Gazette of Federal People's Republic of Yugoslavia 54/1946). The law was further amended and revised in 1947 (OG of FPRY 104/1947) and twice in 1948 (OG of FPRY 88/1948 and 105/1948).
3   'The Law on the Deprivation of Citizenship for Officers and Non-Commissioned Officers of the Former Yugoslav Army Who do not Want to Return to the Homeland, and for the Members of Military Forces Who Have Served for the Enemy and Have Defected Abroad' (this law also entailed the confiscation of goods; it was invalidated in 1962), Official Gazette of FPRY 88/1948 and 22/1962.
4   Official Gazette of FPRY 104/1947.
5   The citizenship of these groups was later defined by the Memorandum of Understanding between the Government of Italy, the United Kingdom and Yugoslavia which divided the Free Territory of Trieste (1947–1954) between Italy and Yugoslavia (Official Gazette of FPRY Supplement 6/1954). Their status was later regulated by the 1975 Osimo Treaty between Italy and Yugoslavia (Jovanović 1977: 27–31; Medved 2007: 215; Medvedović 1998: 32).

6   See, for instance, *Narodne Novine* [Official Gazette of Socialist Republic of Croatia], No. 7/1990.
7   The only exception to the general rule of republic-level registers of citizens was the case of foreigners granted Yugoslav citizenship at a Yugoslav embassy who were residing abroad. Once they established their residence in Yugoslavia, they were also entered into the register of the republic in which they resided.
8   Official Gazette of Socialist Federal Republic of Yugoslavia 38/1964 (corrections in 42/1964).
9   Official Gazette of SFRY 58/1976.
10 *Narodne novine* (Official Gazette of People's Republic of Croatia) 23/1950.
11 Official Gazette of Socialist Republic of Croatia 13/1965.
12 Official Gazette of Socialist Republic of Croatia 32/1977.
13 Obviously, between 1965 and 1977 the automatic acquisition of republican citizenship was not the rule if only one parent had Croatian citizenship, even if a child was born in Croatia. On changes in the Croatian law on republican citizenship and administrative practices between 1950 and 1991, see the report on Croatia in UNHCR 1997.
14 The Party's promotion of Yugoslavism in the 1950s and its abandonment in the mid-1960s are discussed below.

Chapter 4

1   These units played the crucial role in 1991 and 1992 during the armed conflicts between by then the Serb-controlled federal army (JNA) and Serb paramilitaries on one side, and Slovenian, Croatian and Bosnian authorities and their territorial defence forces on the other.
2   For incriminating parts of his speech, see the obituary, 'In Memoriam Professor Mihailo Đurić (1925/2011): Jedna tragična paradigma [One Tragic Paradigm]', *Vreme*, 1 December 2011, http://www.vreme.co.rs/cms/view.php?id=1022041 [Accessed 5 October 2014]. See also Haug 2012: 275–280.
3   I slightly amended the translation.
4   Around 80,000 candidates were competing for seats in all chambers of the republics and provinces (2,769 seats) and the communal assemblies (40,279 seats) (Lampe 2000: 306–307).
5   *A Platform for the Preparation of Views and Decisions of the Tenth LCY Congress* [Platforma za pripremu stavova i odluka Desetog kongresa SKJ] (in Kobsa et al. 1978: 364).
6   Interestingly, the Macedonian law on citizenship from 1977 in its first article states that 'for citizens of the Socialist Republic of Macedonia citizenship of the Socialist

Republic of Macedonia is provided', without mentioning the federal citizenship (*Official Gazette of the SR of Macedonia 19/1977*).

7   In Yugoslavia, nevertheless, *residence* never became as important for determining citizenship status as it is, for instance, in the US legislation, or as it was in the USSR. American citizens change their state citizenship *automatically* if they move to another state within the United States. There is also a legal possibility for Americans to posses only federal citizenship if a citizen, for example, lives abroad (Neuman 2003: 152–153). Obviously, this type of legislation is more appropriate to federal nation-states in which the primacy of the federal citizenship is clearly stated.

8   The whole affair is documented in Laura Silber and Alan Little's *The Death of Yugoslavia* (1995) and the BBC's documentary of the same name (1995).

Chapter 5

1   It is interesting to note in the context of linguistic conflicts that at the same time, in April 1967, the Federal Assembly introduced simultaneous translation enabling delegates to speak in their mother tongue if it was one of the languages of Yugoslav peoples or national minorities. Therefore, Yugoslavia, after the Swiss parliament, became the second multilingual parliament in Europe (Hondius 1968: 328–329), a practice that preceded the current multilingual communication in the EU institutions.

2   'The Scholars' Initiative: Confronting the Yugoslav Controversies'; the reports on different aspects of Yugoslavia's dissolution are available at www.cla.purdue.edu/si [Accessed on 5 October 2014].

Chapter 6

1   The fact that Spain was a unitary state before the first elections helped polity-wide parties to emerge. Moreover, these polity-wide parties predated Franco's destruction of the Spanish republic. It is also equally important to note that the Spanish kingdom is a long-standing territorial unit on the map of Europe, whereas the USSR – although one could argue that it was a successor state to the Russian Empire – Yugoslavia and for that matter, Czechoslovakia – which held its first general elections simultaneously with regional elections and also disintegrated – were all established towards the end of the First World War.

2   In 1990, the Yugoslav average unemployment was at 15.9 per cent (in Woodward 1995b: 384): Bosnia (20.6 per cent), Montenegro (21.6 per cent), Macedonia (22.9 per cent), Kosovo (38.4 per cent), Vojvodina (16.6 per cent), Serbia proper (16.4 per cent), Croatia (8.6 per cent) and Slovenia (4.8 per cent).

Chapter 7

1. Among the most relevant and/or most quoted works are Little and Silber (1995), Glenny (1993), Malcolm (1996), Ramet (1992, 2002), Woodward (1995a), Cohen (1995) and Wachtel (1998).
2. This imbalance of power was illustrated by Serbia's insistence on keeping Vojvodina's and Kosovo's seats in the collective Presidency. It became clear that when Milošević had political control over not only Serbia proper, Vojvodina and Kosovo, but also Montenegro, that the balance of power had changed drastically. Serbia now confronted the other four republics with four votes out of eight in the Presidency and hoped furthermore to capitalize from the fact that the Bosnian representative (Bogić Bogićević) was an ethnic Serb, during the critical months in 1991. At the key meeting of the Presidency called by the federal army (JNA) after the demonstrations in Belgrade in March 1991, the JNA demanded that the Presidency declare a state of emergency. Bogićević surprisingly defied both the federal army chiefs and the Serb leaders by refusing to use Bosnia's decisive fifth vote to sanction a large military intervention. This was a rare example of the prevalence of civic over ethnic loyalty. The paralysis of the collective Presidency culminated in Serbia's refusal to recognize the Croatian candidate Stjepan Mesić as President, even though it was Croatia's turn to take over the presidency of Yugoslavia.
3. The Serb Democratic Party (SDS) was established in both Croatia and Bosnia and was under the direct influence of Milošević who was already perceived (and often portrayed himself) as not only the leader of Serbia but of *all* Serbs. Similarly, Tudjman's Croatian Democratic Union (HDZ) founded a Bosnian branch and Tudjman, though the president of the Republic of Croatia, fashioned himself as the 'president of all Croats'. Alija Izetbegović's Party of Democratic Action (SDA) founded Sandžak and Croatian branches as well with a goal of politically representing ethnic Muslims (later Bosniaks) in and outside Bosnia.

Chapter 8

1. According to the exhaustive database of the Research and Documentation Centre in Sarajevo (IDC). For war victims in Croatia see 'Documenta' research centre publications at www.documenta.hr.
2. Russia broke this initial agreement by recognizing Abkhazia and South Ossetia in 2008.

Chapter 9

1. On the citizenship laws of the USSR, see Ginsburgs (1983). For more on new citizenship laws by the Soviet Union successor states, see Brunner (2001) and Shevel (2009).
2. According to the UNHCR (July 1993), there were between 400,000 and 500,000 stateless persons living in Estonia as of 30 March 1993. During the EU accession process, Latvia and Estonia removed some restrictions and amended their citizenship laws to allow non-citizens to apply for citizenship. Nevertheless, language requirements remain a huge problem for non-native speakers (Jackson 2004). There are still 370,000 stateless persons in Estonia and Latvia today, according to the UNHCR, see 'Statelessness in Europe', http://www.unhcr.org/pages/4e12db4a6.html [Accessed 9 October 2014].
3. I am grateful to Rainer Bauböck for this suggestion.
4. The European Union Observatory on Democracy – Citizenship, a research project based at EUI in Florence (for more information on the project see www.eudo-citizenship.com), obtained the official statistics from the Croatian Ministry of the Interior that confirm that between 1991 and 2010, 1.11 million persons acquired Croatian citizenship (800,000 of them originate from Bosnia-Herzegovina). For other sources, see UNHCR (1997) and Omejec (1998).
5. Both Serbia and Montenegro retained old republican-level laws on Serbian citizenship (dating back to 1979; amended in 1983) and Montenegrin citizenship (from 1975). Montenegro changed its law on republican citizenship in 1999 and Serbia only in 2004.
6. According to some estimates, up to 300,000 non-Slovene residents lived in Slovenia in 1991. Obviously, the idea of having such numerous 'non-autochthonous minorities', as they are called in the Slovenian constitution, consisting of Croats, Serbs, Bosnian Muslims, Albanians and Roma from other Yugoslav republics, was problematic for the administration of the first Slovenian independent state. Some 170,000 of this group regulated their status, whereas the status of the others remained unresolved. Many of them left Slovenia (e.g. federal army personnel and their dependents, others with non-regulated status), but those who remained in Slovenia and did not apply for or obtain the new citizenship in time were later *erased*.
7. Although in April 2003 the Constitutional Court of Slovenia ordered the administration to immediately issue permanent residence status to this group, the whole case became highly politicized with the right-wing government showing a lack of will to resolve the issue. In recent years, the centre-left administration apparently started to solve the remaining cases. It is expected that the 'erased' chapter will be closed after the European Court of Human Rights in July 2010

found Slovenia guilty of breaching the European Convention on Human Rights and Fundamental Freedoms in the case *Kurić and others v. Slovenia* (initially known as *Makuc and others v. Slovenia*; see Deželan 2013). The Court's Grand Chamber unanimously confirmed the verdict on 26 June 2012.
8 We should add that Albanians in Macedonia boycotted the referendum on Macedonian independence in 1991, held their own referendum on the creation of their own autonomous region, but eventually, although grudgingly, accepted Macedonian institutions. In 2001, Albanian armed rebellion in Macedonia played again with the prospect of self-exclusion. Both times – either peacefully or violently – the prospect of self-exclusion was mostly used to gain more political rights.
9 Besides minor corrections, the Croatian citizenship law had not been changed since its creation in 1991 until very recently. In late October 2011, during the last session of the outgoing Croatian parliament before the new elections, the right-wing majority voted for new changes to the law without a public or significant parliamentary debate. Among others, these changes make the acquisition of citizenship harder for permanent residents (requiring eight instead of five years of continuous residence) and introduced clearer criteria for ethnic Croat applicants (in terms of documents needed to prove their ethnic belonging) and Croat emigrants (limiting the right to Croatian citizenship to the third generation). In other words, the basic ethnocentric character of Croatian citizenship has not been questioned.
10 Derived from File: Former Yugoslavia 2006.png by Dudemanfellabra at en.wikipedia, author: Ijanderson977.

Chapter 10

1 The first major intervention affecting the totality of Serbian citizens on the territory of internationally administered Kosovo and the first move towards the establishment of a separate body of Kosovo residents/citizens was initiated already in 2000. UNMIK issued a regulation establishing the Central Civic Registry for 'residents of Kosovo' and had been issuing new Kosovo identification cards and travel documents that, as it was stated, did not determine a resident's citizenship (see Krasniqi 2013a).
2 Since the visa liberalization, some EU states such as Belgium and Germany faced the problem of an increased number of asylum seekers from Macedonia (mainly ethnic Albanians), Serbia and Bosnia. The issue of large numbers of (mainly Roma) asylum seekers from Serbia is constantly raised in the European Parliament as well as the possibility of abolishing the visa-free regimes for some states.

3 There is a lot of anecdotal evidence that Kosovans go to southern Serbian municipalities and obtain biometric visa-free Serbian passports there. In a separate development, Albania recently changed its citizenship law paving the way for many ethnic Albanians to acquire Albanian citizenship. However, the amendments explicitly exclude the largest group of ethnic Albanians, namely those from Kosovo (1.8 million), from acquiring visa-free Albanian passports. The move was clearly motivated by a fear (or a threat?) that the EU might put Albania back on the Schengen blacklist. See Krasniqi, G., 'Albania to Grant Citizenship to Ethnic Albanians in the Neighbourhood and Diaspora', *Citizenship in Southeast Europe*, 5 July 2013, http://citsee.eu/blog/albania-grant-citizenship-ethnic-albanians-neighbourhood-and-diaspora [Accessed 10 October 2014].

4 Marušić, S. J., 'More Macedonians Apply for Bulgarian Citizenship', *Balkan Insight*, 5 August 2014, http://www.balkaninsight.com/en/article/more-macedonians-apply-for-bulgarian-citizenship [Accessed 10 October 2014].

5 Thorpe, N., 'Hungary Creating a New Mass of EU Citizens', *BBC*, 7 November 2013, http://www.bbc.com/news/world-europe-24848361 [Accessed 10 October 2014].

Bibliography

Allcock, J. B. (2000), *Explaining Yugoslavia*, London: Hurts & Company.
Amandmani na Ustav Socijalističke Federative Republike Jugoslavije 1981
   [The Amendments to the Constitution of the Socialist Federal Republic of Yugoslavia 1981] (1988), in *Ustavni razvoj socijalističke Jugoslavije* [*The Constitutional Development of Socialist Yugoslavia*], Belgrade: Eksportpres.
Anderson, B. (1992), *Long-Distance Nationalism – World Capitalism and the Rise of Identity Politics*, Amsterdam: Center for Asian Studies.
Anderson, P. (1996), *Passages from Antiquity to Feudalism*, London: Verso.
Banac, I. (1984), *The National Question in Yugoslavia*, Ithaca, London: Cornell University Press.
——. (1988), *With Stalin against Tito – Cominformist Splits in Yugoslav Communism*, Ithaca: Cornell University Press.
Barsova, A. (2007), 'Czech Citizenship Legislation between Past and Future', in R. Bauböck, B. Perchinig and W. Sievers (eds), *Citizenship Policies in the New Europe*, Amsterdam: Amsterdam University Press.
Bauböck, R. (2001), 'Recombinant Citizenship', in M. Kohli and A. Woodward (eds), *Inclusions and Exclusions in European Societies*, London: Routledge.
——. (2008), *Stakeholder Citizenship: An Idea Whose Time Has Come?*, Washington: Migration Policy Institute.
——. (2011), 'Temporary Migrants, Partial Citizenship and Hypermigration', *Critical Review of International Social and Political Philosophy*, 14(5): 665–693.
Bauer, O. (2000 [1907]), *The Question of Nationalities and Social Democracy*, Minneapolis: The University of Minnesota Press.
Bauman, Z. (2005), 'Freedom from, in and through the State: T.H. Marshall's Trinity of Rights Revisited', *Theoria*, 108: 13–27.
Béaud, O. (2002), 'The Question of Nationality within Federation: A Neglected Issue in Nationality Law', in R. Hansen and P. Weil (eds), *Dual Nationality, Social Rights and Federal Citizenship in the U.S. and Europe: The Reinvention of Citizenship*, London and New York: Berghahn Books.
Bellamy, R. (2004), 'Introduction: The Making of Modern Citizenship', in R. Bellamy, D. Castiglione and E. Santoro (eds), *Lineages of European Citizenship: Rights, Belonging and Participation in Eleven Nation-States*, London: Palgrave.
Benhabib, S. (1999). 'Citizens, Residents, and Aliens in a Changing World: Political Membership in the Global Era', *Social Research*, 66(3): 709–744.
Bourdieu, P. (1991), *Language and Symbolic Power*, Cambridge: Harvard University Press.

Bowman, G. (1997), 'Nations, xenophobie et fantasme. La logique de la violence nationale dans l'ancienne Yougoslavie', *Balkanologie* 1(1), http://balkanologie.revues.org/201 [Accessed 20 November 2014].

Brubaker, R. W. (1992), 'Citizenship Struggles in Soviet Successor States', *International Migration Review*, 26(2): 269–291.

——. (1996), *Nationalism Reframed: Nationhood and the National Question in the New Europe*, Cambridge: Cambridge University Press.

Brunner, G. (2001), 'Citizenship and Protection of Minorities in Eastern Europe', in R. Clark, F. Feldbrugge and S. Pomorski (eds), *International and National Law in Russia and Eastern Europe: Essays in Honor of George Ginsburgs*, The Hague, Boston and London: Martinus Nijhoff Publishers.

Budding, A. H. (2008), 'Nation/People/Republic: Self-Determination in Socialist Yugoslavia', in L. J. Cohen and J. Dragović-Soso (eds), *State Collapse in South-Eastern Europe*, West Lafayette: Purdue University Press.

Bunce, V. (1997), 'The Yugoslav Experience in Comparative Perspective', in M. K. Bokovoy, J. A. Irvine and C. S. Lilly (eds), *State-Society Relations in Yugoslavia, 1945–1992*, New York: St. Martin's Press.

——. (1999), *Subversive Institutions: The Design and the Destruction of Socialism and the State*, Cambridge: Cambridge University Press.

Burg, S. L. (1983), *Conflict and Cohesion in Socialist Yugoslavia: Political Decision Making Since 1966*, Princeton: Princeton University Press.

Čepulo, D. (1999), 'Pravo hrvatske zavičajnosti i pitanje hrvatskog i ugarskog državljanstva 1868–1918: Pravni i politički vidovi i poredbena motrišta' [The Right of Croatian Homeland Belonging and the Question of Croatian and Hungarian Citizenship 1868-1918: Legal and Political Aspects and Comparative Views], *Zbornik FPZ* 49(6): 795–825.

Cesarec, A. (1978[1923]), 'Nacionalno pitanje i naši zadaci' [The National Question and Our Tasks], in L. Kobsa, V. Koprivnjak and I. Šaškor (eds), *Nacionalno pitanje u djelima klasika marksizma i u dokumentima i praksi kpj/skj* [*The National Question in the Works of Marxist Classics and in Documents and Practice of CPY/LCY*], Zagreb: Naklada CDD.

Chandler, D. (2010), 'The EU and Southeastern Europe: The Rise of Post-Liberal Governance', *Third World Quarterly*, 31(1): 69–85.

Cohen, E. F. (2009), *Semi-citizenship in Democratic Politics*, Cambridge: Cambridge University Press.

Cohen, L. J. (1989), *The Socialist Pyramid: Elites and Power in Yugoslavia*, London: Mosaic Press.

——. (1995), *Broken Bonds: Yugoslavia's Disintegration and Balkan Politics in Transition*, Second edition, Boulder: Westview Press.

——. (2008), 'Disintegrative Synergies and the Dissolution of Socialist Federations: Yugoslavia in Comparative Perspective', in L. J. Cohen and J. Dragović-Soso (eds), *State Collapse in South-Eastern Europe*, West Lafayette: Purdue University Press.

Čok, V. (1999), *Pravo na državljanstvo* [*The Right to Citizenship*], Beograd: Beogradski centar za ljudska prava & Dosije.

Connor, W. (1984), *The National Question in Marxist-Leninist Theory and Strategy*, Princeton: Princeton University Press.

Constitution of the Federative People's Republic of Yugoslavia (1947), Belgrade: The Government of the Federative People's Republic of Yugoslavia.

Constitution of Montenegro (2007), http://www.skupstina.me/images/documents/constitution-of-montenegro.pdf [Accessed 20 November 2014].

Constitution of the Republic of Kosovo (2008), http://kryeministri-ks.net [Accessed 20 November 2014].

Constitution of the Republic of Macedonia (2001), http://www.minelres.lv/NationalLegislation/Macedonia/Macedonia_Const2001_excerpts_English.htm [Accessed 20 November 2014].

Constitution of the Republic of Serbia (2006), http://www.srbija.gov.rs/cinjenice_o_srbiji/ustav.php [Accessed 20 November 2014].

Constitution of the Socialist Federal Republic of Yugoslavia (1963), Secretariat for Information of the Federal Executive Council: Belgrade.

Constitution of the Socialist Federal Republic of Yugoslavia (1974), Ljubljana: Dopisna delavska univerza.

Culic, I. (2003), 'State Building and Constitution Writing in Central and Eastern Europe after 1989', *Regio*, 3: 38–58.

Cvijić, Đ. (1978 [1923]), 'Predlog rezolucije o nacionalnom pitanju' [A Draft Resolution on the National Question] in L. Kobsa, V. Koprivnjak and I. Šaškor (eds), *Nacionalno pitanje u djelima klasika marksizma i u dokumentima i praksi kpj/skj* [*The National Question in the Works of Marxist Classics and in Documents and Practice of CPY/LCY*], Zagreb: Naklada CDD.

Debeljak, A. (1994), *Twilight of the Idols: Recollections of a Lost Yugoslavia*, translated by Michael Biggins, Fredonia: White Pine Press.

Deželan, T. (2013), 'In the Name of the Nation or/and Europe? Determinants of the Slovenian Citizenship Regime', in J. Shaw and I. Štiks (eds), *Citizenship after Yugoslavia*, Abingdon: Routledge.

Dika, M., Helton, A. C. and Omejec, J. eds. (1998), 'The Citizenship Status of Citizens of the Former SFR Yugoslavia after Its Dissolution', *Croatian Critical Law Review*, 3(1–2): 1–259.

Dimitrijević, V. (1995), 'The 1974 Constitution and Constitutional Process as a Factor in the Collapse of Yugoslavia', in P. Akhavan and R. Howse (eds), *Yugoslavia, the Former and Future: Reflections from Scholars from the Region*, Washington and Geneva: The Brookings Institution & The United Nations Research Institute for Social Development.

———. (1998), 'The Construction of States: Nationalism and the Definition of Nation-States in Post-Communist European Countries', in B. Stern (ed.), *Dissolution, Continuation and Succession in Eastern Europe*, The Hague: Martinus Nijhoff Publishers.

Djilas, A. (1991), *The Contested Country: Yugoslav Unity and Communist Revolution, 1918-1953*, Cambridge: Harvard University Press.

Djilas, M. (1980), *Tito: The Story from Inside*, translated by Vasilije Kojić and Richard Hayes, New York and London: Harcourt Brace Jovanovich.

Djokić, D. (2007), *Elusive Compromise: A History of Interwar Yugoslavia*, London: Hurst & Co.

———. (2003), '(Dis)integrating Yugoslavia: King Alexander and Interwar Yugoslavism', in D. Djokić (ed.), *Yugoslavism: Histories of a Failed Idea 1918-1992*, Madison: The University of Wisconsin Press.

Dragović-Soso, J. (2003), 'Intellectuals and the Collapse of Yugoslavia: The End of the Yugoslav Writers' Union', in D. Djokić (ed.), *Yugoslavism: Histories of a Failed Idea 1918-1992*, Madison: The University of Wisconsin Press.

———. (2008), 'Why Did Yugoslavia Disintegrate? An Overview of Contending Explanations', in L. J. Cohen and J. Dragović-Soso (eds), *State Collapse in South-Eastern Europe*, West Lafayette: Purdue University Press.

Drouet, M. (1997), 'Citoyenneté dans un Etat plurinational: Le Cas de l'ex-Yougoslavie', *Balkanologie*, 1(1): 81-94.

Džankić, J. (2010), 'Lineages of Citizenship in Montenegro', *CITSEE Working Papers Series*, (14).

———. (2013), 'Understanding Montenegrin Citizenship', in J. Shaw and I. Štiks (eds), *Citizenship after Yugoslavia*, Abingdon: Routledge.

Foucault, M. (1975), *Surveiller et punir: naissance de la prison*, Paris: Gallimard.

Fraser, N. (1995), 'From Redistribution to Recognition? Dilemmas of Justice in a "Post-Socialist" Age', *New Left Review*, 1(212): 68-93.

Gagnon, V. P. Jr. (2004), *The Myth of Ethnic War: Serbia and Croatia in the 1990s*, Ithaca: Cornell University Press.

Gellner, E. (1983), *Nations and Nationalism*, Ithaca: Cornell University Press.

Gibson, E. L. (2004), 'Federalism and Democracy: Theoretical Connections and Cautionary Insights', in E. L. Gibson (ed.), *Federalism and Democracy in Latin America*, Baltimore and London: The Johns Hopkins University Press.

Ginsburgs, G. (1983), *The Citizenship Law of the USSR*, The Hague, Boston and Lancaster: Martinus Nijhoff Publishers.

Glenny, M. (1993), *The Fall of Yugoslavia: The Third Balkan War*, London: Penguin.

Gordy, E. (2008), 'Destruction of the Yugoslav Federation: Policy or Confluence of Tactics?', in L. J. Cohen and J. Dragović-Soso (eds), *State Collapse in South-Eastern Europe*, West Lafayette: Purdue University Press.

Groebner, V. (2007), *Who Are You? Identification, Deception, and Surveillance in Early Modern Europe*, New York: Zone Books.

Gyarfasova, O. (1995), 'Slovakia after the Split: Dilemmas of the New Citizenship', in A. Liebich, D. Warner and J. Dragović (eds), *Citizenship East and West*, London and New York: Kegan Paul International.

Habermas, J. (2000), *The Inclusion of the Other: Studies in Political Theory*, Cambridge: MIT Press.

Hale, H. E. (2004), 'Divided We Stand: Institutional Sources of Ethnofederal State Survival and Collapse', *World Politics*, 56(2): 165–193.

Haug, H. K. (2012), *Creating a Socialist Yugoslavia: Tito, Communist Leadership and the National Question*, London and New York: I. B. Tauris.

Hayden, R. (1992), 'Constitutional Nationalism in the Formerly Yugoslav Republics', *Slavic Review*, 51(4): 654–673.

———. (1999), *Blueprints for a House Divided: The Constitutional Logic of the Yugoslav Conflicts*, Ann Arbor: The University of Michigan Press.

Herbst, J. I. (2000), *States and Power in Africa: Comparative Lessons in Authority and Control*, Princeton: Princeton University Press.

Hobsbawn, E. (2001[1973]), *Revolutionaries*, New York: New Press.

Hondius, F. W. (1968), *The Yugoslav Community of Nations*, The Hague and Paris: Mouton.

Horowitz, D. L. (1985), *Ethnic Groups in Conflict*, Berkley, Los Angeles and London: University of California Press.

Horvat, S. and I. Štiks eds. (2015), *Welcome to the Desert of Post-Socialism: Radical Politics after Yugoslavia*, London and New York: Verso.

Imeri, S. ed. (2006), *Rule of Law in the Countries of the Former SFR Yugoslavia and Albania: Between Theory and Practice*, Gostivar: Association for Democratic Initiatives.

Iordachi, C. (2004), 'Dual Citizenship in Post-communist Central and Eastern Europe: Regional Integration and Inter-ethnic Tensions', in O. Ieda, U. Tomohiko (eds), *Reconstruction and Interaction of Slavic Eurasia and Its Neighboring World*, Sapporo: Slavic Research Center.

Irvine, J. A. (1997), 'Introduction: State-Society Relations in Yugoslavia, 1945–1992', in M. K. Bokovoy, J. A. Irvine and C. S. Lilly (eds), *State-Society Relations in Yugoslavia, 1945–1992*, New York: St. Martin's Press.

Isin, E. (2009), 'Citizenship in Flux: The Figure of Activist Citizen', *Subjectivity*, 29: 367–388.

Jackson, L. (2004), 'Nationality, Citizenship and Identity', in M. Bradshaw and A. Stenning (eds), *East Central Europe and the Former Soviet Union: The Post-Socialist States*, Essex: Pearson Education/Prentice Hall.

Jančar, D. (1999 [1990]), 'Farewell to Yugoslavia', in Andrew Zawacki (ed.), *Afterwards: Slovenian Writing, 1945–1995*, Buffalo: White Pine Press.

Joppke, C. (2007), 'Transformation of Citizenship: Status, Rights, Identity', *Citizenship Studies*, 11(1): 37–48

Jovanović, S. Đ. (1977), *Državljanstvo Socijalističke Federative Republike Jugoslavije* [*Citizenship of the Socialist Federal Republic of Yugoslavia*], Belgrade: Službeni List SFRJ.

Jović, D. (2001a), 'Fear of Becoming Minority as a Motivator of Conflict in the Former Yugoslavia', *Balkanologie*, 5(1–2): 21–36.

———. (2001b), 'The Disintegration of Yugoslavia: Critical Review of Explanatory Approaches', *European Journal of Social Theory*, 4(1): 101–120.

———. (2003a), *Jugoslavija, država koja je odumrla: Uspon, kriza i pad Kardeljeve Jugoslavije 1974–1990*, Zagreb, Belgrade: Prometej and Samizdat B92. [Available in English, Jović, D. (2009), *Yugoslavia: A State That Withered Away*, West Lafayette: Purdue University Press].

———. (2003b), 'Yugoslavism and Yugoslav Communism: From Tito to Kardelj', in D. Djokić (ed.), *Yugoslavism: Histories of a Failed Idea 1918–1992*, Madison: The University of Wisconsin Press.

Kacarska, S. (2012), 'Europeanisation Through Mobility: Visa Liberalisation and Citizenship Regimes in the Western Balkans', *CITSEE Working Papers Series*, (21).

Kardelj, E. (1977), *Pravci razvoja političkog sistema socijalističkog samoupravljanja* [*Directions of the Development of the Political System of Socialist Self-Management*], Cyrillic edition, Belgrade: IC Komunist.

Kapović, M. (2010), *Čiji je jezik?* [*To Whom Language Belongs?*], Zagreb: Algoritam.

Kobsa, L., Koprivnjak, V. and Šaškor, I. eds. (1978), *Nacionalno pitanje u djelima klasika marksizma i u dokumentima i praksi kpj/skj* [*The National Question in the Works of Marxist Classics and in documents and practice of CPY/LCY*]. Zagreb: Naklada CDD.

Kordić, S. (2010), *Jezik i nacionalizam* [*Language and Nationalism*], Zagreb: Durieux.

Koska, V. (2013), 'Framing the Citizenship Regime within the Complex Triadic Nexuses: The Case Study of Croatia', in J. Shaw and I. Štiks (eds), *Citizenship after Yugoslavia*, Abingdon: Routledge.

Krasniqi, G. (2013a), 'Overlapping Jurisdictions, Disputed Territory, Unsettled State: The Perplexing Case of Citizenship in Kosovo', in J. Shaw and I. Štiks (eds), *Citizenship after Yugoslavia*, Abingdon: Routledge.

———. (2013b), 'Equal Citizens, Uneven 'Communities': Differentiated and Hierarchical Citizenship in Kosovo', *CITSEE Working Papers Series*, (27).

Kusa, D. (2007), 'The Slovak Question and the Slovak Answer: Citizenship during the Quest for National Self-determination and After', in R. Bauböck, B. Perchinig and W. Sievers (eds), *Citizenship Policies in the New Europe*, Amsterdam: Amsterdam University Press.

Kymlicka, W. (2001a), 'Preface', in W. Kymlicka and M. Opalski (eds), *Can Liberal Pluralism Be Exported? Western Political Theory & Ethnic Relations in Eastern Europe*, Oxford: Oxford University Press.

———. (2001b), 'Reply & Conclusion', in W. Kymlicka and M. Opalski (eds), *Can Liberal Pluralism Be Exported? Western Political Theory & Ethnic Relations in Eastern Europe*, Oxford: Oxford University Press.

Lampe, J. R. (2000), *Yugoslavia as History: Twice There Was a Country*, Second edition, Cambridge: Cambridge University Press.

Lazitch, B. and Drachkovitch, M. M. (1986), *Biographical Dictionary of the Comintern*, Stanford: The Hoover Institution Press.

Lebowitz, M. (2013), 'Some Explanations of the Fall of "Real Socialism"', *Links – International Journal of Socialist Renewal*, http://links.org.au/node/3518 [Accessed 4 October 2014].

Lenin, V. I. (1964 [1913]), *Critical Remarks on the National Question*, in *Collected Works*, translated from the Russian by Bernard Isaacs and Joe Fineberg, Fourth edition, Vol. 20, Moscow: Progress Press.

Liebich, A. (2007), 'Introduction: Altneuländer or the Vicissitudes of Citizenship in the New EU States', in R. Bauböck, B. Perchinig and W. Sievers (eds), *Citizenship Policies in the New Europe*, Amsterdam: Amsterdam University Press.

Linz, J. J. and Stepan, A. (2001 [1992]), 'Political Identities and Electoral Sequences: Spain, the Soviet Union, and Yugoslavia', in A. Stepan, *Arguing Comparative Politics*, Oxford: Oxford University Press.

Little, A. and Silber, L. (1995), *The Death of Yugoslavia*, London: Penguin Books.

Lowinger, J. (2009), *Economic Reform and the 'Double Reform' in Yugoslavia: An Analysis of Labour Unrest and Ethno-nationalism in the 1980s*, Ph.D. Dissertation, Baltimore: Johns Hopkins University

MacDonald, D. B. (2002), *Balkan Holocausts? Serbian and Croatian Victim-Centered Propaganda and the War in Yugoslavia*, Manchester: University of Manchester Press.

Malcolm, N. (1996), *Bosnia: A Short History*, New York: New York University Press.

Malešević, S. (2000), 'Ethnicity and Federalism in Communist Yugoslavia and Its Successor States', in Y. P. Ghai (ed.), *Autonomy and Ethnicity: Negotiating Competing Claims in Multi-ethnic States*, Cambridge: Cambridge University Press.

Mann, M. (2005), *The Dark Side of Democracy: Explaining Ethnic Cleansing*, Cambridge: Cambridge University Press.

Marković, S. (1985 [1923]), *Tragizam malih naroda* [*The Tragedy of Small Nations*], Belgrade: Filip Višnjić.

Marshall, T. H. (1950), *Citizenship and Social Class and Other Essays*, Cambridge: Cambridge University Press.

Matvejević, P. (1984), *Jugoslavenstvo danas* [*Yugoslavism Today*], Paperback edition, Belgrade: BIGZ.

Medved, F. (2007), 'From Civic to Ethnic Community? The Evolution of Slovenian Citizenship', in R. Bauböck, B. Perchinig and W. Sievers (eds), *Citizenship Policies in the New Europe*, Amsterdam: Amsterdam University Press.

Medvedović, D. (1998), 'Federal and Republican Citizenship in the Former SFR Yugoslavia at the Time of Its Dissolution', *Croatian Critical Law Review*, 3(1–2): 21–56.

Meiksins Wood, E. (1995), *Democracy against Capitalism: Renewing Historical Materialism*, Cambridge: Cambridge University Press.

Mill, J. S. (1861), *Considerations on Representative Government*, Second edition, London: Parker, Son and Bourn.

Mujkić, A. (2007), 'We, the Citizens of Ethnopolis', *Constellations*, 14(1): 112–128.
Muminović, E. (1998), 'Problems of Citizenship Laws in Bosnia and Herzegovina', *Croatian Critical Law Review*, 3(1–2): 71–88.
Neuman, G. L. (2003), 'Fédéralisme et citoyenneté aux Etats-Unis et dans l'Union européenne', *Critique Internationale*, 21: 151–169.
Nimni, E. (2000), 'Introduction for the English-Reading Audience', in O. Bauer, *The Question of Nationalities and Social Democracy*, Minneapolis: University of Minnesota Press.
Omejec, J. (1998), 'Initial Citizenry of the Republic of Croatia at the Time of the Dissolution of Legal Ties with the SFRY, and Acquisition and Termination of Croatian Citizenship', *Croatian Critical Law Review*, 3(1–2): 99–128.
Ong, A. (2006), 'Mutations in Citizenship', *Theory, Culture & Society*, 23(2–3): 499–505.
Palous, M. (1995), 'Questions of Czech Citizenship', in A. Liebich, D. Warner and J. Dragović (eds), *Citizenship East and West*, London and New York: Kegan Paul International.
Pateman, C. (1970), *Participation and Democratic Theory*, Cambridge: Cambridge University Press.
Pavković, A. (2003), 'Yugoslavism's Last Stand: A Utopia of Serb Intellectuals', in D. Djokić (ed.), *Yugoslavism: Histories of a Failed Idea 1918–1992*, Madison: The University of Wisconsin Press.
Pejić, J. (1998), 'Citizenship and Statelessness in the Former Yugoslavia: The Legal Framework', in S. O'Leary and T. Tiilikainen (eds), *Citizenship and Nationality Status in the New Europe*, London: The Institute for Public Policy Research/Sweet & Maxwell.
Perović, L. (1984), *Od centralizma do federalizma: KPJ u nacionalnom pitanju* [*From Centralism to Federalism: The CPY and the National Question*], Zagreb: Globus.
Pocock, J. G. A. (1998), 'The Ideal of Citizenship Since Classical Times', in G. Shafir (ed.), *Citizenship Debates: A Reader*, Minneapolis: University of Minnesota.
Popović, S. (2008), 'Raspad Jugoslavije' [The Disintegration of Yugoslavia], *Peščanik*, 29 September 2008, http://pescanik.net/2008/09/raspad-jugoslavije-i-2/ [Accessed 19 November 2014].
Prpa-Jovanović, B. (1997), 'The Making of Yugoslavia: 1830–1945', in J. Udovički and J. Ridgeway (eds), *Burn This House: The Making and Unmaking of Yugoslavia*, Durham & London: Duke University Press.
Ragazzi, F. and Štiks, I. (2009), 'Croatian Citizenship: From Ethnic Engineering to Inclusiveness', in R. Bauböck, B. Perchinig and W. Sievers (eds), *Citizenship Policies in the New Europe*, Second expanded edition, Amsterdam: Amsterdam University Press.
Ragazzi, F., Štiks, I. and Koska, V. (2013), 'Country Report: Croatia', *EUDO Citizenship Observatory*, http://eudo-citizenship.eu/country-profiles/?country=Croatia [Accessed 19 November 2014].

Rajaković, N. (1992), 'Les Ambigüités du "yougoslavisme"', in J. Rupnik (ed.), *De Sarajevo à Sarajevo*, Brussels: Ed. Complexe.

Rakić, V. (1998), 'State Succession and Dissolution: the Example of FR Yugoslavia', *Croatian Critical Law Review*, 3(1-2): 57-70.

Ramet, S. P. (1992), *Nationalism and Federalism in Yugoslavia 1962-1991*, Second edition, Bloomington & Indianapolis: Indiana University Press.

——. (2002), *Balkan Babel: The Disintegration of Yugoslavia from the Death of Tito to the Fall of Slobodan Milošević*, Fourth edition, Boulder and Oxford: Westview Press.

——. (2005a), 'The Dissolution of Yugoslavia: Competing Narratives of Resentment and Blame', http://www.cla.purdue.edu/history/facstaff/Ingrao/si/Team2Report.pdf [Accessed 5 October 2014].

——. (2005b), *Thinking about Yugoslavia: Scholarly Debates about the Yugoslav Breakup and the Wars in Bosnia and Kosovo*, Cambridge: Cambridge University Press.

——. (2006), *Three Yugoslavias - State-Building and Legitimation, 1918-2005*, Washington, Bloomington and Indianapolis: Woodrow Wilson Center Press & Indiana University Press.

Rava, N. (2010), 'Serbia: Elusive Citizenship in an Elusive Nation-State', *CITSEE Working Papers Series*, (8).

Roeder, P. G. (1999), 'People and States after 1989: The Political Costs of Incomplete National Revolutions', *Slavic Review*, 54(4): 854-882.

Rupnik, J. (2000), 'Divorce à l'amiable ou guerre de sécession? (Tchécoslovaquie - Yougoslavie)/Divorce by Mutual Consent or War of Secession? (Czechoslovakia-Yugoslavia)', *Transeuropéennes*, (19/20).

Rusinow, D. I. (1977), *The Yugoslav Experiment 1948-1974*, Berkeley and Los Angeles: University of California Press.

——. (1981), *Unfinished Business: The Yugoslav 'National Question'*, American Universities Field Staff Reports 35.

——. (2003), 'The Yugoslav Idea before Yugoslavia', in D. Djokić (ed.), *Yugoslavism: Histories of a Failed Idea 1918-1992*, Madison: The University of Wisconsin Press.

Sarajlić, E. (2010), 'The Bosnian Triangle: Ethnicity, Politics and Citizenship', *CITSEE Working Papers Series*, (6).

——. (2013), 'Conceptualising Citizenship Regime(s) in Post-Dayton Bosnia and Herzegovina', in J. Shaw and I. Štiks (eds), *Citizenship after Yugoslavia*, Abingdon: Routledge.

Shachar, A. (2009), *Birthright Lottery: Citizenship and Global Inequality*, Cambridge: Harvard University Press.

Shafir, G. (1998), 'Introduction: The Evolving Tradition of Citizenship', in G. Shafir (ed.), *Citizenship Debates: A Reader*, Minneapolis: University of Minnesota.

Shaw, J. (2007), *The Transformation of Citizenship in the European Union: Electoral Rights and the Restructuring of Political Space*. Cambridge: Cambridge University Press.

———. (2010), 'The Constitutional Mosaic across the Boundaries of the European Union: Citizenship Regimes in the New States of South Eastern Europe', *CITSEE Working Paper Series*, (7).

Shaw, J. and Štiks, I. (2010), 'The Europeanisation of Citizenship in the Successor States of the Former Yugoslavia: An Introduction', *CITSEE Working Papers Series*, (1).

———. (2012), 'Citizenship in the New States of South Eastern Europe', *Citizenship Studies*, 16(3–4): 309–321.

——— eds. (2013a), *Citizenship after Yugoslavia*, Abingdon: Routledge.

———. (2013b), 'Introduction: What Do We Talk about When We Talk about Citizenship Rights', in J. Shaw and I. Štiks (eds), *Citizenship Rights*, Farnham: Ashgate.

Shevel, O. (2009), 'The Politics of Citizenship Policy in New States', *Comparative Politics*, 41(3): 273–291.

Shoup, P. (1968), *Communism and the Yugoslav National Question*, New York and London: Columbia University Press.

Skalnik Leff, C. (1999), 'Democratization and Disintegration in Multinational States: The Breakup of the Communist Federations', *World Politics*, 51(2): 205–235.

Smooha, S. (2005a), 'The Model of Ethnic Democracy', in S. Smooha and P. Jarve (eds), *The Fate of Ethnic Democracy in Post-Communist Europe*, Budapest: Open Society Institute.

———. (2005b), 'The Non-emergence of a Viable Ethnic Democracy in Post-Communist Europe', in S. Smooha and P. Jarve (eds), *The Fate of Ethnic Democracy in Post-Communist Europe*, Budapest: Open Society Institute.

Snyder, J. (2000), *From Voting to Violence: Democratization and Nationalist Conflict*, New York and London: W. W. Norton & Company.

Soysal, Y. N. (2000), 'Citizenship and Identity: Living in Diasporas in Post-war Europe', *Ethnic and Racial Studies*, 23(1): 1–15.

Spaskovska, Lj. (2013), 'The Fractured 'We' and the Ethno-national 'I' – The Macedonian Citizenship Framework', in J. Shaw and I. Štiks (eds), *Citizenship after Yugoslavia*, Abingdon: Routledge.

Stalin, J. V. (1953 [1913]), Marxism and the National Question, in *Works*, vol. 2, Moscow: Foreign Languages Publishing House.

Stepan, A. (2004a), 'Towards a New Comparative Politics of Federalism, Multinationalism and Democracy: Beyond Rikerian Federalism', in E. L. Gibson (ed.), *Federalism and Democracy in Latin America*, Baltimore and London: The Johns Hopkins University Press.

———. (2004b), 'Electorally Generated Veto Players in Unitary and Federal Systems', in E. L. Gibson (ed.), *Federalism and Democracy in Latin America*, Baltimore and London: The Johns Hopkins University Press.

Štiks, I. (2006), 'Nationality and Citizenship in the Former Yugoslavia: From Disintegration to the European Integration', *South East European and Black Sea Studies*, 6(4): 483–500.

———. (2011), 'Being Citizen the Bosnian Way: Transformations of Citizenship and Political Identities in Bosnia-Herzegovina', *Transitions*, 51(2): 245–267.

———. (2013), 'A Laboratory of Citizenship: Shifting Conceptions of Citizenship in Yugoslavia and Post-Yugoslav States', in J. Shaw and I. Štiks (eds), *Citizenship after Yugoslavia*, Abingdon: Routledge.

Stokes, G. (2013), 'Independence and the Fate of Minorities (1991-1992)', in Ch. Ingrao and Th. A. Emmert (eds), *Confronting Yugoslav Controversies: A Scholars' Initiative*, Second edition, West Lafayette: Purdue University Press.

Suvin, D. (2014), *Samo jednom se ljubi: Radiografija SFR Jugoslavije* [*You Only Love Once: Radiography of SFR Yugoslavia*], Beograd: Rosa Luxemburg Stiftung Southeast Europe.

Svilanović, G. (1998), 'The New Law on Yugoslav Citizenship: Procedural Provisions and Practice', *Croatian Critical Law Review*, 3(1-2): 243-259.

Tepić, Đ. and Bašić, I. (1969), *Zbirka propisa o državljanstvu* [The Collection of the Citizenship Regulations], Zagreb: Narodne novine.

Thompson, M. (1999), *Forging the War: The Media in Serbia, Croatia, Bosnia and Hercegovina*, Luton: University of Luton Press.

Tito, J. B. (1978), *Josip Broz Tito on the National Question*, Belgrade: BIGZ.

———. (1983), *The National Question*, Belgrade: Socialist Thought and Practice.

Torpey, J. (2000), *The Invention of the Passport: Surveillance, Citizenship and the State*, Cambridge: Cambridge University Press.

Udovički, J. (1995), Nationalism, Ethnic Conflict, and Self-Determination in the Former Yugoslavia, in B. Berberoglu (ed.), *The National Question – Nationalism, Ethnic Conflict, and Self-Determination in the 20th Century*, Philadelphia: Temple University Press.

Ugrešić, D. (1996), *Kultura laži* [*The Culture of Lies*], Zagreb: Arkzin.

UNHCR, Regional Bureau for Europe (1993), *Nationality Laws of the Former Soviet Republics*, 1 July 1993, http://www.refworld.org/docid/3ae6b31db3.html [Accessed 14 January 2015]

UNHCR, Regional Bureau for Europe (1997), *Citizenship and Prevention of Statelessness Linked to the Disintegration of the Socialist Federal Republic of Yugoslavia*. European Series 3(1), Geneva: UNHCR.

Unkovski-Korica, V. (2015), 'Self-Management, Development and Debt: The Rise and Fall of the "Yugoslav Experiment"', in S. Horvat and I. Štiks (eds), *Welcome to the Desert of Post-Socialism: Radical Politics after Yugoslavia*, London and New York: Verso.

Ustav Socijalističke Federativne Republike Jugoslavije i ustavni amandmani I – XLII [Constitution of the Socialist Federal Republic of Yugoslavia and the Constitutional Amendments I – XLII] (1971), Belgrade: Književne novine.

Ustav Socijalističke Federativne Republike Jugoslavije – Ustav Socijalističke Republike Hrvatske [Constitution of the Socialist Federal Republic of Yugoslavia – Constitution of the Socialist Republic of Croatia] (1974), Zagreb: Narodne novine.

Ustavni zakon o osnovama društvenog i političkog uređenja Federative Narodne Republike Jugoslavije i saveznim organima vlasti [*The Constitutional Law on Fundamentals of the Social and Political Formation of the Federal People's Republic of Yugoslavia and the Federal Organs of Government*], 1988[1953], in *Ustavni razvoj socijalističke Jugoslavije* [*Constitutional Development of Socialist Yugoslavia*], Eksportpres: Belgrade.

Vasiljević, J. (2013), 'Imagining and Managing the Nation: Tracing Citizenship Policies in Serbia', in J. Shaw and I. Štiks (eds), *Citizenship after Yugoslavia*, Abingdon: Routledge.

Verdery, K. (1998), 'Transnationalism, Nationalism, Citizenship, and Property: Eastern Europe Since 1989', *American Ethnologist*, 25(2): 291–306.

Višnjić, M. (1977), *Delegatski sistem* [*The Delegate System*], Belgrade: Zajednica klubova samoupravljača Beograda.

Vladisavljević, N. (2008), *Serbia's Anti-Bureaucratic Revolution: Milošević, The Fall of Communism, and Nationalist Mobilization*, Basingstoke: Palgrave Macmillan.

Vlajčić, G. ed. (1974), *Nacionalno i seljačko pitanje u dokumentima Komunističke partije Jugoslavije i Komunističke internacionale* [*The National and Peasant Question in Documents of CPY and the Communist International*], Zagreb: Obrazovni centar saveza omladine Zagreba 'Karl Marx'.

———. (1984), *Jugoslavenska revolucija i nacionalo pitanje 1919–1927* [*The Yugoslav Revolution and the National Question 1919–1927*], Zagreb: Centar za kulturnu djelatnost & Globus.

Vucinich, W. S. (1969), 'Nationalism and Communism', in W. S. Vucinich (ed.), *Contemporary Yugoslavia – Twenty Years of Socialist Experiment*, Berkley and Los Angeles: University of California Press.

Wachtel, A. B. (1998), *Making a Nation, Breaking a Nation: Literature and Cultural Politics in Yugoslavia*, Stanford: Stanford University Press.

———. (2006), *Remaining Relevant after Communism: The Role of the Writer in Eastern Europe*, Chicago: University of Chicago.

Walzer, M. (1983), *Spheres of Justice: A Defense of Pluralism and Equality*, New York, London: Basic Books.

———. (1993), 'Exclusion, Injustice and the Democratic State', *Dissent* 40(2): 55–64.

Woodward, S. L. (1995a), *Balkan Tragedy: Chaos and Dissolution after the Cold War*, Washington: The Brookings Institution.

———. (1995b), *Socialist Unemployment: The Political Economy of Socialist Yugoslavia 1945–1990*, Princeton: Princeton University Press.

Zakon o biračkim spiskovima sa objašnjenjima [*The Voting Registers Law, with explanations*] (1947), Belgrade: Službeni List FNRJ.

Žižek, S. (2009), *Violence*, London: Profile Books.

Zukin, S. (1975), *Beyond Marx and Tito: Theory and Practice in Yugoslav Socialism*, Cambridge: Cambridge University Press.

Index

Note: Locators followed by the letter 'n' refer to notes.

Albanian rebellion (in Macedonia) 140, 165, 190
Alexander (King) 32, 34, 46
Allcock, J. B. 12, 16–17, 78, 121
Alliance of Reform Forces (SRS) 115
Anderson, B. 154
Anderson, P. 133
Anti-Fascist Council of National Liberation of Yugoslavia (AVNOJ) 48–50, 56, 90, 110, 113
asylum seekers 5, 179, 181, 201n. 2
Austro-Marxist ideas 29, 38–40, 195n. 1
Axis powers 3, 18, 32, 35, 47, 49

Bakarić, Vladimir 60, 68, 93
Balkan ghosts (Kaplan) 120
Balkan holocausts (MacDonald) 97
Balkan wars 32
Ban, Matija 194n. 3
Banac, I. 44, 51, 56, 91, 194n. 4
Banovina 34
Barsova, A. 154
Bašić, I. 11, 32, 62, 195n. 7
Bauböck, R. 9, 194n. 1, 200n. 3
Bauer, Otto 39, 40, 42, 195n. 1
Bauman, Z. 8
Béaud, O. 164
Bellamy, R. 194n. 1
Benhabib, S. 194n. 1
bifurcated citizenship in Yugoslavia 17, 19, 62–4, 79, 81
Bled agreement 91
Bogićević, Bogić 199n. 2
Bosnia-Herzegovina
　anti-fascist council 50
　Austria–Hungary's annexation 41
　Brčko, district 177, 180
　citizenship laws 157–9, 161–2
　Croatian citizens 158, 183, 200n. 4

　ethnonational subunits 58, 62, 123, 171, 191
　EU intervention 177–8
　federal union 152
　internal division 146
　in 'New' Yugoslavia 55
　Ottoman rule 32
　symbols and flags 99
　triadic relationship 142
　triggers of violence 139
　two-tier system of citizenship 168
　unemployment (1990) 198n. 2
Bosnian war 97–9
Bourdieu, P. 151
Bowman, G. 98
Brubaker, R. W. 111, 142, 155, 163, 169
Brunner, G. 200n. 1
Budding, A. H. 69, 109
Bunce, V. 13, 16, 77, 78, 84, 104, 121, 122, 144
Burg, S. L. 13, 69, 70, 71, 72, 74, 77

centralist federalism 55, 62
centrifugal federalism 17, 19, 68, 70, 71, 75, 83, 90, 122, 124, 129
Čepulo, D. 33, 195n. 6
Cesarec, A. 44
Chandler, D. 173
citizen
　citizenship regime 4, 7, 10
　cultural identity 7–8
　EU influence on 174
　inter-war Yugoslavia 17
　members 1, 5
　non-citizens 4, 6, 7, 9, 10
　participation 5–6
　in regional communities 9
　rights and duties 4
　'semi-citizens' 5

citizenship
  administrative policies 10–11
  Greek conception 6, 133
  political participation 1, 2, 4–6, 10, 13
  as quality 4–6
  as status 4–6, 10, 12, 194n. 1
citizenship laws
  1976 law on Yugoslav citizenship 65
  in Austria-Hungary 32
  between 1967 and 1974
    (Yugoslavia) 81
  in Bosnia-Herzegovina (1910) 32
  citizenship regimes and 10, 32
  Croatian 182
  in Czech Republic 154
  ethnocentrism 184, 189–90
  in The Kingdom of Montenegro 32
  in The Kingdom of Serbia 32
  Kosovan 176
  Macedonia 140, 178
  in new post-Yugoslav states 3–4, 12,
    20, 151–5, 160, 163, 165, 168–9,
    182, 190
  Peace Treaties regulations 33
  in post-Soviet states 155, 200nn. 1–2
  redefinitions 3–4, 151
  Serbian 73
  in Slovakia 154
  Slovenian 182
  Yugoslav republics 3, 65
citizenship regime
  of Austria–Hungary 39
  civic 192
  concept 4, 9–11, 194n. 3
  Croatian 182
  ethnic grounds 21, 32, 152, 158, 169
  EU influence 18, 174–5, 179, 181–2,
    183–4
  federal and confederal 188–9
  in The Kingdom of Yugoslavia 32, 34,
    46, 192
  Kosovan 163, 167, 177
  Macedonian 178
  in the post-Yugoslav states 18, 133,
    151–2, 168
  Serbian 168
  two-tier 151, 182, 188
  Yugoslav federalism 19, 66, 68, 81, 133
Citizenship and Social Class (Marshall) 7
civic rights 8, 14

Civil code
  of Austria 32
  of the Kingdom of Serbia 32
Clinton, Bill 120
co-citizens 4, 18, 108, 187
'code red' 97–9
Cohen, E. F. 5
Cohen, L. J. 13, 119, 199n. 1
Čok, V. 12
Communist Party of Yugoslavia (CPY)
  35, 37, 41, 43–9, 51, 68, 87,
  195n. 2
confederal citizenship 79–81, 104, 189
Congress of Brno 39
Connor, W. 38, 43, 195n. 6
Constitution of The Principality of
  Montenegro 32
Corfu Declaration (1917) 29
Ćosić, Dobrica 92, 96
Critical Remarks on the National Question
  (Lenin) 40
Croatia
  1950, law on citizenship of the People's
    Republic of Croatia 65
  bourgeoisie 26, 28, 44–5
  citizenship laws 32, 65–6, 157–62,
    165–8
  communist party 46, 77, 87, 93
  conservative decentralists 84
  Croatian crisis 77
  Croatian Democratic Union (HDZ)
    199n. 3
  democratic elections 114–15
  dialects 26–7
  election of delegates 64
  ethnic nationalism 37, 106–7, 109–10,
    153, 190
  EU influence 173, 175, 180–4, 192
  grievances with Yugoslavia 30–1
  Hungarian law on citizenship 32
  independence 35, 45, 128, 134–6, 143,
    188
  Independent State of Croatia (NDH)
    3, 35, 188
  inter-ethnic conflicts 35, 115, 145
  linguistic autonomy 92–3
  mass killings 48
  national minority (Serb) 142–6
  nationalist movements 18, 28, 75
  passport 158, 180

republican citizenship 55, 65–7
secessionist movement 125
Serb rebellion 139, 146, 162, 190
Social-Democratic Party of Croatia
    and Slavonia 41
Sporazum 34
Spring movement 75, 111
statism 78
unemployment (1990) 198n. 2
Culic, I. 152
Cvetković, Dragiša 34
Cvijić, Đ 44

Dabčević-Kučar, Savka 75
Dark Side of Democracy, The (Mann) 111
Dayton Peace Agreement 152, 158, 162, 177–8, 191
Death of Yugoslavia, The (BBC documentary) 123, 198n. 8
Debeljak, A. 83
decentralization
    1974 Constitution 76, 125
    constitutional amendments 72
    in the early 1950s 66–7
    economic field 67–8
    federation vs subunits 77–8
    ideological structure 89–90
    LCY's role 68–70, 92
    liberal democracy and 83
    linguistic policies 178
    in Macedonia 178
    self-management and 66–8
    state apparatuses 78
    unilateral 86–7, 125
'Declaration Concerning the Name and the Position of the Croatian Literary Language' 92
democratization
    citizenship laws 12–13, 184
    Dual Monarchy 42
    ethnically diverse societies 111–13, 116–17, 120–3
    LCY and 68
    minority nationalism and 117
    in the nineteenth and twentieth century 6–8
    political rights 6, 8
    post-communist Europe 125, 168
    in Yugoslavia 17, 19–20, 83, 104, 107–8, 119, 129–30, 132

Deželan, T. 160, 201n. 7
Dika, M. 12, 160
Dimitrijević, V. 12–13, 75–6, 109, 112, 153
Dimitrov, Georgi 91
Djilas, A. 13, 41–4, 46, 56–7, 59, 90
Djilas, M. 66–8, 70, 196n. 7
Djokić, D. 31, 34, 194n. 4
Đorđević, Jovan 61
Drachkovitch, M. M. 195n. 5
Dragović-Soso, J. 85, 96, 119
Drašković, Janko 26
Drouet, M. 12, 77, 79
Đukanović, Milo 137
Đurić, Mihailo 74, 197n. 2
Durrell, Lawrence 1
Džankić, J. 137, 166, 180

Eastern Europe 26, 29, 57, 83, 97, 116, 118, 133, 142, 168, 170, 174
Ekmečić, Milorad 97
Engels, Friedrich 40
'erased' (Slovenia) 160, 164, 165, 174, 181, 200nn. 6, 7
ethnic democracy 169–70
ethnic engineering 18, 20, 151, 156, 159–61, 163, 168–9
ethnocentrism 184, 190, 192
ethnofederalism 191
EU citizens 5–6, 165, 182–4, 202n. 5
EU Council of Ministers 180
EU member states
    citizens 9
    citizenship regimes 183–5
    direct intervention and supervision 176–9
    new 152
    post-accession influence 181–3
    pre-accession influence 181–3
    visa liberalization 179–81
EU Rule of Law Mission (EULEX) 176–7
European/EU citizenship 4, 9, 21, 182, 184, 192
European Convention on Nationality 182
European Court of Human Rights (ECHR) 160, 174, 178, 181, 200n. 7
European Economic Community 78, 97

Farewell to Yugoslavia (Jančar) 96
Fascism 34

federal citizenship
  contract 164
  in Czechoslovakia 154
  in Federal Republic of Yugoslavia
    (FRY) 166, 192
  in socialist Yugoslavia 3, 17, 64, 79,
    111, 129, 183, 188–9, 198n. 6
  in the US 198n. 7
federalism
  and disintegration of Yugoslavia 122–5,
    129
  identity and membership 106
  and inter-war Yugoslavia 18, 44
  in post-war Yugoslavia 16–17, 19, 55,
    57–9, 62, 66, 68, 70–7, 83–4,
    90, 188
  socialist 13, 16, 40
  Soviet multinational 40, 50–1, 58
Federal Republic of Yugoslavia (FRY)
  citizenship 158–9, 165
  Dayton Peace Agreement 139
  dissolution 137
  ethnocentric migrations 159
  EU's influence 176
  exclusion politics 161
  formation 158
  Kosovo citizens 161, 167, 176, 180
  successor states 156, 159
Ferdinand, Franz 1, 25
Filipović, Filip 43
Finci, Jakob 178
First World War 1, 2–3, 18, 28–9, 32, 41–2,
  45, 99, 111, 198n. 1
Foucault, M. 7
Fraser, N. 8

Gagnon, V. P. Jr 113, 120, 127–8
Gaj, Ljudevit 26
Garašanin, Ilija 28–9, 194n. 3
Gellner, E. 7, 25
Gibson, E. L. 16
Ginsburgs, G. 200n. 1
Glenny, M. 199n. 1
Gligorov, Kiro 115
Gligorov, Vladimir 111
Gordy, E. 127, 145
Gorkić, Milan 47
Greater Serbianism 29, 41, 85, 96, 109,
  128, 142, 145, 162, 188
Grimm, Jacob 27

Groebner, V. 7
Gyarfasova, O. 154

Habermas, J. 7
Habsburg Empire 33
Hale, H. E. 124
Haug, H. K. 51, 71, 195n. 4, 197n. 2
Hayden, R. 12, 125–6, 151, 153
Helton, A. C. 12
Herbst, J. I. 103
Hobsbawm, Eric 1, 37
Hondius, F. W. 13, 56, 58, 61, 64, 71, 72,
  198n. 1
Horowitz, D. L. 113
Horvat, S. 193
Hroch, Miroslav 29
Hrvatski tjednik (Croatian Weekly) 75
Hungarian law on citizenship 183

'Illyrian awakening' (1830) 26–7
Imeri, S. 12, 160, 161
International Civilian Mission
  (Kosovo) 176
International Monetary Fund (IMF) 82,
  115, 122, 129
Iordachi, C. 154
Irvine, J. A. 16, 78
Isin, E. 6
Izetbegović, Alija 126, 199n. 3

Jackson, L. 200n. 2
Jančar, D. 96
Joppke, C. 8, 194n. 1
Jovanović, S. Đ 11, 33, 62, 63, 79–80,
  196n. 5
Jović, Borisav 145
Jović, D. 13, 73, 77, 78, 84, 92, 94, 95, 96,
  98, 106, 107, 111, 119

Kacarska, S. 179, 181
Kadijević, Veljko 145
Kapović, M. 27
Karadžić, Radovan 97, 98, 143
Karadžić, Vuk 26
Kardelj, Edvard 15, 38–9, 58, 59, 60,
  61, 66, 69, 73, 76, 77, 78, 82,
  93, 94
Kidrič, Boris 67
Kingdom of Serbs, Croats and Slovenes 3,
  30, 32–3, 194n. 4, 195n. 5

Kingdom of Yugoslavia 31–2
  citizenship regime 18, 32
  communists 18, 30, 37–47
  Constitution of 1921 (*Vidovdanski Ustav*) 30
  disappearance of 35, 48
  map of 31
  political community 188, 192
Kobsa, L. 43, 44, 45, 69, 77, 92, 93, 195nn. 3–4, 197n. 5
Koliševski, Lazar 68
Koprivnjak, V. 195n. 3
Kordić, S. 27
Koska, V. 161, 165
Kosovo
  Albanians in 109, 191–2
  autonomous region 55, 73, 75, 80, 86, 115, 124, 126, 136–7, 141–2, 146, 159, 199n. 2
  citizenship law 33, 163, 165, 167–8, 171
  civil unrest 1981 82
  conservative decentralists 84
  Council of Nationalities 57, 72
  crisis 82, 86, 96
  economic development 67
  ethnic principle 89, 109
  EU influence 173, 175–81, 183
  FRY citizens 161, 200n. 1
  independence 4, 137–8, 167
  international recognition 140, 144
  Milošević's role in 82, 85–6, 96, 161
  minorities 142, 168
  Ottoman subjects 32
  Second World War 35
  semi-protectorate 173
  Serbs in 85, 167–8, 171, 191
  Stabilisation and Association Agreement 176
  unemployment (1990) 198n. 2
  war in 119
Kosovo Liberation Army 162
Krasniqi, G. 161, 167, 168, 201n. 1, 202n. 3
Krleža, Miroslav 27, 93, 96, 196n. 7
Kučan, Milan 84, 114, 126–7
Kusa, D. 154
Kvaternik, Eugen 28
Kymlicka, W. 116, 117

Lampe, J. R. 57, 58, 59, 67, 69, 74, 76, 197n. 4
Latin Bridge (Sarajevo) 1, 99
Lazitch, B. 195n. 5
League of Communists of Serbia 73
League of Communists of Yugoslavia (LCY) 68–9, 77, 82, 87, 92, 104, 114, 131, 145, 195n. 2, 197n. 5
Lebowitz, M. 67
Lenin 39–40
les années 89 133
liberal democracy 8, 13–14, 83, 90, 105–8, 111, 118, 134, 169–70, 189, 193
Liebich, A. 152, 153
Linz, J. J. 17, 106, 113–14, 116
Little, A. 127, 198n. 7, 199n. 1
Lowinger, J. 129

MacDonald, D. B. 97
Macedonia
  Albanian rebellion (2001) 140–1, 165, 190, 201n. 8
  anti-fascist council 50
  Bulgarian citizens 183, 202n. 4
  citizenship law 156, 159, 161, 168, 197n. 6
  conservative decentralists 84
  CPY 45–6
  Croatian citizens 158, 183
  democratic elections 115
  economic competition 67
  education 57
  ethnic issues 109, 137, 167, 171, 191
  EU influence 173, 175, 178–9, 181, 183
  in 'New' Yugoslavia 55
  Ottoman subjects 32
  Peace Treaties 33
  republican sovereignty 59, 68
  Serbian bourgeoisie 45
  Serbian socialists 41
  unemployment (1990) 198n. 2
  visa liberalization 179, 201n. 2
  Yugoslav passports 80
Maček, Vlatko (Croatian Peasant Party) 34
Malcolm, N. 199n. 1
Malešević, S. 126
Mann, M. 111
Marković, Ante 115, 128

Marković, Sima 44–5, 47, 195n. 5, 196n. 8
Marshall, T. H. 7–8, 14
Marx, Karl 40, 66
Marxism
  'bourgeois parliamentarism' 14, 60
  citizenship 11, 14
  on class struggle 11, 44, 60
  national question 37–40, 43, 51
Matica hrvatska (Croatian cultural organization) 75, 92
Matvejević, P. 94, 98
Medved, F. 160, 196n. 5
Medvedović, D. 12, 62, 80, 196n. 5
Meiksins Wood, E. 6, 15
Mesić, Stjepan 199n. 2
Meštrović, Ivan 29–30
Mihailović, Draža 48
Mill, J. S. 117
Milošević, Slobodan 82, 84–7, 96, 98, 105, 107, 109, 115, 119, 124–8, 137, 145, 159, 199nn. 2–3
modern citizenship
  development 7, 194n. 2
  national integration 32
  political constitutions 4
  status and *quality* 1, 4–6
  Tanzimat reforms 32
  various forms 2
Montenegro
  Albanians 159
  anti-bureaucratic revolution 86
  anti-fascist council 50, 56
  citizenship law 32–3, 158–9, 165–6, 168, 192, 200n. 5
  civic principle 166, 168, 190, 192
  conflict 135–6, 139, 141, 145
  conservative recentralizers 84, 87
  Constitution of The Principality of Montenegro 32
  democratic elections 115
  education 57
  ethnonational subunits 58, 125
  EU membership and influence 173, 175, 176, 179–81, 183
  Federal Republic of Yugoslavia (FRY) 139, 158–9
  ijekavian dialect 27
  independence 4, 28, 45, 137–8, 146, 166–7
  Kosovo crisis, impact on 82
  Milošević's control 82, 87, 109, 115, 125, 199n. 2
  in 'New' Yugoslavia 55–6
  Sandžak 56, 142, 196n. 9
  Serb refugees 159
  unemployment (1990) 198n. 2
Mujkić, A. 178
Muminović, E. 79, 158

nation-building process
  citizenship's role 17–20
  communist rule 117
  double coding 7
  in Eastern Europe 26, 29, 57
  federalism 106
  'integral' Yugoslavism 30
  nationalist movement 25
  socialist Yugoslav 90, 93
  Yugoslav 45
National Assembly
  Serbian 165
  Yugoslav 67
nationalist movements (creation of Yugoslavia) 18, 28, 38
Nazism 34, 48
Neuman, G. L. 198n. 7
new states
  citizenry 20, 64–5, 151, 156, 163, 165, 175
  citizenship 4, 156
  conflict 134–5, 139–40
  creation 119
  ethnonationalism 98, 105, 151, 193
  peace treaties 33
  territorial shape 139, 141
Nikola, Pašić 30
Nimni, E. 39
North Atlantic Treaty Organization (NATO) 137–8, 161, 176
Nova Revija (journal) 96
Novi Sad agreement 91–2

October revolution 37, 51
Office of High Representative (OHR) 177
Ohrid Framework Agreement 165, 175, 178, 190
Omejec, J. 12, 200n. 4
Ong, A. 9
Ottoman nationality law (1869) 32

Palous, M. 154
Party of the Rights (Croatia) 28
Pateman, C. 15, 67
Pavković, A. 95
Peace Treaties 33
Peasant Party (Croatia) 30, 34
Pejić, J. 12, 79, 80, 158, 163
Perović, L. 195
Pijade, Moša 56, 59, 196n. 1
Pirjevec, Dušan 92, 96
Pirker, Pero 75
Pocock, J. G. A. 133, 194n. 2
political communities
   citizenship laws 151
   civic 118, 189
   ethnic 118, 189
   EU's influence 174
   ideological regimes 14
   modern citizenship 1–2
   multiethnic 192
   overlapping 75, 168
   in Yugoslavia and the post-Yugoslav states 1–2, 157
   in Yugoslav republics 55, 129
political rights 6, 8, 130, 169, 178, 184, 191, 201n. 8
Popović, S. 145
Preradović, Petar 26
Princip, Gavrilo 25
Provinces Illyriennes (Napoleon) 26
Prpa-Jovanović, B. 29, 31
Pucar, Djuro 68

Question of Nationalities and Social Democracy, The (Bauer) 39, 195n. 1

Račan, Ivica 114
Rački, Franjo 28
Radić, Stjepan 30–1
Ragazzi, F. 157, 165
Rajaković, N. 29
Rakić, V. 79
Ramet, S. P. 13, 17, 69, 71, 74, 77, 83, 84, 85, 86, 89, 97, 119, 124, 199n. 1
Ranković, Aleksandar 62, 69–70, 72, 92–3
Rapallo Treaty 33, 195n. 5
Rava, N. 159
refugees
   break-up of Soviet Union, impact on 163
   citizenship issues 164
   Croat 161
   EU citizenship 184
   rights 5
   Roma 180
   Serb 159, 161, 165
Renner, Karl 39, 40
residents
   categories 5
   citizenship regimes and 21, 33, 152
   in Croatia 160–1, 201n. 9
   elections 20, 64
   ethnic democracy 169
   of the FPRY 62
   FRY 158
   Kosovan 176, 179, 201n. 1
   metics, status 163–4
   naturalization process 155–6
   non-citizen 6, 9
   permanent 33
   in the republics (SFRY) 20–1, 64, 131, 152, 156, 158, 160–1
   rights 5
   in Slovenia (the 'erased') 160, 164, 165, 174, 181, 200nn. 6, 7
   zero option model 155
Resistance movement (Second World War) 3, 18, 35, 48–9, 52, 56, 188
Roeder, P. G. 118
Rupnik, J. 144
Rusinow, D. I. 1, 13, 16, 28, 29, 58, 60, 61, 67, 68, 69, 70, 71, 72, 75, 76, 78, 81, 94

Sarajevo
   Assassination of Franz Ferdinand 1, 25
   ethnocentric migrations 159
   Latin Bridge in 99
   war (siege) 98–9, 134
   Winter Olympic Games (1984) 82
Sarajlić, E. 32, 158, 178
Šaškor, I. 195n. 3
Second World War 14, 34, 38, 51–2, 90, 97, 131, 188
Sejdić, Dervo 178
Sekelj, Laszlo 76
self-determination 40, 43–5, 47, 56, 59, 61, 68, 87, 108–9, 169
self-management 15, 59–61, 66–9, 75, 89, 108, 111, 129, 189

'semi-citizens' 5
Serb rebellion (in Croatia) 139, 146, 162, 190
Serbia
　anti-fascist council 50, 56
　autonomous provinces (Vojvodina and Kosovo) 16, 55, 72–3, 75, 78, 86, 124–6, 136, 143, 161
　'AVNOJ' borders 113
　bourgeoisie 43–5
　Chetniks 48, 188
　citizenship law 32–3, 157–8, 165–6, 175–6, 192, 200n. 5, 201n. 1
　collaborationist regime 35, 48
　conflict 135–7, 139, 141–4
　congress of the Communist Party of Serbia (1945) 51
　Constitution (1990) 115, 126
　constitutional amendments 72
　education 57
　ethnic sovereignty 106, 109, 124–7, 138–9, 153, 190–1
　EU membership 173, 175–6, 181, 183
　Federal Republic of Yugoslavia 139, 158, 161, 176, 190, 192
　'Greater Serbianism' 29, 85, 96, 109, 128, 145, 162, 188
　independence 4, 28, 165
　Kosovo crisis, impact on 96
　Kosovo secession 165, 167–8
　The League of Communists of Serbia 73
　military power 30, 138
　Milošević, Slobodan 82, 84–7, 109, 119, 125, 128, 159, 199n. 3
　minorities 141–2
　Novi Sad agreement 91
　passports 80, 180
　Presidency (SFRY) 87, 199nn. 2–3
　pro-fascist formations 48
　recentralization 84, 86–7, 125–6, 128
　refugees 159, 161
　republican borders 75, 162
　Sandžak 196n. 9
　Social Democratic Party 41
　standard language 26–7
　unemployment (1990) 198n. 2
　Vichy-like regime 3
　visa liberalization 179–81, 201n. 2
　Yugoslav unification 29–30, 42

Serbian Academy of Arts and Sciences (SANU) 84–5, 96
Shachar, A. 5
Shafir, G. 14, 194n. 2
Shaw, J. 8, 9, 10, 12, 174, 194n. 3
Shevel, O. 155, 200n. 1
Shoup, P. 41, 46, 48, 57, 59, 68, 69
Silber, L. 127, 198n. 8, 199n. 1
Skalnik Leff, C. 97, 104, 112, 113
Slovenia
　administrative exclusion 160
　anti-fascist council 50
　class struggle 44
　Communist Party 45–6
　decentralisation policies 84–7
　economic issues 69, 129
　education 57
　elections 114–15
　'erased' 160, 164, 165, 174, 181, 200nn. 6, 7
　ethnic sovereignty 109, 126, 153, 159, 190
　EU membership/citizenship 4, 165, 173–5, 181–2, 184, 192
　Kosovo crisis, impact on 96
　literary traditions 26
　metics and *aliens* 164
　minorities 63, 190
　nationalist movements 28–9
　in 'New' Yugoslavia 55
　road building project (*cestna afera*) 77
　secessionist movement 125
　Slovenian Writers' Union 96
　unemployment (1990) 198n. 2
　White Guards 48
　Yugoslav army's (JNA) intervention 135, 145, 197n. 1
　Yugoslav citizenship 33
　Yugoslav Social Democratic Party 41
Smodlaka, Josip 28
Smooha, S. 169–70, 190
Snyder, J. 111, 113
Social-Democratic Party of Croatia and Slavonia 41
social rights 5, 8, 14, 160, 194n. 1
socialist citizenship 14, 68
socialist/federal Yugoslavia (also FNRJ/FPRY and SFRJ/SFRY)
　1953 Constitutional Law 58–60, 63

1946 Constitution 56–8, 63
1963 Constitution 60–3, 69, 70, 73
1974 Constitution 63, 71, 73–7, 79, 84–7, 108, 125
borders (internal) 51, 56, 73, 75, 80, 83, 87, 94, 113, 131
citizenship 13, 62–4, 66, 79–80, 104, 159
collapse of multinational socialist federations 122–3
constitutional amendments (1967–1971) 70, 71–7
constitutional amendments (1989) 125–6
Council of Nationalities, also Chamber of Nationalities (*Vijeće naroda*) 57, 59, 61, 71–4
Council of Producers (*Vijeće proizvođača*) 59
creation of separate republics 55–6
Federal Assembly 61, 72, 76, 198n. 1
Federal Chamber 72, 76–7, 86
Federal Executive Committee/Council (SIV) 60–1, 74, 76–7
federalized citizenship 19, 35
Presidency 74, 76, 77, 85–7, 115, 199n. 2
republican citizenships 19, 34
Soviet Constitution 58
successor states 12, 20, 27, 81, 119, 131, 151, 156, 163–4, 168
South Slavs
  dialects 26
  inter-war experience 17
  national unification 25, 29–30, 42, 97, 123
  nationalist programmes 28, 97, 99
  socialists 38–9, 41
  Yugoslavia 1, 18, 25, 93, 123
  Zagreb 28
Soviet Union (USSR) 1, 16, 47–8, 51, 58, 60, 66, 104, 112, 113–14, 122–4, 136, 140, 144, 146, 154–5, 163, 196n. 7, 198n. 7, 198n. 1, 200n. 1
Soysal, Y. N. 9
Spaskovska, Lj 161, 178
Sporazum 34
Stalin 37, 39–40, 45, 47, 58, 66, 91, 194n. 1, 195n. 5, 196n. 7
Starčević, Ante 28

States and Power in Africa: Comparative Lessons in Authority and Control (Herbst) 103
statism 78
Stepan, A. 13, 17, 106, 113–14, 116, 123–4
Štiks, I. 8, 10, 12, 13, 18, 151, 157, 165, 178, 193, 194n. 3
Stokes, G. 111
Strossmayer, Bishop Josip Juraj 28–9
Strugar, Colonel Vlado 56
Supilo, Ante 28
Suvin, D. 16, 67
Svilanović, G. 159

Telegram (Zagreb-based newspaper) 92
Tepić, Đ 11, 32, 62, 195n. 7
Thompson, M. 78
Tito, Josip Broz 3, 19, 38, 39, 47, 48, 49, 50, 51, 55, 59, 67, 69, 70, 74, 75, 77, 78, 81, 82, 84, 89, 91, 92, 93, 94, 97, 99, 120, 126, 195n. 6, 196nn. 7–8
  'administrative federalism' 55
  Bled agreement 91
  charisma 89, 94
  death of 3, 19, 81–2, 84
  Fifth Conference of the CPY 47
  national liberation struggle 3, 18, 47–51
  national question 38–9, 47, 50, 69, 195n. 6, 196n. 8
  president 59, 74, 77
  self-management 67
  Stalin, conflict with 91
  on statism 78
  Yugoslav communism 19, 47–9, 69, 75, 93–4
Toholj, Miroslav 112
Torpey, J. 7
Tripalo, Mika 75
Trumbić, Ante 28–9
Tudjman, Franjo 110, 114, 126–8, 143, 161–2, 199n. 3

Udovički, J. 78
Ugrešić, D. 83
Ukrainian crisis 146
UN mission (UNMIK, UN Interim Administration Mission) 176, 201n. 1

University of Zagreb 28
Unkovski-Korica, V. 16, 67

Vasiljević, J. 166
Verdery, K. 12, 112, 153
violence, triggers of 20, 132–4, 138–45
Višnjić, M. 15, 76
Vladisavljević, N. 86
Vlahović, Veljko 69
Vlajčić, G. 195n. 4
Vojvodina
  autonomy 45, 55, 73, 75, 78, 80, 86, 115, 124, 126, 190, 199n. 2
  citizenship, deprivation of 63
  conservative recentralizers 84
  Council of Nationalities 57, 72
  economic competition 67
  ethnonational subunits 58
  Germans in 63
  Hungarian law on citizenship 32
  League of Communists of Vojvodina 73, 114
  Magyars in 109
  minorities 126, 142
  refugees 159
  unemployment (1990) 198n. 2
  yogurt (anti-bureaucratic) revolution 98
  zavičajnost (municipal belonging) 33
Voting Registers Law 63–4
Vraz, Stanko 26
Vucinich, W. S. 50, 92

Wachtel, A. B. 26, 30, 58, 78, 93, 96, 194n. 1, 199n. 1
Walzer, M. 5, 164, 187
White Guards (Slovenia) 48
Winter Olympic Games (1984) 82
Woodward, S. L. 84, 121–2, 129, 198n. 2, 199n. 1
working class 8, 11, 14–15, 44, 59–60, 75, 108, 192–3
Writers' Association of Serbia ('A Proposal for Consideration') 93

Yugoslav Academy of Arts and Sciences 28
Yugoslav citizens
  after Tito's death 82
  confederal citizenship 104
  definition 177
  democratic elections in 1990 64
  disintegration of Yugoslavia 130, 156, 159, 184
  EU policies (post-Yugoslav citizens) 18, 173–4, 183–5
  exclusion policies 159
  Federal Republic of Yugoslavia (FRY) 161
  inclusion policies 156
  internal *migrants* 81
  legal assessment 12, 156
  peace treaties 33, 63
  primacy between federal and republican-level 79
  principle of origin 62
  proof of *zavičajnost* 34, 64
  republican citizenship 64, 80
  rights and duties 64
  Schengen zone 181
  self-management system 66
Yugoslav communists 15, 18, 37–8, 43, 45, 51–2, 89, 114–15, 189, 196n. 7
Yugoslav People's Army (JNA) 105, 125, 128, 135–6, 145, 197n. 1, 199n. 2
Yugoslav Writers' Union 96–7
Yugoslavism
  anti-centralist 31
  Bosnian war 98
  centralist 31, 92
  communist policy 18, 37, 90–1, 197n. 14
  CPY's rejection 46
  Croatian demands 34
  cultural 92
  definitions 94–5
  federalist 18, 30–1, 50, 58, 91–2
  Great War 99
  ideological conviction 19, 89–90
  integral 30, 32, 34
  King Alexander's 32
  Matvejević's definition 94–5, 98
  nation-building process 25, 28, 29–30
  political conflicts 31
  resurrection 90
  royal dictatorship of King Alexander 32, 46
  Serbian 29–30
  socialist 91–3
  South-Slavic nationalisms 28, 37–8

Soviet model 50–1, 58
unitarist 30–1
writers and intellectuals 92, 94–6
Yugoslavism Today (Matvejević) 94

Zagreb
   CPY's Conference (Fifth and Sixth) 47, 68
   creation of the Presidency 77
   Croats to (migrations) 159

cultural capital of South Slavs 28
liberation 51
linguistic unity 92
Tito 51, 77
Tudjman's government 143, 162
zavičajnost (municipal belonging) 33–4, 63, 195n. 6
zero option model (citizenship) 155
Žižek, S. 98
Zukin, S. 67

www.ingramcontent.com/pod-product-compliance
Lightning Source LLC
Chambersburg PA
CBHW062216300426
44115CB00012BA/2082